Agricultural Markets Instability

T0361163

Since the financial and food price crises of 2007, market instability has been a topic of major concern to agricultural economists and policy professionals. This volume provides an overview of the key issues surrounding food prices volatility, focusing primarily on drivers, long-term implications of volatility and its impacts on food chains and consumers.

The book explores which factors and drivers are volatility-increasing and which others are price level-increasing, and whether these two distinctive effects can be identified and measured. It considers the extent to which increasing instability affects agents in the value chain, as well as the actual impacts on the most vulnerable households in the EU and in selected developing countries. It also analyses which policies are more effective to avert and mitigate the effects of instability.

Developed from the work of the European-based ULYSSES project, the book synthesises the most recent literature on the topic and presents the views of practitioners, businesses, NGOs and farmers' organizations. It draws policy responses and recommendations for policy makers at both European and international levels.

Alberto Garrido is Professor of Agricultural and Natural Resource Economics and a Researcher at the Research Centre for the Management of Agricultural and Environmental Risks (CEIGRAM), Technical University of Madrid, Spain.

Bernhard Brümmer is a Professor in the Department of Agricultural Economics and Rural Development at Georg-August University Göttingen, Germany.

Robert M'Barek is an Agricultural Economist and leader of the "Agricultural trade and market analysis" group at the European Commission's Joint Research Centre (IPTS) in Seville, Spain.

Miranda P. M. Meuwissen is Associate Professor in the Business Economics group at Wageningen University, the Netherlands.

Cristian Morales-Opazo is an Economist in the Agricultural Development Economics Division at the Food and Agriculture Organization of the United Nations (FAO), Rome, Italy.

Seasonal Workers in Mediterranean Agriculture
The social costs of eating fresh
Edited by Jörg Gertel and Sarah Ruth Sippel

Food Security, Food Prices and Climate Variability
Molly E. Brown

Depolarizing Food and Agriculture
An economic approach
Andrew Barkley and Paul W. Barkley

Cities and Agriculture
Developing resilient urban food systems
Edited by Henk de Zeeuw and Pay Drechsel

Agricultural Markets Instability
Revisiting the recent food crises
Edited by Alberto Garrido, Bernhard Brümmer, Robert M'Barek,
Miranda P. M. Meuwissen and Cristian Morales-Opazo

The Sociology of Food and Agriculture
Second Edition
Michael Carolan

Food Security, Gender and Resilience
Improving smallholder and subsistence farming
Edited by Leigh Brownhill, Esther M. Njuguna, Kimberly L. Bothi,
Bernard Pelletier, Lutta W. Muhammad and Gordon M. Hickey

For further details please visit the series page on the Routledge website:
http://www.routledge.com/books/series/ECEFA/

Agricultural Markets Instability

Revisiting the recent food crises

Edited by
Alberto Garrido, Bernhard Brümmer,
Robert M'Barek, Miranda P. M. Meuwissen
and Cristian Morales-Opazo

Editorial Assistants
Ana Felis and Lucian Stanca

Routledge
Taylor & Francis Group

LONDON AND NEW YORK

from Routledge

First published 2016
by Routledge

2 Park Square, Milton Park, Abingdon, Oxfordshire OX14 4RN
711 Third Avenue, New York, NY 10017

Routledge is an imprint of the Taylor & Francis Group, an informa business

First issued in paperback 2018

British Library Cataloguing-in-Publication Data
A catalogue record for this book is available from the British Library

Library of Congress Cataloging-in-Publication Data
Agricultural markets instability : revisiting the recent food crises / edited by Alberto Garrido, Bernhard Brümmer, Robert M'Barek, Miranda P. M. Meuwissen and Cristian Morales-Opazo.
    pages cm
  Includes bibliographical references and index.
  1. Food prices—Developing countries.   2. Agricultural prices—Developing countries.   3. Food security—Developing countries.   4. Food supply—Developing countries.   5. Agriculture—Economic aspects—Developing countries.   I. Garrido, Alberto, editor.
    HD9018.D44A3656 2016
    338.1'3091724—dc23
    2015027176

ISBN: 978-1-138-93741-3 (hbk)
ISBN: 978-1-138-58894-3 (pbk)

Typeset in Bembo
by Apex CoVantage, LLC

This book is a deliverable of Project ULYSSES, a 3-year project (running from August 2012 to July 2015) co-funded by the European Commission under the Framework Programme 7 (FP7), addressing the Strategic theme: KBBE.2012.1.4–05 "Volatility of agricultural commodity markets." Call ID: FP7-KBBE-2012-6-singlestage.

The views expressed are purely those of the authors and may not in any circumstances be regarded as stating an official position of the participating institutions.

Contents

Contributors

Sergio René Araujo Enciso has been a research fellow at the European Commission's Joint Research Centre – Institute for Prospective Technological Studies (Seville, Spain) since 2013. Between 2008 and 2012, he worked as research assistant at the Department of Agricultural Economics and Rural Development at the Georg-August-Universität Göttingen (Göttingen, Germany); from 2000 to 2006, he worked in private industry in Mexico. He studied Chemistry at the Universidad La Salle (Mexico City, Mexico) and Agricultural Economics at the Georg-August-Universität Göttingen (Göttingen, Germany), where he received his doctorate.

Marco Artavia holds a PhD in Agricultural Economics and has vast experience in economic modelling, market analyses, policy support, climate change and risk/stochastic modelling. Before joining DIW Econ in April 2014, he worked for the European Commission at the Joint Research Centre – Institute for Prospective Technological Studies (IPTS) in Seville, Spain. The main focus of his work at IPTS was the applied economic analysis of agricultural markets and policies under the consideration of uncertainty. At DIW Econ, he has been responsible for the CGE-based study of green growth policies for Kazakhstan.

Tsion Taye Assefa is currently a PhD candidate (since September 2012) in the Business Economics Group and Wageningen School of Social Sciences of the Department of Social Sciences of Wageningen University. Her PhD thesis is on "The impact of food price volatility in European food supply chains and the effectiveness of price risk management strategies in reducing the risk from price volatility." Her research interests include econometrics, industrial organization and risk management in agriculture.

Jean Balié is Senior Economist in the Agricultural Development Economics Division of the Food and Agriculture Organization, where he manages the Monitoring and Analysing Food and Agricultural Policies (MAFAP) Programme. He has over 16 years of experience on policy analysis in developing and developed countries. He also worked for the French Ministry of Agriculture on bilateral cooperation and international trade negotiations.

He wrote several papers, articles and reports on topics such as policy processes, policy monitoring, commodity chain analysis and price volatility.

Isabel Bardají is Professor of agricultural economics in the Department of Agricultural Economy, Statistics and Business Management at Technical University of Madrid. Her fields of interest are agricultural policies and rural development. Her research work deals with the analysis of agricultural policies effects, the factors contributing to the adoption of policies and farmers strategies and in rural development. Currently she is Deputy Director of the Research Centre for the Management of Agricultural and Environmental Risks (CEIGRAM).

María Blanco is an Associate Professor of Agricultural and Natural Resource Economics at the Technical University of Madrid. She is largely experienced in quantitative analysis of agricultural policies, development of agroeconomic modelling tools for policy impact assessment and integrated assessment of environmental and agricultural policies. For two years, she worked as a Senior Researcher for the European Commission Joint Research Centre and contributed to the development of the EU Agricultural Outlook. She contributes to the development of large agroeconomic models and has extensive experience in the linkage of biophysical and economic models, in particular in the fields of water economics and climate change impact assessment. She has been contributing to international research projects for more than 20 years.

Bernhard Brümmer has been a Professor in the Department of Agricultural Economics and Rural Development at the Georg-August-University of Göttingen since 2005. He holds a PhD from Kiel (2001). He has published widely, including for the *American Journal of Agricultural Economics*, *Journal of Development Economics* and *German Journal of Agricultural Economics*; since 2011, he is co-editor of the *Quarterly Journal of International Agriculture*, *Food Policy*, *European Review of Agricultural Economics* and *Agricultural Economics*. His current research focuses on efficiency and productivity analysis of farms and firms in the agricultural supply chain, international agricultural trade and price formation in agricultural output and input markets. He is a policy consultant for the European Commission, the Parliament in Ukraine and the World Bank in Ukraine and Russia, and he is involved in a research partnership in China and Indonesia (Bogor, Jambi).

Stephan von Cramon-Taubadel has held the Chair for Agricultural Policy at the Georg-August University of Göttingen since 1999. He studied agricultural economics at McGill University and the University of Manitoba in Canada and completed his PhD at the University of Kiel in Germany. His research focuses on the analysis of agricultural policies and the empirical study of price transmission and market integration. He has worked as a consultant for the FAO, the World Bank and various national governments.

Mulat Demeke is an Economist at the Agricultural Development Economics Division (ESA) of the Food and Agriculture Organization (FAO). He has several years of teaching and research experience at Addis Ababa University, Ethiopia, where he was the Dean of the Faculty of Business and Economics. His experience at FAO includes coordinating policy-monitoring activities in developing countries and providing technical support in food and agricultural policy formulation to several African countries. He has particular interest in the evolution of food and nutrition security policies since the 2007–2009 food, fuel and financial crisis. He has a PhD in Agricultural Economics from Strathclyde University, UK, and an MSc in Economics Development and Planning from Addis Ababa University, Ethiopia. He has published several articles in various academic journals and coauthored books and manuscripts.

Ayça Dönmez is a Postdoctoral Research Fellow at the European Commission's Joint Research Centre. She completed her PhD and BS in Statistics at Middle East Technical University (METU); she received an MA in Economics at Bilkent University, with a minor degree in Industrial Engineering at METU. Her research interests lie in the area of econometrics and statistics, ranging from theory to design to application, with a focus on computational statistics, estimation theory, survey methodology and longitudinal/panel/survey data analysis. In recent years, she has focused on modelling agricultural commodity price volatility and innovative methods of price data collection.

Ana Felis is a researcher at CEIGRAM (Research Centre for the Management of Agricultural and Environmental Risks, Technical University of Madrid, Spain) and an international research project manager for the ULYSSES Project. Her main research areas are agricultural economics, competition policy, industrial organization and macroeconomics. She has worked as a Visiting Lecturer at the Rey Juan Carlos University (Spain), an international macroeconomic analyst and a consultant. She is a PhD candidate in Economics.

Nicolas Ferenczi is in charge of Economics and International Affairs at AGPB, an organization representing 100,000 French cereal growers. He has been actively involved in the CAP reform processes since 2007. His areas of expertise cover agricultural production, cereal markets, agricultural policies and farm economics. He was trained as an agronomist at AgroParisTech and holds an MBA from HEC Paris. He began his career as a rural development consultant in developing countries. He then served in several agronomy and business development positions with fertilizer and plant protection companies based in Paris, Oslo, Brussels and Pau.

Sol García-Germán is currently a PhD candidate at the Research Centre for the Management of Agricultural and Environmental Risks (CEIGRAM), Technical University of Madrid, Spain. Her research focuses on the impacts of food price instability on consumers, particularly related to their implications for poverty and welfare.

Alberto Garrido is Professor of Agricultural and Natural Resource Economics at the Technical University of Madrid (UPM) and Researcher at the Research Centre for the Management of Agricultural and Environmental Risks (CEIGRAM). He has a master's in Agricultural and Natural Resource Economics from the University of California, Davis (1992), and a doctorate in Agricultural Economics from the UPM (1995). He was visiting scholar at the University of California, Berkeley (2005–2006). His research focuses on agricultural and natural resource economics and policy, sustainability assessments and risk management in agriculture. He has supervised 11 doctoral dissertations and published 160 references, of which 35 are academic articles and 15 are books. Has consulted for the main international organisations (FAO, BID, World Bank); several national governments of Europe, Asia and America; and numerous private companies and foundations.

Itzíar Gómez Carrasco is a political scientist and researcher with over 12 years of experience in international development. She has worked in Africa, Latin America, Central Asia and Egypt with several international organizations, academic institutions and NGOs. In recent years, Itzíar's research interests have focused on food security, social protection and resilience in West Africa. She holds a degree in Politics from the University of Edinburgh, a master's in International Cooperation (Universidad Complutense de Madrid) and an MPhil in Development Studies (IDS, University of Sussex).

Nedka Ivanova is a Professor who teaches econometric modeling and agricultural policy and policy analysis. Her main fields of interest and research are agricultural and economic policy and policy analysis, quantitative impact assessment and modelling of policy impact on producers, production and along the food chain, modelling the policy impact on rural regions developments, price and trade policy modeling and analysis. She has been involved in a number of EU Framework program projects (AGMEMOD, AGMEMOD2020, PRIMA, TEAMPEST, CLAVIER, REAPBALK, etc.), FAO, WB as well as national projects.

Tinoush Jamali Jaghdani holds a PhD in Agricultural Economics (2012), an MSc in the Socioeconomics of Rural Development (2007), a certificate of "Applied Statistics and Empirical Method PhD Certificate Programme" (2007; Georg-August-University Göttingen, Germany), and a BSc in Agricultural Economics (2001; University of Tehran, Iran). He was formerly junior research assistant and currently works as a postdoc researcher in the ULYSSES project, Chair of agricultural market analysis, Georg-August-University Göttingen (Germany).

Wim Kloosterboer has occupied several positions in the area of trade and dairy affairs at the national and international levels since his study of Agricultural Economics at Wageningen University. He is currently the Corporate Manager of Trade and Dairy Affairs at Royal FrieslandCampina.

Olaf Korn is Professor of Finance at Georg-August-Universität Göttingen, Germany. He received his PhD and Habilitation in Business Administration from Mannheim Business School. From 2005 to 2007, he held the Chair of Corporate Finance at WHU – Otto Beisheim School of Management. He is a Research Fellow of the Centre for Financial Research (CFR) at the University of Cologne and a former Dean of the Faculty of Economic Sciences.

Alfons G.J.M. Oude Lansink holds an MSc and PhD from Wageningen University. He is the head of the Business Economics Group of Wageningen University and Director of the Wageningen Graduate School of Social Sciences (WASS). His research focuses on the analysis of technical, economic and environmental performance of farms and agribusiness. He has acted as guest editor of leading international refereed economics journals. He was also a member of the editorial board of *Agronomy Journal* and the *European Review of Agricultural Economics*. He is a visiting professor at the University of Wroclaw (Poland) and the University of Florida.

Emiliano Magrini is an Economist in the FAO Agricultural Development Economics Division, where he is currently working in the Monitoring and Analyzing Food and Agricultural Policies (MAFAP) Programme. His research interests focus on agricultural commodity price volatility and the impact of risk on poverty, vulnerability and food security at both the micro and macro levels. He holds an MSc in International Economics from the University of Sussex (UK) and a PhD in International Monetary and Financial Markets from the University of Rome "Sapienza".

Robert M'Barek is an Agricultural Economist and leader of the Agricultural Trade and Market Analysis group at the European Commission's Joint Research Centre (IPTS) in Seville. He received his PhD on EU trade relations in 2002 from the University of Hohenheim, Germany. Since 2005, he has coordinated the agroeconomic modelling platform and has been involved in analyses related to the Common Agricultural Policy, trade, markets and price volatility. He is co-editor of the book *Methods to Analyse Agricultural Commodity Price Volatility* (Springer, 2011).

Steve McCorriston is a Professor in the Department of Economics at the University of Exeter Business School. He was coordinator of the EU FP7 project on the transparency of food prices. His research has been published widely, including in the *European Economic Review*, the *American Journal of Agricultural Economics* and the *Journal of Empirical Finance*, among others. He has previously served as Associate Editor for the *American Journal of*

Agricultural Economics and is currently the editor of the *European Review of Agricultural Economics*. He has been a consultant to a number of organisations, including the UN FAO and the OECD.

Miranda P. M. Meuwissen is Associate Professor in the Business Economics group of Wageningen University. She did her PhD in risk management in agriculture and was Senior Researcher at the Institute for Risk Management in Agriculture. Her current research area is risk management and finance in food supply chains in both European and international contexts.

Plamen Mishev is Professor in Agricultural Economics and Marketing at the University of National and World Economy, Sofia, and Chairman of the Executive Committee of the National Research Fund. He works in topics related to agricultural policy, agricultural marketing and climate change; participated as a partner in a number of 6th and 7th FM projects; and has more than 130 publications.

Milkana Mochurova is a research fellow at the Economic Research Institute of the Bulgarian Academy of Sciences. Her main research interests and publications are in the fields of environmental economics, integrated water resources management, climate change impacts, renewable energy sources and policy analyses, as well as public participation in environmental decision making.

Cristian Morales-Opazo is an Economist in the Agricultural Development Economics Division of the Food and Agriculture Organization of the United Nations. He has been conducting agricultural and food policy analysis and research for more than ten years. He has published research in the areas of trade and markets, domestic price policy, production and natural resources and nutrition. His PhD is in Agricultural Economics.

Gabriel Pons Cortès has extensive experience working on rural development issues with a special focus on sustainable livelihoods and food security. His main field of expertise is sustainable agriculture, with a special focus on cereal banks and food reserves – an area he has studied for the past 15 years – as well as issues linked to commercialization and trade. He is currently collaborating with the task force for the Regional Food Security Reserve in West Africa.

Fabien Ramos has worked at the Joint Research Centre of the European Commission since 2007. He has been studying the impact of agriculture and rural development on the environment, including issues related to land use change, biodiversity and soil conservation. He is specialised in biophysical modelling for agriculture with a recent focus on assessing the impact of climate change on crop yields and analysing the potential for adapting farming practices to future climate conditions.

Alberto Saucedo is a PhD candidate in the Chair of Agricultural Market Analysis at the Department of Agricultural Economics and Rural Development, University of Göttingen, Germany. He has a degree in Business Administration and an MSc in International Agribusiness. He worked for the banking sector as a risk manager before joining the UN Food and Agriculture Organization and later the Economic Commission for Latin America. His research focus is on agricultural markets, trade and the economics of biofuels.

Kristina Schlüßler has been a PhD candidate and research assistant at the Chair of Finance at Georg-August-Universität Göttingen since October 2012. In October 2006, she started studying business administration, majoring in finance and accounting at Georg-August-Universität Göttingen and the University of Bologna. She received her master's degree in Finance, Accounting and Taxes in September 2011. From January 2012 until September 2012, she worked as a research assistant at the Chair of Managerial Accounting at Hamburg University. Her research focuses on options' implied information and on volatility in commodity markets.

Torsten Staack is the Managing Director of ISN (Interessengemeinschaft der Schweinehalter Deutschlands e.V.), the German board of producers of piglets and fatteners. ISN has about 12,000 pig farmers. He holds a PhD from the University of Göttingen and formerly was head of the Marketing and Communication Department of QS Qualität und Sicherheit GmbH, Bonn.

Lucian Stanca holds a Masters in Economics from Universidad Complutense (Madrid) and a degree in Business Administration from Universidad Autónoma (Madrid). He joined the Department for Agricultural Economics at the Universidad Politécnica (Madrid) in 2014 as a research assistant. His research is focused on agricultural markets, climate change economics, international trade and agroeconomic modelling.

José María Sumpsi Viñas has been Full Professor at the Universidad Politécnica de Madrid since 1980, and is the former Coordinator of de PIDERAL (Spanish Cooperation Regional Project for building Territorial Rural Development Policies in Latin America). Has been an advisor of different national governments in Latin America, a consultant for international agencies (FAO, BID, World Bank) and a member of the advisory board for international institutions and EU research projects. Amongst the former positions, he was Assistant Director-General of the Technical Cooperation Department at FAO, Assistant Director-General of the Agriculture and Consumer Protection Department at FAO and President of Spanish Association of Agricultural Economists. He worked at the Inter-American Development Bank in Washington as an expert in Rural Development. He has published more than 100 papers and 15 books.

Adamo Uboldi received his PhD in Mathematics in 2004, focusing on Mathematical Finance, at University "La Sapienza" of Rome, Italy. After spending some years doing research in academia, he joined the European Commission in 2011. He's currently dealing with agricultural commodities modelling at the Directorate General for Agriculture and Rural Development in the unit taking care of agricultural modelling and outlook.

Benjamin Van Doorslaer is an agricultural engineer specialising in agroeconomics. He works at the European Commission (DG AGRI & IPTS) as a socioeconomic analyst of EU agricultural policy, with a focus on projections in the EU/world meat sector and economic modelling of climate and GHG and trade policy.

Preface

This volume reports some of the results of ULYSSES project (a EU three-year project of 7h Framework Research Programme of the European Commission). ULYSSES stands for "Understanding and coping with food markets voLatilitY towards more Stable world and EU food SystEmS." The project focuses on price volatility and more particularly on the analysis of the volatility drivers, long-term implications and causes of volatility, and the impact of volatility on food chains and consumers, with the final goal to draw policy responses and recommendations to policy makers. The project's scope and focus include both the EU and developing countries.

ULYSSES's partners are the Technical University of Madrid (Spain), Wageningen University (The Netherlands), Joint Research Centre of the European Commission, University of National and World Economy (Sofia, Bulgaria), Georg-August-Universität Göttingen (Germany) and the Food and Agriculture Organization (FAO) of the United Nations.

The goal of this volume is to synthesise the most recent literature on the topic and complement the dissemination effort of ULYSSES with some unpublished results and findings. The output of ULYSSES comprises a collection of six policy briefs, thirteen scientific papers and seven working documents, all of them available from the project's webpage (http://www.fp7-ulysses.eu/). The project's portal includes the materials and presentations of seminars held in Madrid on March 27, 2014; hosted by FAO in Rome on February 11, 2015; held in Brussels on June 24, 2015; and held in the Expo in Milan on July 9–10, 2015, this one co-organised with the Università Cattolica del Sacro Cuore (Italy) and the Joint Research Centre of the European Commission. These seminars provided extremely valuable ideas and results, which ULYSSES partners integrated into their research activities. This monograph thus rounds up a communication strategy that has targeted different audiences and employed various formats, with a view to widen the group of interested listeners and readers.

Three of the 15 chapters of the volume have been authored by members of the Advisory Board of ULYSSES (Torsten Staack, representing the Interest Group of Pig Farmers in Germany [ISN]; Nicolas Ferenczi from the French

Association of Wheat Producers; Wim Kloosterboer from FrieslandCampina, a Dutch Dairy Cooperative). These chapters are diverse in focus, length and approach, and they represent the personal views of the authors on the issue of food and agricultural markets instability. The book also includes a chapter coauthored by S. McCorriston, also a member of the Advisory Board, and S. von Cramon-Taubadel that summarises the policy conclusions of the Project TRANSFOP (7th Framework Programme), and another chapter by G. Pons Cortès and I. Gómez Carrasco, from OXFAM, that discusses the potential of local food reserves to manage and cope with price risks in sub-Saharan Africa. We acknowledge their valuable contributions, not only for this book but also during the entire duration of the project.

We are grateful for the support and continuous assistance of our Scientific Officer in DG Research (European Commission), Barna Kovacs. We also acknowledge the support of the Earthscan editorial team, Ashley Wright and Tim Hardwick. The assistance of Ana Felis and Lucian Stanca in providing the final check for all the chapters, polishing and revising is highly appreciated. Finally, the ULYSSES coordinator wishes to express his most sincere gratitude to CEIGRAM's staff, Esperanza Luque and Katerina Kucerova, and UPM Research officers Eva Báguena and Javier López.

The Editors

Acronyms and abbreviations

AGP	Association Générale des Producteurs de Blé et autres céréales, French Association of Wheat Producers
AMIS	Agricultural Market Information System
APTERR	ASEAN Plus Three Emergency Rice Reserve
CAADP	Comprehensive Africa Agriculture Development Programme
CAP	Common Agricultural Policy
CBOT	Chicago Board of Trade
CIT	Commodity index trader
EMIR	European Market Infrastructure Regulation
EU	European Union
EU-SILC	EU Statistics on Income and Living Conditions
FAO	Food and Agriculture Organization of the United Nations
FEWS NET	Famine Early Warning Systems Network
FIGARCH	Fractionally integrated generalized autoregressive conditional heteroskedastic
GARCH	Generalised autoregressive conditional heteroskedastic
GIEWS	Global Information and Early Warning System on Food and Agriculture
HIC	High income countries
HICP	Harmonised Index of General Consumer Prices
IFPRI	International Food Policy Research Institute
IMF	International Monetary Found
LFR	Local food reserves
LIC	Low income countries
MAFAP	Monitoring and Analysing Food and Agricultural Policies
MAR	Market abuse regulation
MIC	Middle income countries
MIFID	Markets in Financial Instruments Directive
MS	Member State (of the EU)
NBER	National Bureau of Economic Research
NEPAD	New Partnership for Africa's Development
NGO	Non-governmental organisation

NPCA	NEPAD Planning and Coordinating Agency
OECD	Organisation for Economic Co-operation and Development
OTC	Over the counter
P4P	Purchase for Progress
PPP	Private–public partnerships
SMP	Skim milk powder
SNV	Netherlands Development Organisation
SSA	Sub-Saharan Africa
TRANSFOP	Acronym of 7th FP Project, Transparency in Food Prices
ULYSSES	Acronym of 7th FP Project, Understanding and coping with food markets voLatilitY towards more Stable World and EU food SystEmS
USAID	United States Agency for International Development
VAR	Vector autoregression
WFP	World Food Program
WRS	Warehouse receipt systems
WTO	World Trade Organization

1 Scope and objectives

Alberto Garrido, Robert M'Barek, Isabel Bardají,
Miranda P. M. Meuwissen, Cristian Morales-Opazo
and José María Sumpsi Viñas

1 The new policy and agricultural markets context

The spike in world food prices in 2007–2008 was the largest since the food crisis of 1973–1975. While there were price surges for the world's three major cereals (rice, wheat and maize) in the years 2007 to 2008, the behaviour of world rice prices obeyed different factors than did wheat and maize prices, and it had different impacts, too. After the market turmoil of 2007–2008 and the 2011 rebound, at this writing, agricultural markets appear to be stable. According to the World Bank (2015), agricultural prices, which fell 3.4% in 2014, are projected to decline by 5% in 2015, following good harvest projections and stock-to-use ratios expected to increase for wheat and maize and most oilseeds, though decline for rice. This scenario is not conducive to export restrictions (as they were in 2008–2009), and the collapse in oil prices in 2015 (running at 50% of the highest in 2014) erodes one of the main support drivers for biofuel production in recent years. In view of the restoration of stock levels, the Organisation for Economic Co-operation and Development (OECD) also expects reduced risk of market volatility for the next years (OECD-FAO, 2014).

In 2007–2008, the phenomenon of soaring food prices surprised governments, experts and the international community. On all measures, it was a largely unanticipated series of shocks, both in the first spike in 2007 and the 2011 rebound. To find a similar episode of sudden, rapid and large increase of food prices, we have to go back to 1972–1973. The world food crisis of 1972–1973 was rooted in a severe weather shock to global grain production, although subsequent policy actions in the United States and the Soviet Union exacerbated the problem and triggered the price explosion (Falcon and Timmer, 1974). In contrast to the single-factorial and temporary 1972–1973 food crisis with its limited geographical scope, the crisis of 2007–2008 was a global, multi-factorial and sustained crisis (long-standing volatility, followed by recurrent food price spikes in 2010 and 2012).

While tensions in consumer food prices have subsided, domestic price movements have varied widely across countries, and the observed price variation in any particular country does not necessarily respond to changes in world market prices. For developing countries, world market prices are crucially important for import bills, foreign exchange earnings, poverty reduction and food security and as signals to guide resource allocation. But it is well known that changes in world market prices are not always transmitted into changes in domestic prices due to transport costs, government policies, changes in exchange rates and market failures, including imperfect information (Conforti, 2014; Rapsomanikis, 2011; Baquedano and Liefert, 2014; Dawe et al., 2015).

Prompted by the sudden food crisis of 2007, the G20 leaders approved in the 2011 Cannes Summit an 'Action Plan on Food Price Volatility and Agriculture'. The plan had five goals: (a) improve agricultural production and productivity both in the short and long term in order to respond to a growing demand for agricultural commodities; (b) increase market information and transparency in order to better anchor expectations from governments and economic operators; (c) strengthen international policy coordination in order to enhance confidence in international markets and to prevent and respond to food market crises more efficiently; (d) improve and develop risk management tools for governments, firms and farmers in order to build capacity to manage and mitigate the risks associated with food price volatility, in particular in the poorest countries; and (e) improve the functioning of agricultural commodities' derivatives market. This ambitious policy programme presents unequal records of implementation and delivery, as this book will review carefully in many of its chapters. But the fact is that this political initiative was followed up by numerous others from international and supranational organisations, national governments and private foundations. The food crisis shook the foundations of the global food system.

Since the 2011 G20 Summit, uneven progress has been made at global and national levels to put in place policies, measures and initiatives to respond to the challenges of the 2007–2008 global food crisis. Important progress has been made in improving market information and early warning systems. In particular, the Agricultural Market Information System (AMIS) was set up in 2012 and housed in the UN's Food and Agriculture Organization (FAO), complementing its price information at local levels with Global Information and Early Warning System on Food and Agriculture (GIEWS), which dates back to 1975. Famine Early Warning Systems Network (FEWS NET) was launched by USAID. The Food Price Watch, run by the World Bank, was launched in 2010, later followed by the Food Price Crisis Observatory. Notably, AMIS and the Monitoring and Analysing Food and Agricultural Policies (MAFAP, also an FAO initiative) report also detailed policy information. Despite better and more insightful market and policy information systems, key questions still linger in the policy debate: How much can the market be relied upon to provide food security? When and how much should the government intervene on behalf of this objective?

Some progress was made in strengthening the global governance (Committee of Food Security, G20 and WTO), although more enforcement mechanisms and coordination are needed among these three global spheres. Some progress has also been made in reinforcing the regulating financial and commodity markets in the US and the EU, but this is a very difficult task from a technical and legal perspective (Massot, 2013). With hindsight, it appears that the role played by the entry of institutional investors, such as hedge funds, pension funds and investment banks, into food commodity derivatives markets may have been overstated. And yet, the UN Special Rapporteur on the Right to Food claimed that 'Fundamental reform of the global financial sector is therefore required in order to avert another food price crisis'.[1]

Less progress has been made in strengthening the coordination of global and national policies that influence food price volatility and food security, and even less in pushing international trade negotiations in spite of the Bali Agreement signed in December in 2013 (Doha Round of the World Trade Organization). This is perhaps one of the most commonly cited flaws of the international governance, because it goes against any national policy initiative to strike the right balance between food sovereignty, trade openness and domestic farms and consumers' support.

Finally, unsatisfactory progress has been made in increasing public and private investment in agricultural development plans to raise food production in developing countries. Because there is now evidence that price volatility delays gains in productivity (Haile et al., 2015), and that increases in productivity reduce volatility (Alston et al., 2014), it is clear that promoting sustainable intensification is a fundamental goal to make world food systems more stable.

At the European level, just as the new Common Agricultural Policy (CAP) entered into force in the agricultural year 2014–2015, some voices have already been raised to begin considering more flexible support systems with embedded counter-cyclical features (MOMAGRI, 2015). This could be interpreted as a recognition that the new CAP for 2015–2020 was perhaps an evolutionary political outcome of the previous CAPs, but that it still lacks some flexibility, at least from the perspective of budget execution and the types of programmes the EU can implement in the event of systemic market crises.

The end of milk quotas and the upcoming end of the sugar quota have also brought about an intense debate about how these two and other markets should be managed, or whether they should be at all. The 2014 Russian veto tested the safety net mechanisms foreseen in the new CAP and, judged from the most recent assessments, it seems that its budget proved insufficient to compensate all negative impacts. Most agricultural subsectors have been deprived of specific policy mechanisms to address wide price swings. For most of the fundamental commodities in the EU, prices now fluctuate jointly with international prices, unless they drop to the intervention prices, which only apply to wheat and skimmed milk powder and are set at very low levels. It is somewhat understandable that in the EU, in parallel with the dismantling of the quotas in the dairy and sugar sectors, there is now a growing interest in using some untested mechanisms like mutual funds, revenue insurance and other more flexible farm support measures (Cordier, 2014; Bardají et al., 2011).

Perhaps recognizing that income-support and market management policies will always face limitations, not to mention efficiency losses and redistribution effects, a renewed focus has been placed in improving the functioning of the supply chain, both in high-income and low-income countries. Important measures focusing on contractual mechanisms are being enforced in the EU, including the obligation to sign detailed sale and delivery contracts between producers and processors. Most countries in the EU also created 'Price Observatories', not to mention the EU milk market observatory and other national observatories of the food supply chain, which collect prices at different stages of the chain, with a view to enhancing price formation transparency and detecting non-competitive behaviour. A very likely result of all this, as this book clearly shows, is the strengthening of the value chain and the emergence of innovative price risk management strategies.

One final, but by no means unimportant, focus is food demand and the consumption of food and how food prices affect consumption habits. Research shows that the primary influences on people's consumption habits are price, affordability and taste, with trustworthiness and convenience also having an impact. Food prices offer a double-edged perspective: from the health perspective, there are proponents of food taxes to reduce obesity and malnutrition, but the results supporting this recommendation are inconclusive. From another perspective, even in developed countries poor households can be severely hit by rises of food prices. The health effects of variations in food prices have not been established clearly in the literature, but the negative welfare effects of price rises are beyond dispute. How food price volatility affects consumers is still a field of debate in both high- and low-income countries.

2 A growing body of literature that is shaping new research consensus and also sharpening the debates

In the course of the last five to six years, renewed efforts, updated data and new research projects[2] addressing the drivers and the impacts of markets' instability have shaped a corpus of knowledge of significant value for policy makers. To review in full this literature and draw its main conclusions within the length of a typical journal article would leave out too much valuable information. This is one of the main motivations of putting together this collection of essays.

The factors that caused the 2007–2008 global food crisis were not just market fundamentals, but also macroeconomic (rate of exchange and interest rates) and exogenous (increase of oil prices, decrease of real estate prices and the financial crisis) shifters, multiplied by financial and commodity markets' activity, some policy decisions (export restrictions instituted by some important net exporter countries) and climate shocks (see Chapter 2). As a consequence of all these factors, the phenomenon gained such complexity that dealing with this new era of price and market development will be from then on considered a daunting task to be tackled by the international community, with few options for individual countries or regional initiatives to pursue any other policy than merely reinforcing their coping capacity.

At the core of any intellectual endeavour of drawing policy lessons from a past crisis, it stands that regardless of the quality of data, models and inference, there is still the problem of anticipation. Chavas et al. (2014) rightly frames the problem as follows:

> [. . .] if price changes are not anticipated . . . the econometrician needs to distinguish between what is known versus what is not known to market participants. The changes in what is not known is captured by changes in the distribution of price volatility. . . . This raises the issue of empirically evaluating both changes in market conditions and changes in the information available to market participants . . . how much of the 2008 food crisis was due to poor information . . . about food stocks?
>
> (p. 9)

> [. . .] if [a market] shock is not anticipated, the economic implications are quite different. First, the welfare and distributional effects can be stronger. Second, the adjustments must be contingent on the particular shock, implying state-contingent decisions that are in the realm of insurance and risk markets. But insurance and risk markets are known to be incomplete . . . [since] insurance markets do not develop easily . . . the welfare costs of volatility are not large enough to justify paying the full costs of insurance. . . . Is it possible to improve on the welfare outcome-associated current food price volatility? What is the role of markets? What is the role of government policies?
>
> (p. 10)

With these questions in mind and drawing on lessons learned from the global food crisis initiated in 2007–2008, these ten points seem to gather some support from recent studies:

1   Only extreme price movements should be a source of concern. Price changes along a well-established trend reflecting market fundamentals and with known cyclical patterns are less a matter of concern. From the policy perspective, food price volatility matters because it creates uncertainty, namely ex-ante unpredictability, and not because it results from ex-post variability. Risk is determined by exposure to uncertainty or unpredictability. Unanticipated shocks, as opposed to anticipated price movements, should attract most of the attention of policy makers (Munier, 2012; Chavas et al., 2014), because these shape the toughest policy dilemmas and courses of actions in times of market turmoil.
2   There is a need to develop forward-looking risk measures that are able to detect volatile periods (or potentially volatile periods) as early as possible

and that contain useful information for the construction of early warning systems. Nevertheless, it is not enough to rely on a single volatility measure, even if it is forward-looking. Instead, we need several risk measures that are linked to the economic consequences of increased volatility (Brümmer et al., 2014). In this vein, promising work (Baquedano, 2014) shows that price increases can be forecasted with reasonable accuracy based on a number of indices and factors that can now be easily monitored. This facilitates setting up early warning systems and preparedness for managing and coping with extreme price movements. However, 'the better our predictions, the less likely are the spikes, because stocks will tend to adjust in a way that moderates the anticipated spike. In this sense, increased success in improving warning indicators is likely to reduce the evidence of their effectiveness' (Bobenrieth et al., 2012, p. 25).

3   It would thus appear that the probability space of anticipated shocks expands at the expense of the likelihood of unanticipated shocks. This is due to (a) more powerful market information systems and modelling techniques; (b) better data collection systems of market fundamentals all over the world; and (c) the recent development of early warning systems based on market intelligence and almost instantaneous flows of information.

4   Drivers and causes leading to extreme price movements are not necessarily the same as those that sustain upward trends (higher price levels). Recent market developments show that volatility increases with high prices and low stocks, and therefore there is a strong correlation between volatility and high prices. This is partly due to the asymmetrical role of the demand for storage, which contributes to offset price drops but is rendered ineffective if stocks are very low and prices grow suddenly (Brümmer et al., 2014).

5   Initiatives to manage more efficiently supply risks that do not rely on physical stockholding, like virtual reserves (von Braun and Torero, 2009), or the risk of financial importing countries via food import financing facilities (Sarris, 2011), have not been translated into practical applications. Instead, regional and mixed (financial and reserves-based) initiatives like APTERR (ASEAN Plus Three Emergency Rice Reserve[3]), which is the agreement for establishing a pilot regional food reserves network for rice in some countries of Asia, holds promising potential to make the partner countries more food secure. APTERR consists of risk management elements and a combination of national and collective physical and cash reserves, which are available for the partner countries.

6   The stability and predictable behaviour of international markets can be considered a 'public good', from which all trading partners can benefit. However, individually each major producer or exporter would perhaps be better off implementing trade measures in the event of rapid price shocks, a factor identified as having a multiplying effect of market tensions during the crisis. There is a consensus that in the absence of more disciplines at WTO dealing with trade policy measures, there will not be complete trust in international markets (Martin and Anderson, 2012) and, in the event

of a new crisis, countries may again resort to implementing insulation policies.

7 Despite the charges placed on speculation and the use of financial instruments by numerous commentators, which prompted G20 leaders to mandate that financial and derivatives need to be improved, it appears that these effects cannot be held accountable among the most relevant causes and drivers of the large price swings during the crisis (see Chapter 2; Aulerich et al., 2014).

8 The value chain perspective is fundamental. Well-functioning and -greased connecting markets help producers, processors and retailers react to unfavourable price movements and implement market risk management tools. In low-income countries, the lack of markets' infrastructure, transportation and storage is at the root of alarming rates of food waste, weak market incentives, abusing market dominance and poor productivity (see Chapter 13).

9 Short-term impacts of the food crisis were considerable in poor importing countries and in the poorest households in middle-income countries. Years later, higher prices reversed the outcome, increasing small farms' income and wages and helping reduce poverty (Ivanic and Martin, 2014). Recent work suggests that food price spikes may not have increased food insecurity in sub-Saharan Africa as dramatically as initially thought (Verpoorten et al., 2013), but clearly deepened the poverty of the poor, this being the acutest humanitarian consequence (Compton et al., 2010).

10 In developed countries, making nutritious and healthy food affordable to the poorest households has been identified as a key aspect to revert the alarming rates of obesity (Jones et al., 2014; Cockx et al., 2015).

3 Book goals and approach

This book seeks to improve the understanding of what happened (and why) during the food crisis of 2007–2008 on both world and domestic markets. It is the final output of the research project ULYSSES[4] (Understanding and coping with food markets voLatilitY towards more Stable World and EU food SystEmS). This project's goal was to provide general, but sufficiently detailed, responses to the main questions that have been recently posed in the literature and debated in the political sphere: What caused the food crisis of 2007–2008? Why did markets become more volatile? Are there also long-term factors evolving in a way that will make markets more vulnerable to supply or macroeconomic shocks? How do agents in the value chain respond to markets' instability? How do consumer food prices respond to changes in food prices? To what extent are households in Low income countries (LICs) and High income countries (HICs) affected by food price increases?

Covering a wide range of issues (drivers, spill-over effects, fundamentals, transmission, value chain agents' perspective, impact on consumers and policies) and from different time perspectives (short-, medium- and long-term); geographies (EU, low- and middle-income countries and global); and market bases (frequent market data, weekly, monthly and annual prices; EU and international markets), ULYSSES aimed at drawing policy-relevant conclusions.

Underlying the questions and the evolving ideas, growing evidence and unsettled debates found in the academic and grey literature, the book's main contribution is to synthesise the most recent findings about the instability of agricultural markets. Its specific goals are:

1   Report new measurements of price volatility and discuss its magnitude with respect to the immediate period before a crisis.
2   Review the most recent literature on volatility drivers, transparency of food pricing in the EU, transmission of volatility over the supply chain and impacts on consumers in both the EU and developing countries.
3   Showcase the views of agricultural market agents, policy practitioners and NGOs about desirable policy approaches for preventing, managing and coping with the instability of agricultural markets.
4   Report in a concise manner ULYSSES's main findings and draw policy conclusions with a view to informing policy developments within the EU and international spheres.
5   Identify upcoming trends and emerging policy approaches that may call the attention of scholars, senior officers, trade and treaty negotiators and legislators from all over the world.

The volume is intended to help policymakers in answering the set of questions that Trostle (2014) suggested: 'a) Who are you trying to protect? b) What are you trying to protect them from? c) How much of the perceived risk are you trying to protect them from? and d) Over what duration of time are you trying to protect them? That is, are you trying to protect producers and consumers from price swings that occur from week to week, from month to month, from season to season, from year to year or over a multiyear period?' (pp. 367–368).

The book consists of 15 chapters, all of them drafted to meet two criterions. First, they contain the essential information that is needed to gather basic ideas on how markets' instability arises and how to cope with it. Secondly, they are written in a non-technical language, thus facilitating the policy debate to convey the main ideas to a wide readership.

This final output of ULYSSES complements a collection of six policy briefs, thirteen scientific papers and seven working documents, all of them available from the project's webpage (http://www.fp7-ulysses.eu/). On this webpage, one can also download materials from four seminars held in Madrid on March 27, 2014; one hosted by FAO in Rome on February 11, 2015; one in Brussels on June 24, 2015; and one at the Expo in Milan on July 9–10, 2015, this one co-organised with the Università Cattolica del Sacro Cuore (Italy) and the European Commission's Joint Research Centre. It rounds up a communication strategy that has targeted different audiences and employed various formats, with a view to widen the group of interested listeners and readers.

Other edited volumes, published right after the first price spikes, complement our work: Prakash (2011), *Safeguarding Food Security in Volatile Global Markets*; Piot-Lepetit and M'Barek (2011), *Methods to Analyse Agricultural Commodity Price Volatility*; Arezki et al. (2012), *Commodity Price Volatility and Inclusive Growth in Low-Income Countries*; Munier (2012), *Global Uncertainty and the Volatility of Agricultural Commodity Prices*; Galtier (2013), *Managing Food Price Instability in Developing Countries*; and Chavas et al. (2014), *The Economics of Food Price Volatility*. Our work is intended to contribute to this series of relevant monographs with new findings and the voice of stakeholders who have a clear interest in agricultural markets and policies.

4 Volume overview

The book is structured into three parts. After this opening chapter, Part 1 contains six chapters devoted to synthesising the current knowledge, in four domains: volatility drivers, long-term factors, food supply chain and contextual factors, and impacts on consumers. Chapter 2 reviews the literature on volatility drivers published after the food crisis, focusing primarily on empirical works that have attempted to identify the main drivers causing wide price movements in the major agricultural markets. The chapter covers theoretical aspects of volatility analysis and spillover effects (focusing specifically on macroeconomic factors, within commodity markets, between energy and agricultural markets and between spot and futures markets). Chapter 2 provides an overview of the literature qualifying the findings based on the degree of consensus among different authors about similar questions. This chapter's main contribution is to identify questions in need of further investigation.

Chapter 3 reviews the concepts and measurement approaches of price volatility, asks whether agricultural markets' volatility has increased since 2007 and analyses spillovers within products of related markets.

Chapter 4 turns on the major midterm drivers of markets' instability, offering sets of simulations that show the impact of crude oil prices, macroeconomic factors and different projections of climate change on the main commodities' price levels and variability.

Chapter 5 summarises the main conclusions of the EU Project TRANS-FOP[5] and draws some policy lessons coming from very detailed and thorough analyses of the functioning of several food chains in selected EU countries. The chapter looks at the impact of business concentration and food supply consolidation and how these influence price transmission and adjustment. Building on pioneering analyses of retail scanner prices and food supply chains in Europe, Chapter 5 concludes by making four recommendations for improving the EU food supply chain.

Chapter 6 looks at the contextual factors that drive volatility of prices in food supply chains. It reviews the factors affecting price level and volatility transmission that can have desirable effects on one type of transmission, but may have the opposite effect on the other type of transmission. This chapter covers in detail the role of contractual tools to manage price risks.

Chapter 7 reviews the literature on the impacts of increased consumer prices and volatility in both the EU and developing countries. A significant finding is that consumer prices of food and staples behaved quite differently across countries, regardless of their income level or whether they share a common currency (e.g. euro). The chapter reviews the literature on food price behaviour and the welfare effects on consumers in the EU and in low-income countries.

Part 2 provides the views of representatives of agricultural producers and food processors in the EU, one NGO and an officer of the European Commission. These shorter chapters include a piece about the use of financial contracts and derivatives (Chapter 8), commenting on the role and meaning of the so-called financialization of commodities markets. Chapter 9 is a brief policy statement about public interventions in the EU pork sector, including a list of policy requests of the German pig producers for improving the market functioning of this important sector. Chapter 10 reviews present and emerging price risk management instruments used and considered by French cereal growers and discusses the potential use of farmers' savings accounts and revenue insurance within the present CAP. In Chapter 11, the view of a large dairy industry (a Dutch cooperative) is presented, discussing different policy options for the heterogeneous European dairy sector and industry. And finally, Chapter 12 describes the role of local solutions in developing countries to cope with food price volatility. The chapter specifically looks at the role of local food reserves (LFR) and discusses its major risks and difficulties.

Part 3 focuses on the policy sphere and addresses future research priorities. It contains three chapters, starting with Chapter 13, that makes an assessment of national policies in developing countries to mitigate the effects of agricultural markets' excessive volatility. Chapter 14 takes the perspective of the supply agents, identifying the policies that may enable them to better manage and cope with large price movements. The book closes with Chapter 15, which summarises the previous chapters' main conclusions and showcases the findings of project ULYSSES.

Notes

1   Olivier de Schutter, http://www.srfood.org/en/speculation
2   EU Projects Transparency of Food Pricing (TRANSFOP; http://www.transfop.eu/), Foodsecure (http://www.foodsecure.eu/), ULYSSES (http://www.fp7-ulysses.eu/)
3   http://www.apterr.org/
4   ULYSSES is a three-year project (running from August 2012 to August 2015) co-funded by the European Commission under the Framework Programme 7 (FP7), addressing the Strategic theme: KBBE.2012.1.4–05 'Volatility of agricultural commodity markets'. Its webpage is at http://www.fp7-ulysses.eu/
5   http://www.transfop.eu/

References

Alston, J.M., Martin, W.J., and Pardey, P.G. (2014). Influences of agricultural technology on the size and importance of food price variability. In J.-P. Chavas, D. Hummels, and B.D. Wright (Eds.), *The economics of food price volatility* (pp. 13–54). Chicago: The University of Chicago Press.

Arezki, R., Pattillo, C., Quintyn, M., and Zhu, M. (Eds). (2012). *Commodity price volatility and inclusive growth in low-income countries* (pp. 245–295). Washington, DC: International Monetary Fund.

Aulerich, N.M., Irwin, S.H., and Garcia, P. (2014). Bubbles, food prices and speculation. In J.-P. Chavas, D. Hummels, and B.D. Wright (Eds.), *The economics of food price volatility* (pp. 193–253). Chicago: The University of Chicago Press.

Baquedano, F.G. (2014). *Developing a price warning indicator as an early warning tool: A compound growth approach.* Presented at ULYSSES International Seminar Food Price Volatility: Looking for Viable Policy Approaches, Madrid, March 27–28.

Baquedano, F.G., and Liefert, W.M. (2014). Market integration and price transmission in consumer markets of developing countries. *Food Policy, 44*, 103–114.

Bardají, M., Garrido, A., Iglesias, E., Blanco, M., and Bielza, M. (2011). What market measures in the future CAP after 2013? Retrieved from http://www.europarl.europa.eu/RegData/etudes/etudes/join/2011/460044/IPOL-AGRI_ET(2011)460044_EN.pdf [accessed May 2015]

Bobenrieth, E., Wright, B., and Zeng, D. (2012). *Stocks-to-use ratios as indicators of vulnerability to spikes in global cereal markets.* Paper presented at AMIS Global Food Market Information Group, Rome, December 4.

Brümmer, B., et al. (2014). On historical and implied risk measures for major agricultural commodity markets. Scientific Paper 4, ULYSSES project, EU 7th Framework Programme. Project 312182 KBBE.2012.1.4–05.

Chavas, J.-P., Hummels, D., and Wright, B.D. (Eds.). (2014). *The economics of food price volatility.* Chicago: The University of Chicago Press.

Cockx, L., Francken, N., and Pieters, H. (2015). Food and nutrition security in the European Union: Overview and case studies. FOODSECURE Working paper no. 31. Retrieved from http://www.foodsecure.eu/PublicationDetail.aspx?id=77 [accessed in May 16, 2015]

Compton, J., Wiggins, S., and Sharada, K. (2010). *Impact of the global food crisis on the poor: What is the evidence?* London: Overseas Development Institute.

Conforti, P. (2014). Price transmission in selected agricultural markets. Rome: FAO Commodity and Trade Policy Research Working Paper No. 7.

Cordier, J. (2014). Comparative analysis of risk management tools supported by the 2014 Farm Bill and the CAP 2014–2020. EU Parliament. Retrieved from http://www.europarl.europa.eu/RegData/etudes/STUD/2014/540343/IPOL_STU(2014)540343_EN.pdf [accessed May 2015]

Dawe, D., Morales-Opazo, C., Balie, J., and Pierre, G. (2015). How much have domestic food prices increased in the new era of higher food prices? *Global Food Security, 5*, 1–10.

Falcon, W.P., and Timmer, C.P. (1974). War on hunger or new Cold War? *Stanford Magazine,* Fall/Winter, 4–9, 64.

Galtier, F. (2013). *Managing food price instability in developing countries. A critical analysis of strategies and instruments.* Paris: CIRAD-DIST and Agence Française de Développement.

Haile, M.G., Kalkuhl, M., and von Braun, J. (2015). Worldwide acreage and yield response to international price change and volatility: A dynamic panel data analysis for wheat, rice, corn, and soybeans. *American Journal of Agricultural Economics, 87*(3), 1–19.

Ivanic, M., and Martin, W. (2014). Short- and long-run impacts of food price changes on poverty. Policy Research Working Paper 7011. Washington, DC: World Bank Group.

Jones, N.R.V., Conklin, A.I., Suhrcke, M., and Monsivais, P. (2014). The growing price gap between more and less healthy foods: Analysis of a novel longitudinal UK dataset. *PLoS ONE, 9*(10), 1–7.

Martin, W., and Anderson, K. (2012). Trade distortions and food price surges. In Arezki et al. (Eds.), *Commodity price volatility and inclusive growth in low-income countries* (pp. 331–347). Washington, DC: International Monetary Fund.

Massot, A. (2013). Regulating agricultural derivatives markets. EU Parliament. Retrieved from http://www.europarl.europa.eu/RegData/etudes/divers/join/2013/513989/IPOL-AGRI_DV%282013%29513989_EN.pdf [accessed February 1, 2015]

MOMAGRI (2015). *Un nouveau cap stratégique pour la PAC.* Paris: Livre BLANC.

Munier, B. (Ed.). (2012). *Global uncertainty and the volatility of agricultural commodity prices.* Amsterdam: IOS Press.

OECD-FAO. (2014). *OECD-FAO agricultural outlook 2014.* Paris: OECD Publishing.

Piot-Lepetit, I., and M'Barek, R. (Eds.). (2011). *Methods to analyse agricultural commodity price volatility.* New York: Springer.

Prakash, A. (Ed.). (2011). *Safeguarding food security in volatile global markets.* Rome: FAO. Retrieved from http://www.fao.org/docrep/013/i2107e/i2107e.pdf [accessed February 1, 2015]

Rapsomanikis, G. (2011). Price transmission and volatility spillovers in food markets. In A. Prakash (Ed.), *Safeguarding food security in volatile global markets* (pp. 149–168). Rome: FAO.

Sarris, A. (2011). Global food commodity price volatility and developing country import risks. In I. Piot-Lepetit and R. M'Barek (Eds.), *Methods to analyse agricultural commodity price volatility* (pp. 181–206). New York: Springer.

Trostle, R. (2014). Comment to chapter 9. In J.-P. Chavas, D. Hummels, and B.D. Wright (Eds.), *The economics of food price volatility* (pp. 367–366). Chicago: The University of Chicago Press.

Verpoorten, M., Arora, A., Stoop, N., and Swinnen, J. (2013). Self-reported food insecurity in Africa during the food price crisis. *Food Policy, 39*, 51–63.

von Braun, J., and Torero, M. (2009). Implementing physical and virtual food reserves to protect the poor and prevent market failure. IFPRI Policy Brief 10, February.

World Bank (2015). Commodity markets outlook. The World Bank, January. Retrieved from http://www.worldbank.org/content/dam/Worldbank/GEP/GEPcommodities/GEP2015a_commodity_Jan2015.pdf [accessed April 6, 2015]

Part 1

Literature reviews and new findings

2 Volatility in the after-crisis period
A literature review of recent empirical research

*Bernhard Brümmer, Olaf Korn, Kristina Schlüßler,
Tinoush Jamali Jaghdani and Alberto Saucedo*

1 Introduction

In this chapter, we present a literature review of the agricultural and food price volatility patterns observed over the last decade. We focus on studies published in peer-reviewed journals, but also include a selected number of working papers, policy briefs and discussion papers ('grey literature') from international organisations or research institutes. This literature is categorised and analysed from different dimensions in this section. We divided the literature according to its methodological approach into theoretical, descriptive empirical and modelling categories. Besides these categories, we added another dimension regarding the contribution of the papers to the theory behind volatility and its drivers and spillover effects, changes in volatility patterns and summary papers. We present these papers based on different statistical methods, which are used to analyse the volatility phenomenon in food and agricultural prices.

Food price volatility is a major focus of research and policy advising of many international organizations or research institutes, such as FAO, IFPRI, NBER, IMF, World Bank, etc., in particular since the food price crisis of 2007–2008 brought the issue of food price development back to the top of the international political agenda. Two major examples of comprehensive studies on this topic include an FAO book edited by Prakash (2011) and *The Economics of Food Price Volatility* by Chavas et al. (2014).

In general, the food price volatility literature can be categorised in studies aiming at

- theoretical aspects of price volatility analysis,
- empirical analysis of price volatility drivers,
- volatility spillover effects,
- relation between energy markets and agricultural markets,
- interaction between spot and futures price volatility,
- price formation in futures markets.

In the following, we will present a brief overview of empirical studies in each of the above categories. A more detailed analysis can be found in Brümmer et al. (2013).

2 Theoretical aspects of price volatility analysis

Poon and Granger (2003) and Granger and Poon (2005) are two major papers in the area of forecasting volatility in financial markets. In these papers, the authors review different theoretical concepts of price volatility, provide empirical models to estimate the volatility and present some empirical studies. They note that the generalised autoregressive conditional heteroskedastic (GARCH) model class is 'the most popular structure for many financial time series' (Poon and Granger, 2003, p. 484). Gouel (2012) presents a review over the major theoretical studies on the issue of agricultural price volatility.

Symeonidis et al. (2012) analyse the relation between stock levels and the shape of the forward curve. They use daily futures prices on grains and livestock for the US market. As predicted by the theory of storage, they demonstrate that low (high) inventory is related to curves in backwardation (contango) and price volatility is a decreasing function of stock levels for most of the considered commodities. Karali et al. (2011) employ weekly data for soybean, maize and wheat in the US futures market to test whether modelling volatility as a stochastic instead of a deterministic variable leads to improved inference about its relationship with seasonality, storage and time to delivery. The results show that volatility decreases the closer the time to delivery for soybeans and wheat and increases for maize.

Onour and Sergi (2011) compare the performance of models, when considering a normal instead of a t-distribution, to capture volatility in food commodity prices. This implies that the normality assumption of the residuals may lead to unreliable volatility results. Long-term memory or long-term dependence processes in agricultural futures prices are considered by Jin and Frechette (2004). They find that allowing for fractional integration in the variance equation (fractionally integrated generalized autoregressive conditional heteroskedastic, FIGARCH) is suitable for modelling long-term dependence in the volatility component. Sephton (2009) extends the fractional integration idea by considering the leverage effect for the same dataset as in Jin and Frechette (2004). He finds that a fractionally integrated asymmetric power ARCH approach captures the long-term dependence in futures prices for some of the crops better than the FIGARCH model, as some agricultural commodities futures display asymmetric leverage effects.

Egelkraut and García (2006) indicate that the implied forward volatility has better predictive power for agricultural commodities whose uncertainty resolution is concentrated in space and time. Reitz and Westerhoff (2007) develop a simple commodity market model, which explains the cyclical nature of commodity prices (agricultural and nonagricultural) by considering the behaviour of two types of heterogeneous agents, the fundamentalists and the technical traders. The results show that technical traders progressively enter the market as price deviates from its long-run equilibrium. This trend-following pattern initially enforces mispricing in the market. However, simultaneously the fundamentalists become more active, forcing the price back to its fundamental value and leading to cyclical motions.

3 Empirical analysis of price volatility drivers

There are some studies, which, despite being based on empirical results, do not present explicitly quantitative estimates. For instance, Gilbert and Morgan (2010) recognise that the volatility levels during the recent crisis period were not as high as they were in the 1970s (except for rice). Nevertheless, they argue that factors like global warming–related climate shocks, oil price volatility transmitted via biofuel production and the relative large investment in index funds of futures markets may permanently increase volatility, especially in grain markets. Anderson and Nelgen (2012), using annual prices for major agricultural crops, assess the trade responses of 75 countries to provide empirical evidence on how governments, both in developing and developed countries, reacted during the past price spikes. The responses of agricultural-importing and agricultural-exporting countries are offsetting; therefore, the domestic price-stabilizing effect of their interventions was ineffective.

Nissanke (2012) states that the financialisation of commodity markets served as a transmission channel of the financial crisis from the developed to the developing world. He proposes more regulation and transparency for futures markets, minimal stockholding of essential commodities and innovative market-oriented stabilization mechanisms like virtual reserve holdings or multitier transaction taxes. Wright (2011) identifies as a major cause of food price volatility the low grain stock levels due to mandated diversions for biofuels. He concludes that accumulated shocks, such as the long drought in Australia and further biofuels boost due to an oil price spike, would have caused panic leading to a cascade of export bans and taxes.

The last group of selected literature uses different statistical methods to examine the food price volatility drivers. Zheng et al. (2008) apply an exponential GARCH (EGARCH) model to examine whether unexpected news affects food price volatility. They use monthly prices for 45 foodstuffs in the United States. The results confirm that the amplifying effect of the news is present only in one-third of the products. They argue that the increasing concentration of the distribution and retailing of food on large firms is absorbing the price volatility. Hayo et al. (2012) measure, using a GARCH model, the impact of the US monetary policy on the price volatility of different commodities (agricultural, livestock, energy and metals). They arrive at the conclusion that expected target interest rate changes and communications decrease volatility, whereas unexpected interest rate movements and innovative measures increase it. Du et al. (2011) use a model of stochastic volatility with Merton jump (SVMJ) in returns to investigate the role of speculation on crude oil price variability and to what extent the volatility in oil price transmits to agricultural commodity markets. Using weekly futures prices on oil, maize and wheat, they conclude that scalping,[1] speculation and petroleum inventories explain crude oil price volatility. Oil price shocks appear to trigger sharp price changes in agricultural commodities, especially on the maize and wheat markets, arguably because of the tightening interconnection between the energy and food markets.

Geman and Ott (2014) have measured the intra-annual and inter-annual price volatility for maize, soybeans and wheat from the US market and rice from Thailand. They have used coefficient of variation (CV) as a measure of volatility. The fixed effect panel model is used to run CV on explanatory variables as potential drivers. Results show that there are quantitatively important differences between inter- and intra-annual volatilities. The historically low stock-to-use ratio of wheat, soybeans and especially maize since the beginning of the 2000s explains a major part of the intra-annual volatility and the inter-annual volatility. However, it is quantitatively less important. Macro factors, such as trade restrictions, exchange rate depreciations against the US dollar and oil prices, seem to play a more important role in explaining the inter-annual volatility. The open interest of futures markets as a proxy for speculation activity fails to find a positive impact on commodity prices volatility.

3.1 Volatility spillover effects

A considerable share of the literature on food price volatility covers volatility spillover effects between markets, with different foci. One strand of the literature analyses linkages between commodity markets and macroeconomic variables, a second strand looks into the transmission of volatility along the supply chain and yet another strand concentrates on spillovers between closely related commodity markets.

Macroeconomic factors

The interaction among food commodity prices and macroeconomic variables has been an important area of research on food price volatility. Udoh and Egwaikhide (2012) considered the theory of Dutch Disease Syndrome to be a theoretical framework for analysing the effects of oil price fluctuations on food price volatility in Nigeria. They conclude that oil price volatility has a complementary relation with domestic inflation in food prices of Nigeria.

The potential effects of short-run deviations between relative food prices and specific macroeconomic factors on food price volatility are investigated by Apergis and Rezitis (2011). They find cointegration between relative food prices and macroeconomic variables (real public deficit, real money supply, real exchange rate and per capita income), and all macroeconomic variables exerted an effect on relative food prices. Moreover, results are valid with and without the presence of a structural break (1992 CAP restructuring). Apergis and Rezitis (2003) investigate the volatility spillover effects between food and macroeconomic fundamentals. They find significant and positive effects of macroeconomic volatility on food prices volatility.

Serra (2011a) assesses the linkages between price volatility at different levels of the Spanish beef marketing chain resulting from the Spanish bovine spongiform encephalopathy (BSE) crisis. She concludes that during turbulent times, price volatilities can be negatively correlated, hence stabilizing one market might trigger additional instability in other related markets.

Rezitis and Stavropoulos (2011) examine the implications of rational expectations in a primary commodity sector with the use of a structural econometric model with endogenous risk. They apply a multivariate GARCH model for major meat markets in Greece (beef, lamb, pork and broiler). They conclude that uncertainty caused by price volatility is a restrictive factor for the growth of the Greek meat industry. Hernandez et al. (2014) consider the potential bias that may arise when considering agricultural exchanges with different closing times in the three geographical areas of the United States, Europe and Asia. They used futures prices of maize, wheat and soybeans. The results show that the agricultural markets included in their study are highly interrelated. There are both own- and cross-volatility spillovers and dependence between most of the exchanges. They have recognised a higher interaction between the United States (Chicago) and both Europe and Asia compared with Europe and Asia. Furthermore, Chicago plays a major role in terms of spillover effects over the other markets, especially for maize and wheat. China and Japan also show important cross-volatility spillovers for soybeans.

The interconnection between the energy market and the cereal market and the volatility spillovers among these markets has been an important issue, which has attracted the attention of researchers more and more during recent years. The results of these studies are sometimes contradicting, depending on the approaches they followed or the markets they analysed. It could be the case that by following different statistical approaches for analysing spillover effects in the same market, no volatility spillover can be found or one-way volatility spillover from energy market to cereal market can be recognised. Different strands in the literature on interconnectivity between agricultural commodities and energy markets can be identified. In one group of studies, e.g. Busse et al. (2011) or Liu (2014), the pure correlations between energy and cereal market volatilities are analysed without any attempts to determine the direction of these volatility linkages. The larger part of the literature includes analyses of the direction of spillover effects between the commodity markets (e.g. Serra et al., 2011; Serra, 2011b; or Trujillo-Barrera et al., 2012). A critical issue in this type of analysis is the sample period selection. Some studies, such as those of Du and McPhail (2012) and Nazlioglu et al. (2013), have found critical points in time at which the spillover effects were significantly different before or after that critical period. Multivariate GARCH models are the major statistical tools in this field of research, but other approaches are also used to deal with the relation between the energy market and cereal market volatility. Furthermore, some studies have considered additional exogenous variables as potential drivers of price volatility in both markets simultaneously.

Two examples of volatility cross-correlation studies are by Liu (2014) and Busse et al. (2011). Liu (2014) has tested the nonlinear cross-correlations between crude oil (West Texas Intermediate) and agricultural commodities in the United States for the period of January 1994 to December 2012 with the help of daily spot prices. The results of Podobnik's Q test shows a highly significant cross-correlation between oil and agricultural commodity volatility series. The results show that during the period of crisis, cross-correlation coefficients between crude oil and agricultural commodity markets are stronger than those during a common period. He concludes that the high oil prices partly contribute to the food crisis. Busse et al. (2011) analyse the behaviour of price volatility of the EU biofuel markets during and after the 2006–2008 event. They mention that the model does not allow for conclusions about causal mechanisms of volatility spillovers, neither is it suitable for assessing the magnitude of influence of one market on the other. They found a nonstable and increasing correlation between the returns of rapeseed at MATIF (Marché à Terme International de France) and crude oil prices. They concluded that the correlations of rapeseed price returns with vegetable oil and soybean price returns on the spot market are much lower than those with crude oil. Du and McPhail (2012) and Nazlioglu et al. (2013) separated the sample period into two subsamples, before and after the food price crisis, and also found spillover effects from agricultural or biofuel markets to the energy market.

The main body of literature found only unidirectional spillover effects from energy markets to agricultural markets or no spillover effects. Serra (2011b) analyses the volatility spillovers between weekly prices of crude oil, ethanol and sugar in Brazil. She finds that shocks in crude oil and sugar markets cause an increase in the volatility of the ethanol price and the ethanol price volatility increases as a response to the increased sugar price volatility. Moreover, ethanol markets are found to have a reduced capacity to increase instability in the sugar and crude oil markets.

Serra et al. (2011) analyse the volatility spillovers among ethanol and sugar from the Brazilian market and crude oil from international markets by using spot prices. They find that increases in crude oil prices lead to higher ethanol prices and that the adjustment process is slow, which ends up in higher volatility in the ethanol market. Additionally, increases in sugar prices are also found to increase ethanol price levels and volatility.

Trujillo-Barrera et al. (2012) test the volatility spillovers among crude oil, maize and ethanol markets in the United States by using futures prices. The results show volatility transmission from crude oil to the maize and ethanol markets and volatility spillovers from the maize to the ethanol market. They find no evidence of volatility spillovers from ethanol to maize. They conclude that the maize and ethanol markets have been closely connected during this period.

Simultaneous analysis of volatility spillovers between the energy market and agricultural markets by including the effects of exogenous drivers is followed by Serra and Gil (2013). They study the monthly volatility spillovers between maize and biofuel spot prices. Additionally, they use the stock-level forecasts of maize and interest rate as exogenous drivers of food price volatility. The stock-to-disappearance forecasts are found to reduce maize price instability. Additionally, the instability in ethanol markets destabilises maize markets, and interest rate variability brings more volatile food prices.

Interaction between spot and futures price volatility

The major focus of some of the studies is the relation between futures and spot markets. Will et al. (2012) conclude, based on a review of 35 empirical studies, that according to the current state of research, the alleged financial speculation in commodity futures markets does not have a significant impact on spot prices' level or volatility. They find that changes in the fundamental factors seem to be the real drivers of price volatility.

Further studies test the causal effects of futures price speculation on spot prices using different methods, data and assumptions. Algieri (2012) looks for relationships between excessive[2] speculation and price volatility, using as proxies for speculation the share of total open interest positions held by noncommercial traders and speculative pressure. She applies Granger causality tests to find reciprocal effects between futures markets and volatility in spot markets for wheat, maize, soybean, palm kernel, palm oil, barley and rice. Her findings show no significant relationships for rice and soybeans. In the case of wheat, volatility leads the speculation, whereas for maize there is a more complex bidirectional relation. Bohl and Stephan (2012) use expected and unexpected speculative open interest as explanatory variables, controlling for aggregate trading volume and aggregate open interest. They apply a GARCH model using weekly spot and futures prices for maize, soybeans, soft red wheat and sugar. Their results reveal that even though futures prices tend to lead spot prices in agricultural markets, the speculation seems not to hinder the price discovery process. Von Braun and Tadesse (2012) used a seemingly unrelated regression model to test the impact of supply shocks (production), oil price shocks and futures market speculation on spot returns and volatility. They consider monthly spot prices for maize, wheat, rice and soybeans. The realized volatility is calculated as the standard deviation from the long run average price. The trading volumes of commercial and noncommercial positions in futures markets are used as a proxy for speculation. The results show that speculation has a larger impact than oil and supply shocks on spot price spikes, and oil shocks have a larger impact than speculation and supply shocks on spot price volatility.

Beckmann and Czudaj (2014) investigate the volatility spillover between various agricultural futures markets. They used futures for maize, cotton and wheat in the United States and found that the impact of the volatility of maize futures returns on the returns of cotton and wheat futures is statistically significant, but differs for both markets. The authors indicate that potential speculation effects on one market could be contagious for other markets and cause an increase in volatility in agricultural futures markets. They conclude that the recent rise in the interdependence of futures markets could be held responsible for the increase in volatility in agricultural prices in the past few years.

The role of index fund speculation

A number of studies concentrate on the impact of index fund speculation on the level and volatility of futures prices. Although most of the authors arrive at similar conclusions, their methodologies, data sets and assumptions differ widely. Brunetti et al. (2011) also apply Granger causality tests using generalized methods of moments with Newey-West robust standard errors. They use five commodities, but only maize from agricultural futures markets and data from the Large Trader Reporting System (LTRS). Their findings demonstrate that speculators do not lead price changes; rather, they reduce market volatility and add liquidity to the system.

Irwin and Sanders (2012) test the 'Masters hypothesis',[3] applying the Fama-MacBeth cross-sectional regression test. They argue that the variation of index funds across markets at a given point in time may be more informative than the behaviour of one market across time. They use quarterly data for maize, soybeans, soybean oil, wheat, cotton, live cattle, feeder cattle, lean hogs, coffee, sugar and cocoa futures prices. The findings fail to demonstrate the Masters hypothesis. There is no significant evidence of index funds activity affecting returns or volatility in the considered futures prices, implying that the markets are sufficiently liquid and futures traders do not confuse index fund position changes with changes in markets' fundamentals. Sanders and Irwin (2011) look into the impact of index fund investment in the US commodity futures market. They use log relative returns of weekly nearby futures contracts for wheat, soybean, maize and commodity index trader (CIT) data. They use Granger causality tests and long-horizon regression. The results do not show any evidence of linking commodity index positions with the grain futures market prices.

Gilbert (2012) focuses on the impacts of speculative trading on grain price volatilities. He uses the cash prices and four front futures contracts on the Chicago Board of Trade (CBOT) for soft wheat, maize, soybeans and soybean oil.

Additionally, he uses position data from the CBOT Commitments of Traders report. The results do not present any statistically significant effects of financialisation on cash and futures returns of Chicago grains and vegetable oil markets.

Manera et al. (2012) conduct a detailed study on the speculation spillover issue. They use four energy commodities from the New York Mercantile Exchange (NYMEX) and five agricultural commodities. The returns of futures price series are taken from Thomson Financials. Working's (1960) T index is calculated by using Commodity Futures Trading Commission (CFTC) data. This index measures the excess of speculation relative to hedging activity. Macroeconomic data consists of Moody's corporate bond yield, the Treasury bill, the S&P 500 index and a weighted exchange rate index of the US dollar. The results of econometric model show that speculation, which is measured by Working's T index, does not seem to significantly affect returns. Additionally, the results show that a depreciation of the US dollar increases futures prices. The S&P 500 has a significant and positive effect on the returns. They do not detect a relevant impact of speculation on the returns in their own market or other markets.

4 Conclusions

Price volatility on agricultural and food markets has attracted considerable attention in the literature, both in mainstream agricultural economics and in related fields. This attention is reflected in a growing number of studies published in peer-reviewed journals, as well as in a number of high-profile reports from relevant organisations. In addition, the scientific community has responded to policymakers' concerns by publishing many working papers and technical reports (so-called grey literature), a substantial number of which will go to the journal over the course of the next years.

This already rich (and still expanding) body of literature allows for developing a relatively clear picture about the driving factors of price volatility patterns in the past years. The literature seems in broad agreement that the fundamental factors explain most of the observed price volatility increases in recent times. Supply and demand factors, which in the short run lead to thinner markets and thus make the price-finding mechanism more susceptible to the arrival of new information, can be identified as the major drivers. Many of these drivers will continue to play out in the medium and long run. On the supply side, climate change might increase the frequency of rare detrimental weather events, which will generally lead to higher price volatility. The stagnation in terms of productivity growth in agriculture, in particular in OECD countries, exacerbated by land diversion for nonagricultural purposes, will certainly not help in mitigating the susceptibility of agricultural and food markets for episodes of high price volatility. On the demand side, population and income growth are often mentioned as long-run driving factors. These long-term trends will be difficult to change, in contrast to another major driver, biofuel policies.

The specific instruments employed in this policy field often lead to additional demand, which is very price-inelastic. Given that current biofuel policies are not responsive in their requirements to short- and medium-run price changes in the main input markets, price volatility will be elevated.

However, information on stocks is an important factor, too. Much of the decentralised stockholding is not regularly monitored; even if public or private entities have the necessary information, these are still often treated as state secrets (public bodies) or as potentially very rewarding private information (private bodies). With increasingly integrated agricultural markets worldwide, national-level information on carryover stocks, in particular in key exporting or importing countries, spills over to global markets. Country-specific statistical information systems have an important role to play in the future, as does the global coordination of information on available stocks, which is now pushed forward within the AMIS initiative.

Agriculture nowadays is integrated into the overall economy (even though most countries interfere in agricultural markets much more intensively than in other sectors of the economy). The interdependencies with nonagricultural markets exist both on the input and output sides. Increasing integration implies also that price volatility from input markets will have repercussions on agricultural and food markets. This mechanism has been established in the literature for fossil fuel price volatility (and is exacerbated through biofuel policies). However, as a part of the overall economy, agricultural price formation will also be subject to the impacts of overall economic policy, in particular monetary policy. Inflationary risks will affect price volatility directly and indirectly (because many investors view agricultural assets as relatively safe from inflation).

The role of speculation and financialisation for price volatility on agricultural and food markets, however, is less clearly identified in the literature. This is not surprising since speculation itself is a very broad phenomenon, which is difficult to capture quantitatively. Financialisation, on the other hand, is a relatively new phenomenon, but again is not always consistently defined across different studies. However, the literature seems to have reached a broad consensus on one specific aspect of financialisation, namely, the role of index funds for price volatility on futures markets. As of today, there is no sound scientific evidence in favour of a volatility-increasing impact of index funds' trading activities on agricultural futures. On the contrary, there is a tendency to find price volatility reducing impacts of index fund trading for major cereals. Reforms to the regulatory framework for futures markets should hence be applied rather carefully, so as not to hamper the price discovery and hedging functions of those markets, although additional transparency requirements should be imposed as swiftly as possible.

A much less debated driver of volatility is the wide field of trade policies. The experience from the 2007–2008 food price crisis showed that policy responses from both importing and exporting countries have the potential to increase price volatility in international markets. Initially triggered by concerns about domestic food price inflation, both the reduction of import barriers and the implementation of export restrictions are essentially attempts to export domestic problems to the international market. Unfortunately, the current WTO regime is not adequate to tackle these issues. A renewed impetus for the multilateral trade negotiations looks like a promising pathway toward better functioning of the international markets during a food price crisis. From our point of view, the multilateral framework is better suited for imposing self-discipline in such trade policies than is the approach via negotiations on bilateral and regional trade preferences (which seems to be currently the first choice by many important trading blocs).

Notwithstanding the quite substantial body of literature reviewed in this study, there are still some important research needs. A first set of issues is related to the methodological dimension. Price volatility is inherently unobservable and has thus to be estimated. Such estimation requires many conceptual choices. The estimates for and the interpretation of price volatility depends crucially on these choices. Even if conceptual clarity has been reached, there are many estimation methods available. In order to apply these, additional assumptions are necessary, which often turn out to be rather restrictive. The impact on the generated volatility estimates is not always clear, and there is a danger that some of the estimated price volatility patterns might be driven by inappropriate estimation methods.

In terms of product coverage, there is a strong focus in the existing literature on cereal markets. On the one hand, this is perfectly understandable since cereal prices are still the key prices for agricultural and food markets. On the other hand, the lack of attention toward livestock and noncereal staple crops is unsatisfactory, since livestock products and staple crops are nowadays often more important for farmers and consumers than cereal prices. Farmers in the European Union generate a substantial share of their revenues from livestock production; rural households in developing countries crucially depend on price development for local staple crops. Lack of appropriate data and heterogeneous product quality are two standard excuses for the focus on the relatively liquid international cereal markets, but researchers should view this as a challenge, not a hindrance, for further analyses of price volatility in agricultural and food markets.

Finally, the identification of policy impacts with the goal to establish causal links between policy intervention and price volatility developments is also not yet settled in the existing literature. Instead of focusing too strongly on causality, the concept of predictability might prove to be more fruitful in applied research. In particular, if certain factors are useful in predicting future price volatility, then these are also natural candidates for inclusion in medium- and long-term models, with the aim of also capturing observable price volatility patterns in these models.

Notes

1   Scalping refers to a trading strategy that opens and closes contract positions within a very short period of time to realize small gains.
2   Defined as the level of speculation that surpasses the need of hedging transactions and market liquidity.
3   The Masters hypothesis was named after the hedge fund manager Michael Masters, who argues that the large buy-side positions from index funds created a bubble in commodities, moving prices far away from their fundamental values.

References

Algieri, B. (2012). Price volatility, speculation and excessive speculation in commodity markets: Sheep or shepherd behaviour? (No. 166). Discussion Papers. Bonn.

Anderson, K., and Nelgen, S. (2012). Trade barrier volatility and agricultural price stabilization. *World Development, 40*(1), 36–48. doi:dx.doi.org/10.1016/j.worlddev.2011.05.018

Apergis, N., and Rezitis, A. (2003). Food price volatility and macroeconomic factor volatility: "Heat waves" or "meteor showers"? *Applied Economics Letters, 10*(3), 155–160.

Apergis, N., and Rezitis, A. (2011). Food price volatility and macroeconomic factors: Evidence from GARCH and GARCH-X estimates. *Journal of Agricultural and Applied Economics, 43*(1).

Beckmann, J., and Czudaj, R. (2014). Volatility transmission in agricultural futures markets. *Economic Modelling, 36*, 541–546.

Bohl, M.T., and Stephan, P. M. (2012). Does futures speculation destabilize spot prices? New evidence for commodity markets. *SSRN Electronic Journal.* doi:http://dx.doi.org/10.2139/ssrn.1979602

Brümmer, B., Korn, O., and Schlüßler, K. (2013). Volatility in the after crisis period – A literature review of recent empirical research (pp. 1–46). ULYSSES Project, EU 7th Framework Programme, Project 312182 KBBE.2012.1.4–05, Göttingen.

Brunetti, C., Buyuksahin, B., and Harris, J.H. (2011). Speculators, prices and market volatility. *SSRN Electronic Journal.* doi:http://dx.doi.org/10.2139/ssrn.1736737

Busse, S., Bruemmer, B., and Ihle, R. (2011). Emerging linkages between price volatilities in energy and agricultural markets. In A. Prakash (Ed.), *Safeguarding food security in volatile global markets* (1st ed., pp. 107–121). Rome, Italy: Food and Agriculture Organization of the United Nations (FAO).

Chavas, J-P., Hummels, D., and Wright, B.D. (Eds.). (2014). *The economics of food price volatility*. Chicago and London: The University of Chicago Press.

Du, X., and McPhail, L.L. (2012). Inside the black box: The price linkage and transmission between energy and agricultural markets. *Energy Journal, 33*(2), 171–194.

Du, X., Yu, C.L., and Hayes, D.J. (2011). Speculation and volatility spillover in the crude oil and agricultural commodity markets: A Bayesian analysis. *Energy Economics, 33*(3), 497–503. doi:10.1016/j.eneco.2010.12.015

Egelkraut, T.M., and García, P. (2006). Intermediate volatility forecasts using implied forward volatility: The performance of selected agricultural commodity options. *Journal of Agricultural and Resource Economics, 31*(3), 508–528.

Geman, H., and Ott, H. (2014). A re-examination of food price volatility (No. 6). ULYSSES project, EU 7th Framework Programme, Project 312182 KBBE.2012.1.4–05, Göttingen.

Gilbert, C.L. (2012). *Speculative impacts on grains price volatility*. 123rd Seminar, Dublin, Ireland, February 23–24.

Gilbert, C.L., and Morgan, C.W. (2010). Food price volatility. *Philosophical Transactions of the Royal Society B, 365*, 3023–3034. doi:10.1098/rstb.2010.0139

Gouel, C. (2012). Agricultural price instability: A survey of competing explanations and remedies. *Journal of Economic Surveys, 26*(1), 129–156.

Hayo, B., Kutan, A.M., and Neuenkirch, M. (2012). Communication matters: US monetary policy and commodity price volatility. *Economics Letters, 117*(1), 247–249.

Hernandez, M.A., Ibarra, R., and Trupkin, D.R. (2014). How far do shocks move across borders? Examining volatility transmission in major agricultural futures markets. *European Review of Agricultural Economics, 41*(2), 301–325.

Irwin, S.H., and Sanders, D.R. (2012). Testing the Masters hypothesis in commodity futures markets. *Energy Economics, 34*(1), 256–269.

Jin, H.J., and Frechette, D.L. (2004). Fractional integration in agricultural futures price volatilities. *American Journal of Agricultural Economics, 86*(2), 432–443. doi:10.1111/j.0092–5853.2004.00589.x

Karali, B., Power, G.J., and Ishdorj, A. (2011). Bayesian state-space estimation of stochastic volatility for storable commodities. *American Journal of Agricultural Economics, 93*(2), 434–440.

Liu, L. (2014). Cross-correlations between crude oil and agricultural commodity markets. *Physica A: Statistical Mechanics and Its Applications, 395*, 293–302.

Manera, M., Nicolini, M., and Vignati, I. (2012). Returns in commodities futures markets and financial speculation: A multivariate GARCH approach (No. 170). Quaderni di Dipartimento.

Nazlioglu, S., Erdem, C., and Soytas, U. (2013). Volatility spillover between oil and agricultural commodity markets. *Energy Economics, 36*, 658–665.

Nissanke, M. (2012). Commodity market linkages in the global financial crisis: Excess volatility and development impacts. *Journal of Development Studies, 48*(6), 732–750.

Onour, I.A., and Sergi, B.S. (2011). Modeling and forecasting volatility in the global food commodity prices. *Agricultural Economics, 57*(3), 132–139.

Poon, S.-H., and Granger, C.W.J. (2003). Forecasting volatility in financial markets: A review. *Journal of Economic Literature, 41*(2), 478–539.

Poon, S.-H., and Granger, C.W.J. (2005). Practical issues in forecasting volatility. *Financial Analysts Journal, 61*(1), 45–56. DOI: http://dx.doi.org/10.2469/faj.v61.n1.2683

Prakash, A. (Ed.) (2011). *Safeguarding food security in volatile global markets* (1st ed.). Rome, Italy: Food and Agriculture Organization of the United Nations (FAO).

Reitz, S., and Westerhoff, F. (2007). Commodity price cycles and heterogeneous speculators: A STAR–GARCH model. *Empirical Economics, 33*(2), 231–244. doi:10.1007/s00181–006–0100–7

Rezitis, A., and Stavropoulos, K.S. (2011). Price volatility and rational expectations in a sectoral framework commodity model: A multivariate GARCH approach. *Agricultural Economics, 42*(3), 419–435.

Sanders, D.R., & Irwin, S.H. (2011). New evidence on the impact of index funds in U.S. grain futures markets. *Canadian Journal of Agricultural Economics/Revue Canadienne D'agroeconomie, 59*(4), 519–532.

Sephton, P.S. (2009). Fractional integration in agricultural futures price volatilities revisited. *Agricultural Economics, 40*(1), 103–111. doi:10.1111/j.1574–0862.2008.00363.x

Serra, T. (2011a). Food scare crises and price volatility: The case of the BSE in Spain. *Food Policy, 36*(2), 179–185.

Serra, T. (2011b). Volatility spillovers between food and energy markets: A semiparametric approach. *Energy Economics, 33*(6), 1155–1164. doi:10.1016/j.eneco.2011.04.003

Serra, T., and Gil, J.M. (2013). Price volatility in food markets: Can stock building mitigate price fluctuations? *European Review of Agricultural Economics, 40*(3), 507–528.

Serra, T., Zilberman, D., and Gil, J. (2011). Price volatility in ethanol markets. *European Review of Agricultural Economics, 38*(2), 259–280. doi:10.1093/erae/jbq046

Symeonidis, L., Prokopczuk, M., Brooks, C., and Lazar, E. (2012). Futures basis, inventory and commodity price volatility: An empirical analysis. *Economic Modelling, 29*(6), 2651–2663.

Trujillo-Barrera, A., Mallory, M.L., and Garcia, P. (2012). Volatility spillovers in US crude oil, ethanol and maize futures markets. *Journal of Agricultural and Resource Economics, 37*(2), 16.

Udoh, E., and Egwaikhide, F.O. (2012). Does international oil price volatility complement domestic food price instability in Nigeria? An empirical enquiry. *International Journal of Economics and Finance, 4*(1), 235–246. doi:10.5539/ijef.v4n1p235

Von Braun, J., and Tadesse, G. (2012). Global food price volatility and spikes: An overview of costs, causes, and solutions (No. 161). Discussion Papers. Bonn.

Will, M.G., Prehn, S., Pies, I., and Glauben, T. (2012). *Is financial speculation with agricultural commodities harmful or helpful? A literature review of current empirical research* (No. 2012–27). Halle: Martin-Luther-Universität Halle-Wittenberg, Lehrstuhl für Wirtschaftsethik.

Working, H. (1960). Speculation on hedging markets. *Food Research Institute Studies, 01*(02), 36.

Wright, B.D. (2011). The economics of grain price volatility. *Applied Economic Perspectives and Policy, 33*(1), 32–58.

Zheng, Y., Kinnucan, H.W., and Thompson, H. (2008). News and volatility of food prices. *Applied Economics, 40*(13), 1629–1635.

3 Has agricultural price volatility increased since 2007?

Bernhard Brümmer, Ayça Dönmez, Tinoush Jamali Jaghdani, Olaf Korn, Emiliano Magrini and Kristina Schlüßler

1 Introduction

In this chapter, we assess the development of price volatility in major agricultural markets over the past years. We base this analysis on univariate GARCH models for the commodities under consideration and then analyze these estimated volatilities further, with a specific focus on spillovers between closely related agricultural markets. These volatility dynamics are captured in vector autoregression (VAR) models for five different groups of key agricultural markets. Since volatility is inherently unobservable (and hence must be estimated), we first introduce the major conceptual choices which the researcher faces when conducting analyses of agricultural price volatility. In particular, we discuss the issues of time horizons, ex-ante versus ex-post perspectives, and estimation methods. We then take a closer look at the development of price volatility on key agricultural markets and put those into context with the recent literature. Finally, we provide some additional results on the distinction between short- and long-term volatility.

2 Volatility concepts and measurement

Any attempt to identify the factors that govern volatility in agricultural commodity markets depends on the volatility concept that is applied. Throughout the literature, the following definition is commonly employed: Volatility is the standard deviation of relative price changes (log returns).[1] This definition has several important implications. (i) Since the standard deviation is the square root of the expected squared deviation between the actual (relative) price change and the expected price change, such a volatility concept clearly distinguishes between expected price changes and unexpected price changes. Andersen et al. (2010, p. 69) define volatility as "the component of a given price increment that represents a return innovation as opposed to an expected price movement". (ii) Since volatility expresses the magnitude of deviations from the expected price movement, any attempt to measure volatility empirically requires in addition the modelling of the price process, e.g., by modelling trends, seasonality, or cyclical components. For example, the popular assumptions of zero expected returns, or expected returns that are constant over time, imply the absence of any trend, or a simple linear trend, respectively. These simple trend models may be perfectly appropriate for short time intervals like a minute or a day. However, for longer time intervals it is important to deal both with long-term trends and cycles as well as with seasonalities according to harvest cycles. (iii) Since volatility addresses potential price changes, it inevitably refers to a period (over which a price change can happen) and not only to a single point in time. (iv) According to the above definition, volatility is not a directly observable quantity, like a price, but has to be estimated (see e.g., Poon and Granger, 2003, or Andersen et al., 2010).

The concrete measurement or estimation of volatility based on this definition involves a number of additional choices. Because different choices could lead to different volatility estimates, which in turn could lead to different conclusions about volatility drivers and policy implications, we briefly discuss these choices.

Time horizon: Volatility always refers to a time period. The end of this time period defines the time horizon. The selection of an appropriate time horizon depends on the goal of the analysis. For example, for an understanding of the effects of volatility on producers and consumers, a time horizon of at least one month seems appropriate. The time horizon does not necessarily coincide with the frequency of the data, which is used to estimate volatility. On the contrary, some estimation methods require that data is available at a higher frequency than the time horizon under study.

Ex-post measurement versus ex-ante prediction: It is important to distinguish between ex-post volatility and ex-ante volatility. In general, ex-post measurement of volatility can use all available information, including the price changes that occurred in the time period of interest (see the previous discussion on the time horizon above) and even price changes that occurred later. In contrast, measurement of ex-ante volatility is entirely based on information up to the beginning of the time period. This distinction has several implications: (i) The preferred approach depends on the objectives of the volatility assessment. Ex-post volatility is most useful in an analysis that aims to explain what has driven volatility in the past, whereas ex-ante volatility helps us to understand expectations about future volatility. Both perspectives are economically relevant. In terms of policy implications, ex-post analyses can be used to guide longer-term reforms, whereas ex-ante measures could provide an early warning system that may indicate the need for immediate action. (ii) Ex-post volatility can be interpreted as an in-sample volatility, whereas ex-ante volatility can be seen as a forward-looking out-of-sample volatility. Ex-ante approaches hence require that the estimated volatility model continues to be valid for the time horizon outside the observation sample. (iii) Different estimation methods are available for ex-post volatility and ex-ante volatility. In particular, implied volatilities based on the expectations of options markets participants can be used as measures of ex-ante volatility.

Estimation method: The most common approach is to use a parametric vol-atility model and to estimate it with historical data. The major approaches are models in the GARCH class[2] and stochastic volatility models.[3] A GARCH model explains (squared) volatility by past return innovations and past (squared) volatilities (plus potentially some exogenous explanatory variables [GARCH-X]). A stochastic volatility model treats volatility as a random vari-able and models its evolution via a stochastic process. GARCH models are the most common choice for the analysis of volatility in agricultural commodity markets. Model specification in this context involves several specific choices: (i) To obtain the return innovations, a model for the expected price change has to be specified (see discussion above). In the discussion that follows, we concentrate, however, on the volatility part of the model. (ii) Some general specification issues involve the questions of whether a univariate GARCH model is applied to each market under consideration or several markets are treated simultaneously via a multivariate GARCH model, the integration property of the volatility (stationary, integrated, or fractionally integrated GARCH models), and the question of whether the volatility response to past return innovations is asymmetric (GJR–GARCH) or depends on cer-tain thresholds (TGARCH). For storable agricultural commodities, the fact that demand for storage tends to become more and more elastic at low price levels suggests that asymmetry or threshold effects are likely present. (iii) Lag lengths have to be fixed for both the return innovations and the past vola-tilities, i.e., the order of the GARCH model has to be chosen. (iv) The data frequency to be used for the estimations has to be selected. And (v) the his-torical data period has to be selected, too. One disadvantage of the parametric approach inherent to GARCH models is the assumption that the structure of the model remains constant over the whole data period, including any possible forecast horizon.

An alternative to parametric volatility models is a nonparametric approach often called "realized volatility".[4] The basic idea is that the volatility of a certain time period can be estimated from data of this period only, which is available, however, on a higher frequency. For example, the volatility referring to a cer-tain month is estimated from the daily price changes within this month. The major advantage of this approach is that it does not require the assumption of a fixed model structure over a quite long period of time (the data period used for GARCH models usually contains several years). One disadvantage of the approach is its need for price data measured at relatively high frequencies, which might not be available. Moreover, the issue of how volatility scales over different frequencies appears. For example, if daily data is used to estimate the volatility for a time horizon of one month, we have to convert the daily vola-tility into a monthly one. Simple scaling rules for the volatility, like the square root of time rule, might not work very well because of dependencies in the daily price changes.[5]

Parametric and nonparametric methods based on historical price data can in principle be used both for the ex-post measurement of volatility and for ex-ante predictions. Prediction is rather straightforward with parametric models. Given the parameter estimates, volatility forecasts for different time horizons are easily obtained from the model. The nonparametric approach delivers a time series of realized volatilities that can build the basis for out-of-sample predictions of volatilities. The specification of the concrete prediction model, however, is an additional task that again entails many choices to be made by the researcher. A completely different approach to ex-ante volatility prediction is the use of options data to back out the volatility expectations of market participants. This leads to the concept of implied volatility. This concept relies on the idea that volatility is an input variable in standard option pricing models. Given observed market prices for options, the corresponding pricing formula can be inverted to obtain a volatility estimate that is in line with observed market prices. A drawback of this approach is its reliance on a particular option pricing model. For example, a standard approach uses Black's (1976) model for options on futures or a corresponding discrete-time approximation. Alternatively, model-free approaches to estimate implied volatilities have been developed by Britten-Jones and Neuberger (2000) and Bakshi et al. (2003). These are computationally more complex but do not require the assumption of any specific pricing model. The major advantage of the implied approach to volatility estimation is that it does not require any historical data, which might no longer be representative for the future, but relies only on current option prices. It can therefore exploit the most recent information available to market participants in derivatives markets and often leads to better predictions than alternative methods based on historical price data.

3 Estimating volatility on key agricultural markets

Price volatility in agricultural and food markets should not be viewed in isolation. Substitution possibilities between agricultural products in consumption, competition for scarce land in production, and vertical price transmission along the supply chains lead to complex relations between prices. Therefore, we conduct our analysis not in isolated markets but instead form groups of commodities; volatility transmission along the supply chain will be discussed later in Chapter 6 of this volume.

Group one is called "grains" and consists of wheat, corn, bioethanol, and ammonia, all prices taken from the US spot markets. Bioethanol is added to this group because it is supposed to be affected by grain price volatility, as it is extracted from corn in the United States. Wheat is included because it is usually deemed the lead market for price formation in the grains complex (e.g., Goodwin and Schroeder, 1991). Additionally, ammonia as a main nitrogenous fertilizer is chosen because nitrogen is the main nutrient in wheat production (Piesse and Thirtle, 2009). Therefore, it may influence grain price formation.

Group two is called "oilseeds" and consists of soybeans from the United States and rapeseed from the European Union. These prices are likely related both in levels and volatilities, as the protein component in both oilseeds serves as a major source of meal for animal husbandry feed. The oil component is used for human consumption and industrial uses. The latter includes, predominantly in the EU, the use of vegetable oils for biodiesel production. Hence, the markets for oilseeds are characterized by a high extent of substitution possibilities in consumption (Busse et al., 2012).

These potentially strong linkages via substitution in consumption are at the core of the composition of our third group, "vegetable oils". It contains palm oil from Malaysia, soybean oil from Argentina, rapeseed oil from Northwest Europe, sunflower oil from Argentina, and biodiesel from Germany. These agricultural markets are considered jointly with the market for biodiesel as a major use of vegetable oils in the EU.

As sugar plays an important role in bioethanol and biofuel production in South America, we have considered a fourth group for sugar and bioethanol from Brazil. The final group is called "meat" and includes pork from Germany,[6] as well as corn and soybean meal imported into the European Union. The analysis of the volatility spillover effects among meat markets and feed grains is the major objective of the volatility analysis for this group, which includes the major exportable meat together with two major feedstock components.

As discussed above, modelling and data choices matter in volatility analyses. For our investigation, we chose a monthly data frequency because it is supposed to be a relevant horizon for decision makers in commodity markets. The GARCH (1,1) model[7] is chosen as the most appropriate model for our study because implied volatilities can only be calculated for some commodities due to a lack of sufficient options data, and realized volatilities require higher frequency data to be robust estimators, which are also not available for all commodities.

Price volatilities for all commodities in our study are estimated by fitting a GARCH (1,1) model to monthly continuously compounded returns. The source of the price data and the unit of each series are presented in the appendix. If data are available at a weekly or daily frequency, the latest available price within a month is taken for the return calculation. The lengths of the time series for the volatility calculations are different for different commodities, starting with the first available data for each commodity, but not earlier than January 1990. This is done even if the time series used in the VAR model starts at a later point in time due to data unavailability of other commodities in that group.

The mean process of the returns is modelled either as an AR(12) or AR(1) process, depending on the seasonality of the commodity prices.[8] In case of an

AR(1) mean process, Ljung-Box tests with lags 10, 15, and 20 are applied and indicate in all cases that residuals are free of autocorrelation.

The error distribution used for the GARCH estimations is student-t. The resulting GARCH models lead to a stationary volatility process for all selected commodities ($\alpha+\beta<1$). Finally, the monthly volatility estimates resulting from the GARCH are annualized by multiplying them with $\sqrt{12}$. Table 3.1 summarizes the GARCH estimations for the different commodities and provides some descriptive statistics for the resulting volatilities.

In order to analyze volatility spillovers, we employ the econometric framework of vector autoregressive (VAR) models, as pioneered by Sims (1980), by including lagged volatilities of all the commodities in a system as explanatory variables. The VAR approach provides specific tools for the analysis of spillovers, in particular the impulse-response function, which shows how a volatility shock in a certain commodity is transmitted through the whole system and potentially affects the volatilities of other commodities. We estimate a separate VAR for each of the commodity groups and include a number of additional exogenous potential drivers of price volatility. For details on this latter aspect, see Brümmer et al. (2014).

In the following, we describe the detailed findings for agricultural price volatility group by group.

Table 3.1 Description of annualized GARCH (1,1) volatility estimations

Commod.	Group	Region	Start	End	Mean process	Mean	SD	Min.	Max.
Wheat (soft)	1	US	Feb. 1990	Dec. 2012	AR(12)	33.14%	8.17%	22.99%	58.07%
Corn	1	US	Feb. 1990	Dec. 2012	AR(12)	28.72%	11.71%	17.72%	79.69%
Bioethanol	1	US	Feb. 1990	Dec. 2012	AR(1)	26.72%	9.16%	13.67%	49.85%
Ammonia	1	US	Oct. 1991	Dec. 2012	AR(1)	53.12%	25.37%	36.88%	251.47%
Soybean	2	US	Feb. 1990	Dec. 2012	AR(1)	26.22%	9.43%	14.96%	70.95%
Rapeseed	2	Europe	Feb. 1990	Dec. 2012	AR(1)	18.18%	2.97%	14.34%	30.62%
Palm oil	3	Malaysia	Feb. 1990	Dec. 2012	AR(1)	23.48%	6.11%	17.11%	54.91%
Soybean oil	3	Argentina	Dec. 1995	Dec. 2012	AR(1)	28.34%	3.70%	22.10%	42.51%
Rapeseed oil	3	Northwest Europe	Oct. 1995	Dec. 2012	AR(12)	22.58%	9.15%	15.63%	67.73%
Sunflower oil	3	Netherlands	Feb. 1990	Dec. 2012	AR(12)	22.04%	4.73%	18.71%	64.44%
Biodiesel	3	Germany	Aug. 2002	Dec. 2012	AR(1)	11.59%	2.19%	7.67%	15.62%
Sugar (raw)	4	World	Feb. 1990	Dec. 2012	AR(12)	30.17%	7.83%	19.52%	62.12%
Bioethanol	4	Brazil	Dec. 2002	Dec. 2012	AR(12)	36.56%	27.94%	0.05%	140.93%
Pork	5	Germany	Feb. 1990	Dec. 2012	AR(12)	24.25%	8.93%	14.34%	73.22%
Soybean meal	5	Europe	Feb. 1990	Dec. 2012	AR(1)	19.14%	4.66%	13.86%	45.28%
Corn	5	Europe	Mar. 2000	Dec. 2012	AR(12)	26.18%	7.7%	20.64%	61.6%

Source: Own estimates.

4 Volatility spillovers across commodity markets

4.1 Group 1: grains

Grains: Figure 3.1 shows the estimated volatility for four commodities in the grain group. The fertilizer (ammonia) shows the most volatile price development during the estimated period. For all four products in this group, we observe that the own lagged volatility is significant with the expected positive sign in the VAR model illustrating the volatility persistence inherent to the GARCH model. For wheat and corn, no lagged volatility of any other product is significant, i.e., there is no indication of a volatility spillover from any of the markets to the wheat or corn markets. Bioethanol and ammonia show a different picture. There are some significant coefficients for the lagged volatilities of other markets. However, the specific effects are difficult to judge because the coefficients have different signs and more than one other market is involved. We therefore have to study the dynamics of the whole system. The impulse-response functions are very instructive in this respect. They are presented in Figure 3.2. The reactions of wheat and corn to volatility shocks confirm the lack of volatility spillovers. The only significant effect is a shock in the own volatility. For bioethanol, we observe a significant volatility increase due to a volatility shock in the wheat market. However, the effect is not immediate but materializes with some time lag due to system effects. For ammonia, we observe an immediate volatility increasing effect of a shock in the corn market.

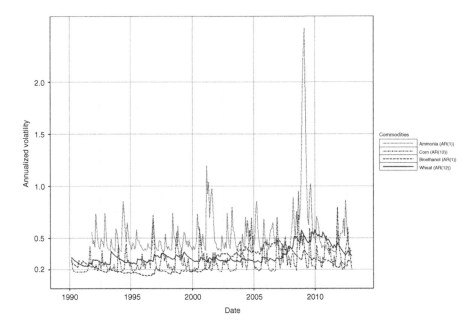

Figure 3.1 GARCH (1,1) volatility estimation for group 1: wheat, corn, ammonia, and bioethanol.

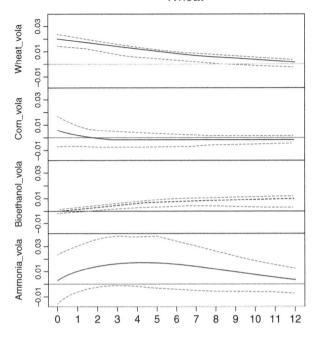

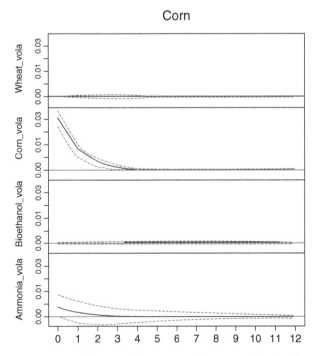

Figure 3.2 Impulse-response functions for group 1 (wheat, corn, bioethanol, ammonia).

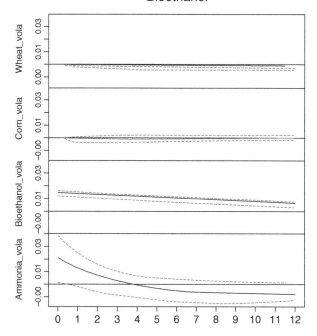

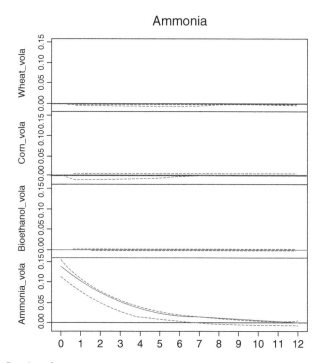

Figure 3.2 Continued

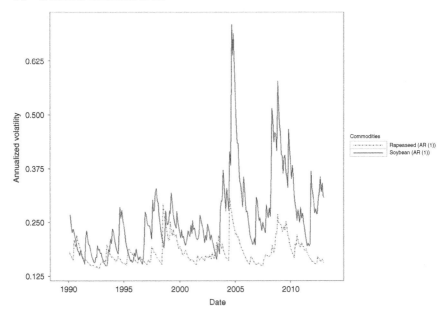

Figure 3.3 GARCH (1,1) volatility estimation for group 2: rapeseed and soybean.

4.2 Group 2: oilseeds

Oilseeds: Figure 3.3 shows the estimated volatility for the two commodities in the oilseeds group. The rapeseed price shows increased volatility after 2003. The dynamic effects of volatility shocks in this group are rather straightforward. There is volatility persistence for both soybeans and rapeseeds, a lagged impact of rapeseed volatility on the volatility of soybeans and vice versa, and a contemporaneous effect. The relative sizes of soybean and rapeseed markets should imply a leading position of the former in volatility spillovers. Hence, we attribute the contemporaneous effects to a shock in the soybean market for the impulse-response analysis in Figure 3.4. As the impulse-response functions show, there are significant spillover effects in both directions. This statement holds even with changed ordering.

4.3 Group 3: vegetable oils

Vegetable oils: Figure 3.5 shows the estimated volatility for five commodities in the vegetable oil group, with remarkably different volatility patterns for the commodities. The vegetable oils group has the most complicated dynamic structure of all groups. For each of the five products, there is at least one lagged volatility of another product that shows a statistically significant impact. The impulse-response functions are shown in Figure 3.6. Because of some high contemporaneous correlations in the residuals, the ordering of the markets is particularly important. The results in Figure 3.6 are based on the

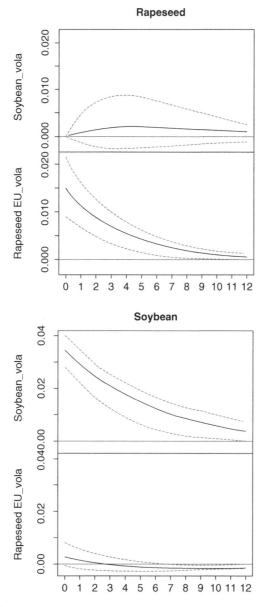

Figure 3.4 Impulse-response functions for group 2 (soybean and rapeseed).

following ordering of contemporaneous effects: palm oil, soybean oil, rapeseed oil, sunflower oil, and biodiesel. The first product in this list (palm oil) affects all other products contemporaneously, but not vice versa. The second product (soybean oil) affects rapeseed oil, sunflower oil, and biodiesel but is not affected by them, etc.

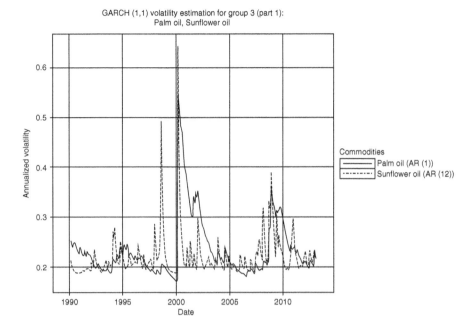

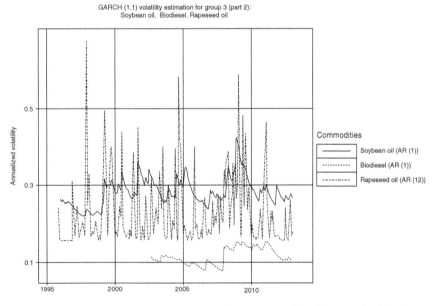

Figure 3.5 GARCH (1,1) volatility estimation for group 3: palm oil, rapeseed oil, biodiesel, soybean oil, sunflower oil.

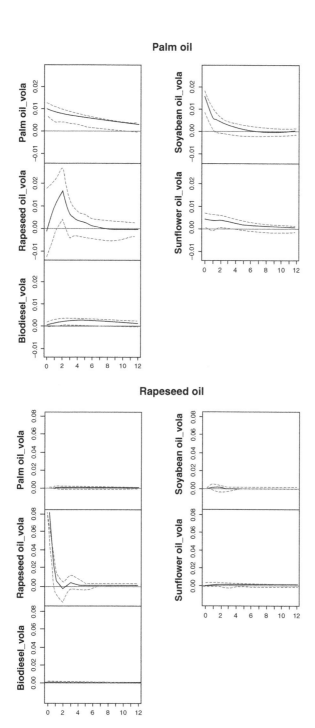

Figure 3.6 Impulse-response functions for group 3 (palm oil, rapeseed oil, biodiesel, soybean oil, sunflower oil).

Biodiesel

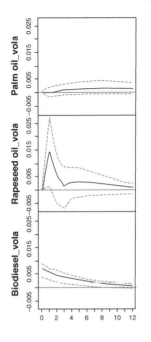
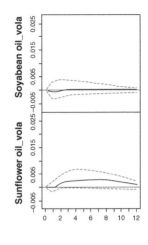

Soybean oil

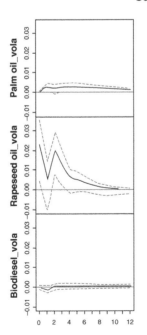
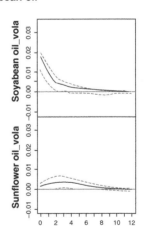

Figure 3.6 Continued

Sunflower oil

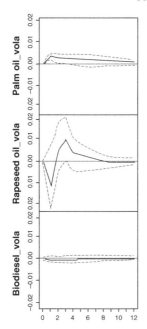

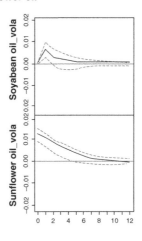

Figure 3.6 Continued

According to the impulse responses, there are significant effects of palm oil volatility on all other products. However, the impact on rapeseed oil and biodiesel price volatility is not immediate but shows a delay of two months. A shock in soybean oil volatility significantly increases the volatilities of sunflower oil and rapeseed oil. Sunflower oil has an impact on rapeseed oil. In summary, our results show a very high interconnectedness between the five products in terms of volatility spillovers.

4.4 Group 4: sugar

Sugar: Figure 3.7 shows the estimated volatility for two commodities in the sugar group. The dynamic structure of the resulting VAR model is very simple for the group with sugar and bioethanol. There is persistence in both volatilities and no spillover, neither via lagged volatilities nor via a contemporaneous correlation of the residuals. This observation is fully confirmed by the impulse-response functions as provided in Figure 3.8.

4.5 Group 5: meats

Meat: Figure 3.9 shows the estimated volatility for three commodities in the meat group. Different volatility patterns for prices can be recognized among

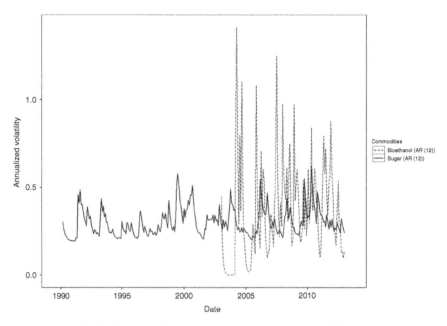

Figure 3.7 GARCH (1,1) volatility estimation for group 4: sugar and bioethanol.

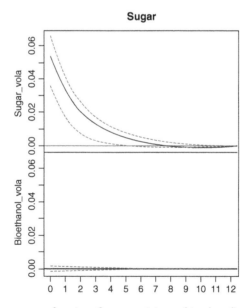

Figure 3.8 Impulse-response functions for group 4 (sugar, bioethanol).

Bioethanol

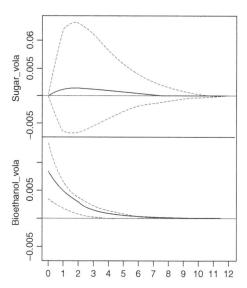

Figure 3.8 Continued

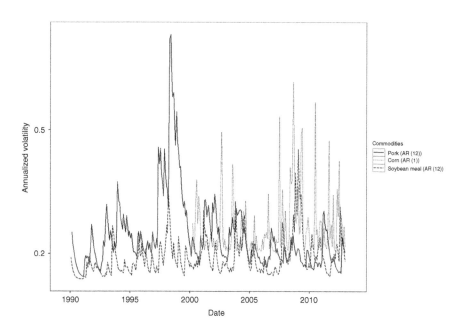

Figure 3.9 GARCH (1,1) volatility estimation for group 5: meat (pork), corn, soybean meal.

meat as output and corn and soybean meal as input. An interesting question for this group is whether volatility in pork prices is affected by volatilities in the major feeds soybean meal and corn. The answer given by our VAR model is that no significant spillovers exist. This result is confirmed by the impulse-response functions (Figure 3.10). There are spillovers in both directions, from soybean meal to corn and from corn to soybean meal.

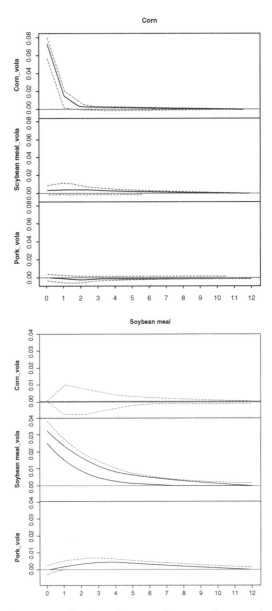

Figure 3.10 Impulse-response functions for group 5 (corn, soybean meal, pork).

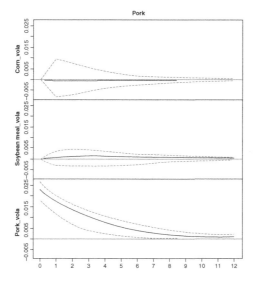

Figure 3.10 Continued

5 High- and low-frequency components of price volatility

This section focuses on models based on realized volatility with an ex-post analysis perspective in order to investigate alternative methods for questioning what has driven the agricultural price volatility. Section 2 summarized the different estimation methods using GARCH models. In this section, we focus on the GARCH-MIDAS model of Engle et al. (2013), in order to take into consideration high- and low-frequency components of volatility. The mixed data sampling (MIDAS) filtering of Ghysels et al. (2005) is used to model the unconditional variance in this special type of GARCH model, which basically allows for combining the information provided by high-frequency (e.g., daily) prices and low-frequency (e.g., monthly) drivers. The overall interest for using the GARCH-MIDAS model comes from its potential to: (i) reduce the trade-off between the accuracy of the volatility measurement provided by the high-frequency data on prices and the necessity to match it with low-frequency variables and avoid loss of efficiency due to multistep procedures; (ii) analyze the causal relationship between price volatility and its determinants in a dynamic perspective, going beyond the usual contemporary analysis;[9] (iii) enable ranking the importance of the drivers of price volatility, individuating which are the most sensible key drivers to be addressed by the policy makers. In order to utilize and test those benefits, we consider the grains (wheat and corn) and oilseeds (soybean) markets among the markets listed in section 3 over the period 1986–2012.

According to the GARCH-MIDAS model, the unexpected returns can be presented as:

$$r_{i,t} = \mu + \sqrt{\tau_t \, g_{i,t}} \varepsilon_{i,t}, \quad \forall i = 1,...,N_t \tag{1}$$

where $r_{i,t}$ is the log return on day i during month/quarter/year t ($i = 1,\ldots, N_t$; N_t is the number of days in period t); μ is the conditional expectation given information at day ($i - 1$) of any arbitrary period t; and the conditional distribution of the errors is assumed to be normal with zero mean and unit variance. Volatility is decomposed into two separate components as in the tradition of the component GARCH models introduced by Engle and Lee (1999). Namely, $g_{i,t}$ characterizes daily fluctuations associated with transitory or short-lived effects of volatility, while the secular or low-frequency component τ_t represents the unconditional volatility and it is aimed to capture slowly varying deterministic conditions in the economy.

In the GARCH-MIDAS model, the $g_{i,t}$ component is assumed to be a (daily) GARCH (1,1) process, namely:

$$g_{i,t} = (1 - \alpha - \beta) + \alpha \frac{(r_{i-1,t} - \mu)^2}{\tau_t} + \beta g_{i-1,t} \tag{2}$$

where $\alpha > 0$, $\beta > 0$ and $\alpha + \beta < 1$.

The MIDAS regression is facilitated to model the low-frequency τ_t component in (1). It is the key element for the analysis as it allows for using data sampled at different frequencies:

$$\tau_t = m + \theta \sum_{k=1}^{K} \varphi_k(\omega_1, \omega_2) RV_{t-k} \tag{3}$$

where RV_t is the fixed time span realized volatility at time t calculated by the square sum over high-frequency index i of log returns and $\varphi_k()$ is the function defining the weighting scheme of MIDAS filters. Engle et al. (2013) proposed two different functions for the weighting scheme: the *Beta* and the *exponentially weighted* lag structures. Following Joyeux and Girardin (2013) and Engle et al. (2013), who showed that they yield similar results, we decided to use the Beta lag structure due to its flexibility to accommodate various lag structures:

$$\varphi_k(\omega_1, \omega_2) = \frac{(k/K)^{\omega_1 - 1}(1 - k/K)^{\omega_2 - 1}}{\sum_{j=0}^{K}(j/K)^{\omega_1 - 1}(1 - j/K)^{\omega_2 - 1}} \tag{4}$$

Different combinations of ω_1 and ω_2 values in (4) can accommodate monotonically increasing, monotonically decreasing, and also unimodal hump–shaped weighting schemes with nonnegative weights resulting in positive estimates of volatility.[10] In this study, we use $\omega_1 = 1$ and $\omega_2 > 1$ in order to have a monotonically decreasing pattern over the lags, which is typical of volatility filters.

It is worth emphasizing that the GARCH-MIDAS model presented in (1)–(4) has a fixed parameter space, which makes it more parsimonious compared to other component volatility models. This feature is exploited to compare different models with various time spans t (e.g., month, quarter, annual) and different number of lags K. In particular, we choose the time period t by comparing the values of log-likelihood functions and, subsequently, define the optimum number of lags K through the minimization of the Bayesian information criteria (BIC). For estimating the parameters, we use the conventional quasi-maximum likelihood estimation (QMLE) method.

In order to calculate realized volatility, we use daily settlement prices of the first nearby futures contracts traded at the Chicago Board of Trade (CBOT) from 1 January 1986 to 31 December 2012 for calculating the returns. We are interested in using futures prices instead of spot prices since: (i) they are standardized and promote accuracy; (ii) they perform as a risk-transfer tool for hedgers and speculators; (iii) they provide information to the market over the price formation; and (iv) they are sampled at high frequency (Hernandez and Torero, 2010). In order to build a unique series for the futures prices and combine different contracts with a limited life span, we conduct some data processing. First of all, we take the nearest contract up to the first day of its maturity month and then we roll over to the next contract (e.g., Gilbert and Morgan, 2010; Gutierrez, 2012) in order to avoid the Samuelson effect supporting that the price volatility increases as the contract approaches its delivery date (Samuelson, 1965). Moreover, as suggested by Ghysels et al. (2006), we take into consideration the effect of seasonality induced by the harvest cycles during a calendar year[11] by seasonally adjusting the monthly and quarterly RV (realized volatility) series before fitting MIDAS regression. We remove the periodic pattern using a multiplicative-type of adjustment via regression on monthly/ quarterly dummies.

As mentioned before, building a GARCH-MIDAS model requires finding the optimum time span t and the MIDAS lag years K that are used in the specification of the low-frequency component τ. Our estimations lead us to monthly specification, since it always outperforms the quarterly and annual representations of τ. Following to the time span selection, we use the BIC criteria to define the lag number. Figure 3.11 displays the estimated lag weights of the GARCH-MIDAS model with monthly RV for one (k = 12) to three (k = 36) MIDAS lag years. Figure 3.11 shows that the optimal weights decay to zero around 20 months of lags for wheat and soybean, regardless if we select two or three years of MIDAS lags. The model with a one-year MIDAS lag is not proper for exploiting all the information provided by the past values of RV, since the weights do not converge to zero. Corn shows a different pattern, where the optimal weights decay to zero with both one and two years of MIDAS lags while the model with three years of MIDAS lags does not converge to zero. Nevertheless, the BIC criteria for the three crops suggest that two years of MIDAS lags achieves the best fit, implying that the best representation is given by the model with t = month and k = 24.

After defining t and k, we use the QMLE method to estimate parameters. For an overall view, the annualized volatility components of the GARCH-MIDAS models are displayed for all crops in Figure 3.12. It is observed that the MIDAS

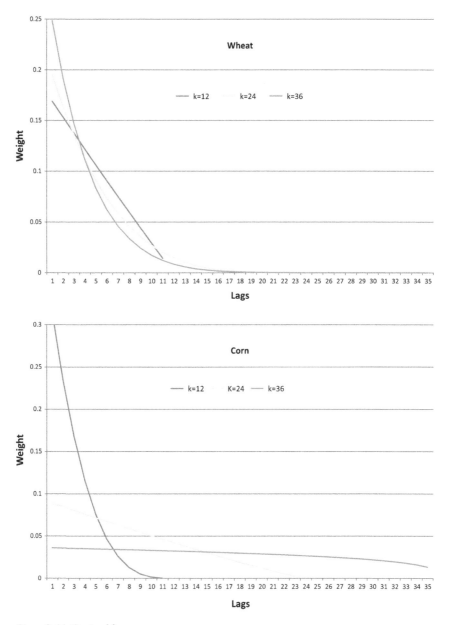

Figure 3.11 Optimal lag structures.

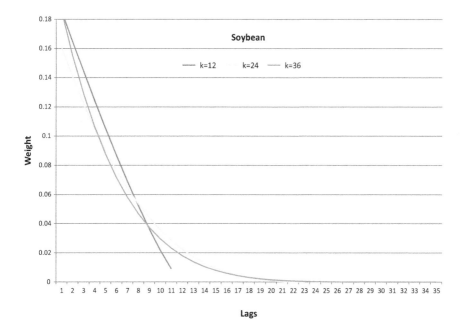

Figure 3.11 Continued

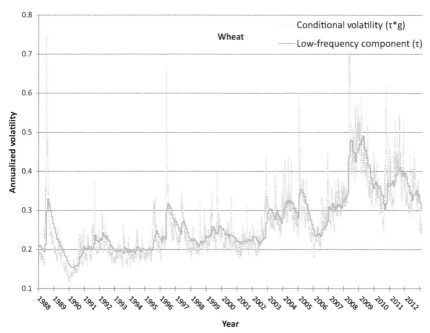

Figure 3.12 Conditional volatility and its low-frequency component for wheat, corn, and soybean.

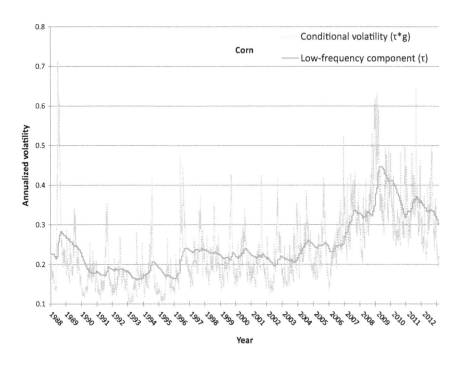

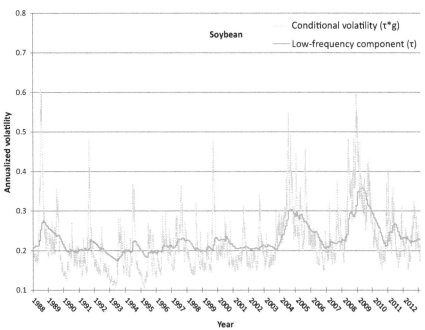

Figure 3.12 Continued

filter applied to the realized volatility allows for extracting a τ component, which is smoother than the total price volatility as it was expected. Nevertheless, the τ component still follows the path of the total volatility and increases substantially in the last decade, especially for wheat and corn.

The parameter estimates of the GARCH-MIDAS model with realized volatility are presented in Table 3.2. For each crop, the first row of the parameters indicates the estimates and the second row shows the robust t-statistics computed by Bollerslev and Wooldridge (1992) standard errors. All of the statistically significant estimates respect the expected sign. Especially, the estimates of θ for all crops are significant and positive, indicating that the information contained in the last two years of RV contributes to explain the low-frequency component of the price volatility. Not surprisingly, the higher the level of past RV, the higher the level of τ. We also estimate a restricted specification of equation (4) with $\theta = 0$ which reduces the GARCH-MIDAS model to a GARCH (1,1) model with constant unconditional variance (Conrad et al., 2012). The GARCH (1,1) model is nested in the GARCH-MIDAS specification, therefore the comparison of the two models is straightforward. The seventh column of Table 3.2 gives the value of the log likelihood function (LLF) and below the BIC while the last column presents the value of the LLF of the GARCH (1,1) and below the chi-square test statistic of the log likelihood ratio test with respect to the GARCH-MIDAS model. According to this test statistic, the GARCH-MIDAS models outperform the standard GARCH (1,1) model. This result supports that a time-varying unconditional variance model accommodates better the analysis of historical agricultural price volatility. It is also worth noting that while the sum of α and β is always close to one in the GARCH model, in the GARCH-MIDAS model the sum is significantly lower, indicating a lower persistence in the low-frequency volatility component. This result is in line with other works based on component models such as Engle and Rangel (2008) and Engle et al. (2013). It can be concluded that modeling the agricultural price volatility as the product of high- and low-frequency components could be further explored. In this respect, an additional effort has already been made by Donmez and Magrini (2013), who studied the

Table 3.2 The GARCH-MIDAS model with realized volatility for the period 1986–2012

Crop	μ	α	β	m	θ	ω_2	LLF/BIC	GARCH (1,1)
Wheat	−0.0004	0.0667	0.8779	0.0000	0.0002	4.9853	17055.58	17038.1888
	−2.19	7.37	38.53	2.29	9.85	1.82	−5.42	34.77
Corn	−0.0002	0.0858	0.8857	0.0000	0.0002	2.1433	17935.83	17916.9234
	−1.39	8.44	57.69	1.08	5.68	2.91	−5.69	37.82
Soybean	0.0000	0.0722	0.9027	0.0001	0.0001	4.0278	18228.01	18224.6246
	0.07	8.70	66.21	2.36	2.98	8.67	−5.79	6.76

Note: The 5% critical value for the chi-square with two degrees of freedom is equal to 5.99.

effect of potential drivers on the low-frequency component of volatility and found that the global business cycle, weather shocks, and the degree of market financialization are the most important determinants.

6 Discussion

The after-crisis period (starting from the second quarter of 2008) is generally characterized by high price volatility for many agricultural commodities. However, in comparison to the 1970s, recent volatility spikes remain well below their historical peaks for most of the commodities. Gilbert and Morgan (2010) conclude that the volatility for agricultural products, with the exception of rice, is lower over the past two decades than in the 1970s and 1980s, and although volatility is high over the 2007–2009 period for many foodstuffs, in the case of groundnut oil, soybeans, and soybean oil, their conditional variances increase significantly. Despite no increasing tendency toward food volatility during recent years, volatility of the main grains does increase. Gilbert and Prakash in Prakash (2011) argue that the periods of extreme volatility in agricultural markets are seldom. They distinguish the 1973–1974 episode as a "crisis" with extreme high price levels and volatility on commodity markets, whereas the recent 2006–2007 episode – despite showing relative high price levels and volatility – is not comparable in size and effects (about five million malnutrition-related deaths) to the former one. Huchet-Bourdon (2011) finds from the analysis of ten products (1957–2010) that agricultural price volatility is on average low for beef and sugar. She also arrives at the conclusion that volatility is higher in the last decade than in the 1990s but not higher than in the 1970s. However, same as Gilbert and Morgan (2010), she finds that recent volatility is higher than in the 1970s only for cereals. The recent literature on the analysis of the volatility of major crops (maize, rice, wheat, and soybean) shows that the distinction between the period of lower volatility before 2006–2007 and higher volatility after that until today is still recognizable (for instance, Geman and Ott, 2014, p. 37). However, the latest OECD-FAO agricultural outlook for the period 2014–2023 forecasts a reduction in the risk of volatility because of the recovery in the stock levels (OECD-FAO, 2014).

Notes

1   The only alternative concept that is used in some papers is the coefficient of variation; however, this measure contains the standard deviation in the numerator.
2   The approach dates back to the seminal work by Engle (1982) and Bollerslev (1986). A comprehensive review of the most important ARCH and GARCH variants can be found in Bollerslev et al. (1994).
3   An early example of a model that treats volatility itself as stochastic is Clark (1973). A very popular stochastic volatility model is the one by Heston (1993). For a review paper that covers both GARCH models and stochastic volatility models see Andersen et al. (2010).

4 This approach was first introduced and applied by French et al. (1987), Schwert (1989, 1990a, 1990b), and Schwert and Seguin (1990). It was later formalized by Andersen and Bollerslev (1998).

5 See Lo and MacKinlay (1988) for an analysis of the scaling of volatility in the stock market.

6 German pork prices have a leading role in European pig price formation, in particular for EU export prices (Serra et al., 2006).

7 See Bollerslev (1986).

8 The results are robust against controlling for seasonality by using monthly dummy variables in the volatility estimation model.

9 The mixtures of different frequencies were provided by the other models, such as Roache (2010) and Karali and Power (2013), which exploit the Spline-GARCH model by Engle and Rangel (2008). Their estimation uses a two-step procedure averaging daily/monthly data at monthly/annual level, generally leading to information loss, and the unconditional variance is modelled in a deterministic and nonparametric manner, preventing the possibility to incorporate directly the potential drivers (Ghysels and Wang, 2011). Moreover, not taking into consideration the impact of the lags of the drivers on price volatility imposes exclusively a contemporary relationship which is hardly the case in the agricultural commodity markets.

10 See Ghysels et al. (2007) for a broad discussion on the different patterns that can be obtained through Beta lags.

11 The presence of seasonality in the agricultural commodity price volatility has been largely acknowledged by the literature. For example, see Piot-Lepetit and M'Barek (2011) and Karali and Power (2013).

References

Andersen, T.G., and Bollerslev, T. (1998). Answering the skeptics: Yes, standard volatility models do provide accurate forecasts. *International Economic Review, 39*(4), 885–905.

Andersen, T.G., Bollerslev, T., and Diebold, F.X. (2010). Parametric and nonparametric volatility measurement. In Y. Aït-Sahalia and L.P. Hansen (Eds.), *Handbook of financial econometrics* (pp. 67–137). Amsterdam: North-Holland.

Bakshi, G., Kapadia, N., and Madan, D. (2003). Stock return characteristics, skew laws, and the differential pricing of individual equity options. *The Review of Financial Studies, 16*(1), 101–143.

Black, F. (1976). The pricing of commodity contracts. *Journal of Financial Economics, 3*, 167–179.

Bollerslev, T. (1986). Generalized autoregressive conditional heteroskedasticity. *Journal of Econometrics, 31*, 307–327.

Bollerslev, T., Engle, R.F., and Nelson, D.B. (1994). ARCH models. In R. F. Engle and D. McFadden (Eds.), *Handbook of econometrics*, Vol. IV (pp. 2959–3038). Amsterdam: North-Holland.

Bollerslev, T., and Wooldridge, J. (1992). Quasi-maximum likelihood estimation and inference in dynamic models with time-varying covariances. *Econometric Reviews, 11*, 143–172.

Britten-Jones, M., and Neuberger, A. (2000). Option prices, implied price processes, and stochastic volatility. *The Journal of Finance, 55*(2), 839–866.

Brümmer, B., Korn, O., Schlüßler, K., and Jamali Jaghdani, T. (2014). Volatility analysis: Causation impacts in retrospect (2007–2011) and preparing for the future (p. 41). ULYSSES Project, EU 7th Framework Programme, Project 312182 KBBE.2012.1.4–05, Göttingen.

Busse, S., Brümmer, B., and Ihle, R. (2012). Price formation in the German biodiesel supply chain: A Markov-switching vector error-correction modeling approach. *Agricultural Economics, 43*(5), 545–560.

Clark, P.K. (1973). A subordinated stochastic process model with finite variance for specula-tive prices. *Econometrica, 41*(1), 135–155.

Conrad, C., Loch, K., and Rittler, D. (2012). On the macroeconomic determinants of the long-term oil-stock correlation. University of Heidelberg, Department of Economics, Discussion Paper No. 525.

Donmez, A., and Magrini, E. (2013). Agricultural commodity price volatility and its mac-roeconomic determinants: A GARCH-MIDAS approach (p. 38). Working Paper 5, ULYSSES project, EU 7th Framework Programme, Project 312182 KBBE.2012.1.4–05.

Engle, R.F. (1982). Autoregressive conditional heteroscedasticity with estimates of the vari-ance of United Kingdom inflation. *Econometrica, 50*(4), 987–1007.

Engle, R.F., Ghysels, E., and Sohn, B. (2013). Stock market volatility and macroeconomic fundamentals. *The Review of Economics and Statistics, 95*(3), 776–797.

Engle, R.F., and Lee, G. (1999). A permanent and transitory component model of stock return volatility. In R. F. Engle and H. White (Eds.), *Cointegration, causality, and forecasting: A festschrift in honor of Clive W.J. Granger* (pp. 475–497). Oxford, UK: Oxford University Press.

Engle, R.F., and Rangel, J.G. (2008). The Spline-GARCH Model for low-frequency vola-tility and its global macroeconomic causes. *Review of Financial Studies, 21*(3), 1187–1222.

French, K.R., Schwert, G.W., and Stambaugh, R.F. (1987). Expected stock returns and vol-atility. *Journal of Financial Economics, 19*, 3–29.

Geman, H., and Ott, H. (2014). A re-examination of food price volatility (No. 6). ULYSSES project, EU 7th Framework Programme, Project 312182 KBBE.2012.1.4–05.

Ghysels, E., Santa-Clara, P., and Valkanov, R. (2005). There is a risk-return trade-off after all. *Journal of Financial Economics, 76*, 509–548.

Ghysels, E., Santa-Clara, P., and Valkanov, R. (2006). Predicting volatility: Getting the most out of return data sampled at different frequencies. *Journal of Econometrics, 131*, 59–95.

Ghysels, E., Sinko, A., and Valkanov, R. (2007). MIDAS regression: Further results and new directions. *Econometric Reviews, 26*, 53–90.

Ghysels, E., and Wang, F. (2011). Statistical inference for volatility component models. UNC discussion paper.

Gilbert, C.L., and Morgan, C.W. (2010). Food price volatility. *Philosophical Transactions of the Royal Society B, 365*, 3023–3034. doi:10.1098/rstb.2010.0139

Goodwin, B.K., and Schroeder, T.C. (1991). Price dynamics in international wheat markets. *Canadian Journal of Agricultural Economics, 39*, 237–254.

Gutierrez, L. (2012). Speculative bubbles in agricultural commodity markets. *European Review of Agricultural Economics, 40*(2), 217–238.

Hernandez, M., and Torero, M. (2010). Examining the dynamic relationship between spot and future prices of agricultural commodities. International Food Policy Research Insti-tute (IFPRI), Discussion Paper No. 988.

Heston, S.L. (1993). A closed-form solution for options with stochastic volatility with appli-cations to bond and currency options. *The Review of Financial Studies, 6*(2), 327–343.

Huchet-Bourdon, M. (2011). Agricultural commodity price volatility – Papers – OECD iLibrary (No. 52). Paris. doi:10.1787/18156797

Joyeux, R., and Girardin, E. (2013). Macro fundamentals as a source of stock market vola-tility in China: A GARCH-MIDAS approach. *Economic Modelling*, forthcoming, available online.

Karali, B., and Power, G.J. (2013). Short- and long-run determinants of commodity price volatility. *American Journal of Agricultural Economics, 95*(3), 724–738.

Lo, A.W., and MacKinlay, A.C. (1988). Stock market prices do not follow random walks: Evidence from a simple specification test. *The Review of Financial Studies, 1*(1), 41–66.

OECD-FAO. (2014). *OECD-FAO agricultural outlook 2014.* Paris: OECD Publishing.

Piesse, J., and Thirtle, C. (2009). Three bubbles and a panic: An explanatory review of recent food commodity price events. *Food Policy, 34*(2), 119–129.

Piot-Lepetit, I., and M'Barek, R. (2011). *Methods to analyse agricultural commodity price volatility.* New York: Springer.

Poon, S.-H., and Granger, C.W.J. (2003). Forecasting volatility in financial markets: A review. *Journal of Economic Literature, 41*(2), 478–539.

Prakash, A. (Ed.) (2011). *Safeguarding food security in volatile global markets* (1st ed.). Rome, Italy: Food and Agriculture Organization of the United Nations (FAO).

Roache, S.K. (2010). What explains the rise in food price volatility? International Monetary Fund (IMF) Working Papers 10/129. Washington DC: International Monetary Fund.

Samuelson, P. (1965). Proof that properly anticipated prices fluctuate randomly. *Industrial Management Review, 6*, 41–49.

Schwert, G.W. (1989). Why does stock market volatility change over time ? *The Journal of Finance, 44*(5), 1115–1153.

Schwert, G.W. (1990a). Stock market volatility. *Financial Analysts Journal, 46*, 23–34.

Schwert, G.W. (1990b). Stock volatility and the crash of '87. *The Review of Financial Studies, 3*(1), 76–102.

Schwert, G.W., and Seguin, P.J. (1990). Heteroskedasticity in stock returns. *The Journal of Finance, 45*(4), 1129–1155.

Serra, T., Gil, J.M., and Goodwin, B.K. (2006). Local polynomial fitting and spatial price relationships: Price transmission in EU pork markets. *European Review of Agricultural Economics, 33*(3), 415–436.

Sims, C. (1980). Macroeconomics and reality. *Econometrica, 48*(1), 1–48.

Appendix: The data source of the selected commodities prices and their units

Commodity	Group	Data source	Datatstream Code	Unit
Wheat (soft)	1	Datastream	WHEATSF	US cent/bu
Corn	1	Datastream	CORNUS2	US cent/bu
Bioethanol	1	Datastream	USNEETHP	US$/gallon
Ammonia	1	Datastream	AMMUSGO	US$/Ton
Soybean – No 1 Yellow	2	Datastream	SOYBEAN	US cent/bu
Rapeseed	2	Alfred C. Toepfer International	–	US$/Ton
Palm oil	3	Datastream	HWWIPO$	US$/Ton
Rapeseed oil	3	Datastream	RPOLDNE	Euro/Ton
Soybean oil	3	Datastream	ARGSBOI	US$/Ton
Sunflower seed oil	3	Datastream	HWWISO$	US$/Ton
Biodiesel	3	Agrarmarkt Informations- Gesellschaft mbH	–	Euro cent/lit
Sugar (raw)	4	Datastream	WSUGDLY	US cent/lb
Bioethanol	4	Centro de Estudos Avançados em Economia Aplicada (CEPEA)	–	US$/lit
Pork	5	Marktbericht der Agrar Markt Austria	–	Euro/100 kg
Soybean meal	5	Alfred C. Toepfer International	–	US$/Ton
Corn	5	Alfred C. Toepfer International	–	US$/Ton

4 Medium-term drivers of food markets' variability and uncertainty

Sergio René Araujo Enciso, María Blanco, Marco Artavia, Fabien Ramos, Robert M'Barek, Benjamin Van Doorslaer, Lucian Stanca and Ayça Dönmez

1 Introduction

The evolution of agri-food prices in the last decade has led to increasing concerns about the development of agricultural markets, with many forward-looking studies expecting future price levels above the historical trends and higher price variability (von Lampe et al., 2014; OECD-FAO, 2013). From global food security and farm income perspectives, it is crucial to understand how different drivers of change and their underlying uncertainties could shape future agri-food markets.

Different factors affecting the development of agricultural commodity prices work together and could lead to large price fluctuations, as observed during the food crisis in 2006–2008. Amongst those drivers, the literature mentions harvest failures, exports restrictions, biofuels policies, climate change, declining stocks, speculation, low economic growth, currencies exchange rates, population growth, and diet changes, among others (see Chapter 3 and Brümmer et al., 2013; Headey and Fan, 2008; Trostle, 2008; Baffes and Haniotis, 2010; Naylor and Falcon, 2010; FAO, 2009; FAO et al., 2011; Gilbert, 2010). Broadly speaking, these drivers can be classified into two major groups: socioeconomic (e.g., macroeconomic and socio-demographic indicators, including policies) and biophysical (e.g., climate change, land use, pressure on natural resources, etc.). Previous studies, such as those quoted above, have addressed the impact of several drivers mostly based on econometric approaches. However, the analysis of the potential development of agri-food systems cannot depend on the observed past only, but has to take into account also different assumptions on policies and the economic agents' view of the future. A plausible way to incorporate also future expectations on specific factors is by employing agro-economic models.

Agroeconomic models cover a relatively large number of variables affecting agri-food markets while capturing the complexity of the relations between them. In addition, these models include a forward-looking perspective on agricultural markets called "baseline". The baseline comprises a set of assumptions based on the consensus of different market experts, which feeds the economic models, such that the result is a coherent projection of the market's development for the forthcoming years. The main purpose of agroeconomic models, in addition to the projection (baseline), is the usage for scenario analysis. The interest is to observe the changes with respect to a reference scenario or "baseline" when the assumptions are different. The scenarios can include a modification of one or different variables feeding the model and can be deterministic or stochastic.

With a view to contribute to the current debate about the likely development of price level and variability on agri-food markets in the medium-term (10 to 15 years), we examine in this chapter the main drivers and their associated uncertainties. For this purpose, we implement two approaches:

- The analysis of socioeconomic and policy drivers, together with yield fluctuations, by means of a partial stochastic approach: In a baseline scenario for 2023, we consider the main sources of uncertainty affecting the agri-food markets. We use the 2013 version of the AGLINK-COSIMO model as employed for the European Commission's baseline.
- The analysis of climate change drivers by means of a bioeconomic assessment: We explore the consequences of climate change scenarios on agricultural markets at a highly disaggregated spatial scale combining the biophysical modelling platform BioMA and the agroeconomic model CAPRI.

Both analyses are complementary. On the one hand, the partial stochastic analysis considers the main sources of systematic uncertainty around the macroeconomic market drivers, oil price, and yield. On the other hand, the scenario analysis with CAPRI-BioMA explores how the EU and world agri-food markets could be affected by climate change toward the year 2030, when climate experts expect tangible impacts. Several scenarios of crop yield developments under climate change are included in the analysis, taking into account also the degree of carbon fertilization. The use of both types of analyses allows us to have a broader understanding of potential drivers of price variability in the future.

2 Impact of macroeconomic and yield uncertainty on global prices

Among the socioeconomic drivers affecting price volatility, macroeconomic indicators and the oil price are often identified as having an important impact (Artavia et al., 2014; Brümmer et al., 2013; Abbott and Borot de Battisti, 2011; Baffes and Haniotis, 2010; Magrini and Donmez, 2013; Swinnen and Squicciarini, 2012; Tangermann, 2011). The vast literature has a strong focus on time series analysis using different types of autoregressive models. However, the interactions among drivers, market fundamentals, and policy are only partly addressed. Research work by Gohin and Chantret (2010) using a computable general equilibrium (CGE) seeks to account for the macroeconomic linkages together with oil price shocks.

Aiming at complementing previous research, we address in a comprehensive way different sources of macroeconomic, oil price, and yield uncertainties, which might have an impact on the development of agri-food markets. For this purpose, we employ the stochastic version of AGLINK-COSIMO, a multi-region, recursive-dynamic partial equilibrium model. This approach has been implemented in previous publications, mainly the yearly agricultural outlooks published by DG Agriculture and Rural Development and OECD-FAO (EC, 2012, 2013, 2014; OECD-FAO, 2013, 2014). The methodology for estimating the uncertainty is described in Burrell and Nii-Naate (2013). For this exercise, we include 40 country-specific macroeconomic variables and 79 country- and commodity-specific yields as sources of uncertainty. Following the previous analyses with this tool, we use the coefficient of variation in the last year of the ten years projection period (CV2023) for the presentation of the model output.

The partial stochastic analysis allows for analyzing the variation of world market prices. The results for the main agricultural commodities are shown in Figure 4.1.

Among the crops, oilseeds have the highest level of variation, followed by its subproducts protein meal and vegetable oils. This is partially explained by the use of these crops in the feed industry. Oilseeds cannot be substituted that easily as they provide different levels of protein and oil (energy); supply shocks in high-protein content oilseeds (e.g., soybean) can only be offset by the use of other high-protein inputs, such as fish meal or milk powder, which are

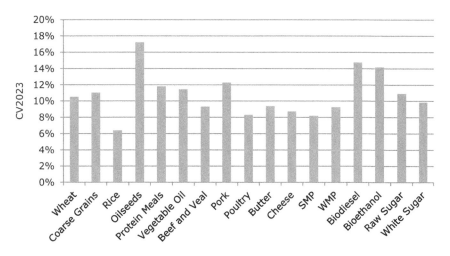

Figure 4.1 Coefficient of variation of world market prices in 2023.

more expensive than soybean meal. In contrast, coarse grains and wheat are homogeneous in the sense that they are substitutes for the provision of energy. As grains can be easily substituted among them, supply shocks are offset, and the impact on variation is diluted. Along with this, there is a rapid economic growth surrounded by high levels of uncertainty in Brazil, Russia, India, and China (BRIC), increasing in particular the demand for meat and dairy, which affects the demand for oilseeds and grains.

High levels of uncertainty coming from large meat importers (BRIC) are transmitted into the different meat markets. Pork meat is exposed to uncertainty, which can be attributed to the increasing demand coming mainly from China. Dairy products, with most of the growth in demand for milk expected to come from India, exhibit similar levels of variation and are in general less variable than meats and crops. Finally, biofuels and sugar prices follow the oilseeds and subproducts (oils and meals) in terms of variation, strongly related to the biofuel policies.

The outcome of the overall uncertainty analysis provides a broad picture of the variation for the main commodities. Nonetheless, it does not allow discerning the main potential sources of uncertainty for each commodity. In order to analyze the impact of yield and macroeconomic uncertainty in isolation, the AGLINK-COSIMO model is run for each category of uncertainty separately. Figure 4.2 shows the results for macroeconomic and yield-related uncertainty alone, as well as the overall uncertainty outcome.

Macroeconomic uncertainty in general drives most of the price variation in the world market prices. This is because world prices are determined by trade, for which exchange rates and transport costs play a major role. The commodities

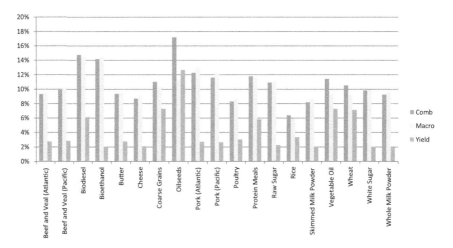

Figure 4.2 Coefficient of variation of world market prices by partial stochastic scenarios in 2023.

most affected by the macroeconomic uncertainty are biofuels and pork meat. In the case of biofuels, the linkage is through the oil price, which drives the demand for fossil fuel; notably binding mandates serve as a vehicle to pass the oil price uncertainty to biofuels. Concerning pork meat, economic growth in China and Russia is assumed to put more pressure on imports and the world demand. Yield uncertainty affects oilseeds the most; this is in part due to the past high levels of variation in Argentina, one of the main exporters of oilseeds and protein meals. In addition, other important exporters such as Ukraine and Kazakhstan (with large fluctuations in their oilseed yields) are expected to have an increasing share on the world markets, adding more uncertainties and variation to world prices. It should be noted that yield and macroeconomic uncertainty are not additive. The reason is that these two sources of uncertainty are assumed to be independent, and their effects can offset each other.

Separating the analysis by source of uncertainty permits identifying the main drivers of price variation. Next, we want to determine which macroeconomic indicator drives variation the most. For this purpose, we run different sources of macroeconomic uncertainty separately, although this approach deserves some words of caution. Macroeconomic variables are interrelated and this is omitted when they are used one-by-one in the model. Thus, our exercise is a sensitivity analysis that can help to identify the impact of specific sources of uncertainty while keeping the remaining ones constant. The results are shown in Figure 4.3.

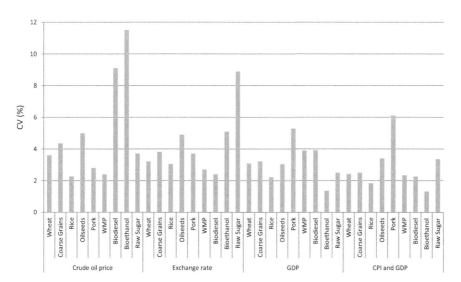

Figure 4.3 Coefficient of variation of world market prices by macroeconomic partial stochastic scenarios in 2023.

The first outcome is the reduction of the variation when looking at the macroeconomic indicators separately, in part reflecting that macroeconomic indicators do not tend to offset their effects. The groups with the largest impact on the price variation are crude oil price and exchange rate. Crude oil price is particularly relevant for biofuels, as biofuels and fossil fuel consumptions are linked. Oil price affects all the commodities by means of the cost of production, more specifically energy, fertilizer, and transport costs. The exchange rate plays a more important role in ethanol than in biodiesel, because there is substantial trade of ethanol in world markets, mainly involving Brazil and the United States. The main driver is the uncertainty of the exchange of the Brazilian Real against the USD. Other commodities largely affected by the exchange rates are oilseeds, coarse grains, and pork meat. Oilseeds and coarse grains are mainly produced in South America (in particular, Argentina and Brazil), for which large fluctuations of exchange rates are recorded; moreover, the main importers for meat and oilseeds are rapid-growing economies, such as Russia and China. The fluctuations in the exchange rate lead to different levels of competitiveness in the world markets, which impact the global trade and the world prices. The third most affecting item is the GDP, which is linked to the production and economic growth. Finally, the consumer price index and GDP deflator uncertainty are more likely to affect through the demand, by affecting the prices for consumers and the purchasing parity power. In general, it can be concluded that price variation will depend on how large the exogenous uncertainty is, the number of linkages that it has along the agri-food chain, and in the global markets how important is the country where the uncertainty comes from.

Together with the analysis of price volatility drivers, it is of interest to analyze if the price variation will differ depending on the price level. In order to do so, we run a scenario with imposed export taxes in Russia, Ukraine, and Kazakhstan (RUK region) for wheat. This restriction causes a decrease on the global supply, thus putting pressure on prices. The baseline projection for the world wheat price in 2023 is 270 USD/ton. Imposing the restrictions on exports in the RUK region causes the price to increase to 338 USD/ton in the same year, which represents an increase of 25% with respect to the baseline. The range for the 10th–90th percentiles goes from 215 to 326 USD/ton in the reference scenario (baseline). With the restrictions, the range values go from 274 to 405 USD/ton, which is broader than the reference scenario. Nevertheless, the increase in the price level does not translate into a higher coefficient of variation, which remains close to levels of 10% (Figure 4.4).

The results presented above are based on certain assumptions. First, the uncertainty accounted for is exogenous; it is neither increased nor decreased by higher taxes on exports. Second, the supply, demand, stocks, and own-price elasticities remain constant for the different shocks, and they are not triggered by the price level. Finally, the uncertainties are affecting the price volatility through different channels, which are not affected by assuming higher export

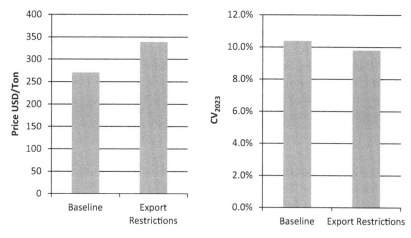

Figure 4.4 Price level (left graph) and variation (right graph) for wheat price in 2023.

taxes. Potentially, prices might serve to activate or enforce policies (support prices), which can weaken or strengthen the connection between the uncertainty and the markets, thus affecting the level of price variation. Nonetheless, the impact of these policies, while significant at the domestic level, might be diluted in the world markets.

3 Influence of climate change on midterm agri-food market developments

3.1 Introduction

In this section, we turn our attention to the environmental drivers. Climate change is acknowledged for being one of the most determining environmental drivers for the future development of agricultural markets. There is a growing body of literature on the biophysical and economic effects of climate change on agriculture (Parry et al., 2004; Nelson et al., 2009; IPCC, 2014). In a recent review of the main contributions, Fernández and Blanco (2014) highlight that results from different studies are not easily comparable and often contradictory, showing that there is a wide range of uncertainty linked to climate projections, crop productivity effects, and market adjustments.

Above all, future crop yield developments are subject to considerable uncertainty, particularly with regard to climate projections and the degree of carbon fertilization effect (Rosenzweig et al., 2013). To assess the influence of these uncertainties in the development of agricultural markets over the next 20 years (from 2010 to 2030), we defined a set of simulation scenarios, all based on the same Shared Socioeconomic Pathway, SSP2 (Kriegler et al., 2012), and the highest Representative Concentration Pathway, RCP 8.5 (van Vuuren et al., 2011). The scenarios differ in (1) the influence of CO_2 effects, based on the extreme cases with and without carbon fertilization, and (2) the climate projection, based on two different global circulation models (GCMs), HadGEM2[1] and IPSL-CM5A-LR.[2] The former represents a warmer and dryer climate while the latter implies relatively milder temperature and higher precipitation. The resulting simulation scenarios[3] were chosen in order to disclose as much information as possible from the uncertainties related to climate change effects on crop production and prices.

3.2 Bioeconomic approach

The bioeconomic modelling approach used in this study consists of combining global biophysical and agroeconomic models. Biophysical models project crop yield effects of climate change under various climate scenarios (defined by GCMs) and those yield effects are incorporated into the agroeconomic model CAPRI in order to evaluate impacts on production and prices. CAPRI represents a unique combination of regional supply-side models with a global market model for agricultural products that provides simulated results for the EU at subnational level, whilst, at the same time, simulating global agricultural markets (Britz and Witzke, 2014). This modelling approach allowed for assessing the biophysical and economic effects of climate change on agriculture both at the global and regionalized levels within the EU.

At the European level, we used the WOFOST (World Food Studies) crop model (Van Diepen et al., 1989) to simulate the biophysical effects of climate change and the carbon fertilization on crop yields throughout the European Union. Biophysical simulations performed at a 25km grid resolution provided changes in crop yields for nine of the most widely grown crops in the EU. The results of the simulations were aggregated at regional, national, and EU28 levels, using regional statistics on crop areas.

For non-EU regions, climate-induced changes on crop yields were taken from available projections from the ISI-MIP modelling initiative, in particular from simulations with the LPJmL model (Bondeau et al., 2007).

3.3 Dealing with climate change uncertainties

Biophysical effects of climate change

Overall, as Figure 4.5 illustrates, crop yields tend to rise over the baseline when the CO_2 effect is taken into account and to fall with no carbon fertilization. On average, maize presents the lowest range of variation, with a decrease down to -1.4% and an increase up to 2%, while soybean displays the highest variability (between -5.2% and 12%).

Taking a closer look at the EU, we observe similar patterns (except for maize and potatoes, which seem to be more affected by climate change regardless of the carbon fertilization effect), with decreasing yields in all scenarios. Average results hide, however, significant regional disparities both at the global and EU levels.

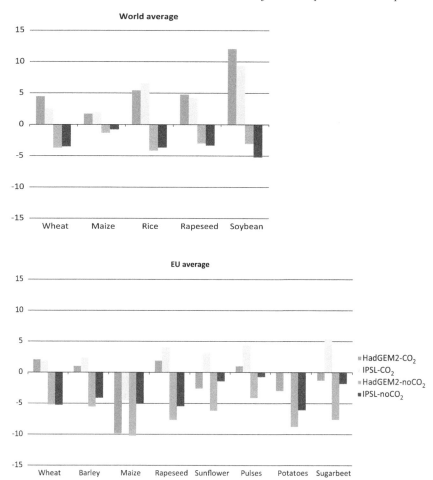

Figure 4.5 Percentage change on simulated actual yields between 2010 (present climate) and 2030 (world and EU averages).

Socioeconomic impacts

In this section, we discuss the climate-induced effects on agri-food markets by comparing – for the time horizon 2030 – the four simulation scenarios to the baseline or reference scenario.

In scenarios accounting for CO_2 effects, the exogenous increase in crop yields globally will be counterbalanced by a decrease in crop prices. In absence of carbon fertilization, the exogenous decrease in crop yields will drive up crop prices. Price effects will lead to interregional adjustments in production, consumption, and trade. Thus, the result of the diverging effects on crop yields and prices will determine the level of production and price for each region or country.

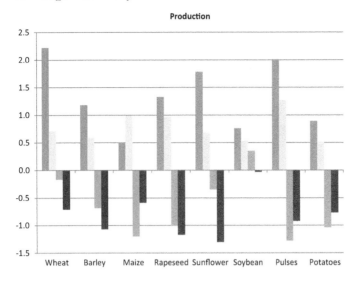

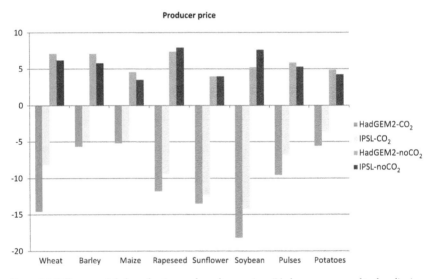

Figure 4.6 Effects on global production and producer prices (% change compared to baseline).

As shown in Figure 4.6, global crop price increases in scenarios without CO_2 effects fall in the range −3.5% to −8.0%, depending on the crop and the climate projection. Price increases partially offset the negative productivity effects. In general, the patterns of global production follow the simulated yields changes, with the exception of soybean in the HadGEM2 scenario, where production increases.

Focusing on scenarios with CO_2 effects, we find opposite results. Global crop prices decreases in the range of −3.7% to −18.2% result in global production increases in the range 0.5% to 2.2%. The degree of carbon fertilization is, therefore, a major driver of climate effects and determines the direction of changes. While the influence of CO_2 fertilization is generally acknowledged, and the scenarios without CO_2 are rather unlikely, there is considerable uncertainty on the degree of the CO_2 effect.

Contrary to what we would have expected from the observed biophysical effects, a high variation in productivity, like in soybean, is not a sufficient condition for high variation in production, since it can be buffered by market effects (e.g., price variation). The considerable price responses to modest production variations reflect the relatively low demand elasticity for most of the agri-food products. Therefore, it is important to highlight that, besides yield changes, other factors – such as food demand – seem to have a strong influence on food production.

Focusing on the European Union, average EU yield effects – with carbon fertilization – are less positive than global yield effects and, because of market-driven adjustments, effects on EU production are more negative (Figure 4.7).

Due to differences in productivity shocks and market-driven adjustments, the comparative advantage of European agriculture will deteriorate in all scenarios. Impacts are unevenly distributed, however, across EU regions and crops. Figure 4.8 illustrates the regional heterogeneity of climate impacts on wheat production, the most cultivated crop in EU, for the HadGEM2 scenario.

Diverging regional impacts of climate change in agricultural productivity lead to adjustments in production, consumption, and trade flows. Particularly

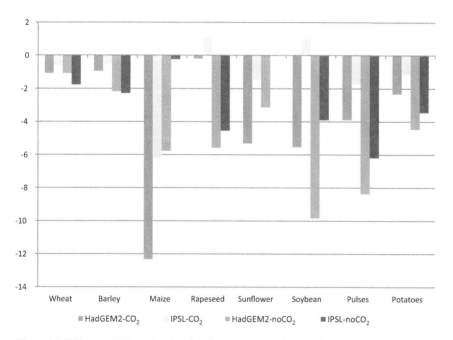

Figure 4.7 Effects on EU production (% change compared to baseline).

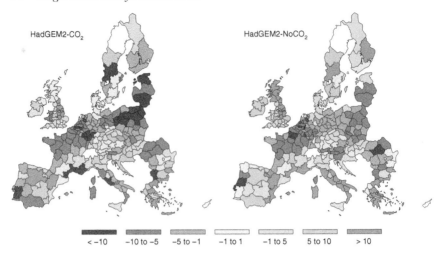

Figure 4.8 Wheat production (% change compared to baseline).

for internationally traded products, this will lead to changes in regional self-sufficiency rates.[4] In this sense, international trade could represent an important mechanism to buffer the effects of climate change.

As highlighted in Figure 4.9, wheat self-sufficiency will decrease in all simulation scenarios in those regions more negatively affected by climate change (i.e., Europe, Australia, and New Zealand), while it will increase in those regions less negatively affected (America).

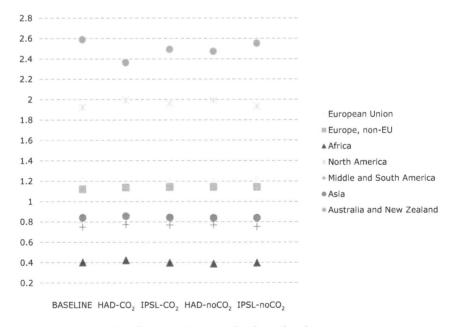

Figure 4.9 Wheat self-sufficiency indicator under the analyzed scenarios.

4 Conclusions and outlook

The functioning of agricultural markets is driven by biophysical and socioeconomic factors, as well as different policies. As these drivers are linked to different sources and levels of uncertainty, understanding how such uncertainties can influence future agricultural markets is crucial in facing food security challenges. Agroeconomic models identify crude oil prices and macroeconomic indicators, especially exchange rates, as main sources of price variability. Other drivers also have an influence, namely the GDP and consumer price index, the stocks levels, as well as weather shocks and climate change.

While market drivers have an impact on the price levels and the variation, the impact differs among markets and products. The commodities with high price variation linked to macroeconomic indicators are oilseeds (and its derivatives), because of their strong connections to biofuels and the meat/dairy markets; biofuels, whose variation is linked mainly to fossil fuels uncertainty; and meat, particularly pork, which is affected by exchange rates and increasing demand in emerging markets. In the world markets, the exogenous sources of uncertainty have similar impacts on price variation regardless of the price level.

Concerning the impacts of climate change on agriculture, both biophysical and economic results vary widely across scenarios, regions, and sectors. The carbon fertilization effect strongly influences the direction of effects for both EU and non-EU regions, leading to crop price increases in the absence of carbon fertilization and to price decreases when CO_2 effects are accounted for. Economic simulations show that crop prices will react to yield changes, attenuating the effects of climate change at the global level, but originating significant distribution effects across regions and sectors. Results suggest that agri-food market projections to 2030 are very sensitive to changes in crop productivity and, therefore, to the uncertainties linked to climate change.

Notes

1   The Hadley Centre Global Environmental Model version 2 (HadGEM2) developed by UK Meteorological Office Hadley Centre.
2   Institut Pierre-Simon Laplace Coupled Model version 5 (IPSL-CM5A-LR) developed by Institute Pierre-Simon Laplace in France (Dufresne et al., 2012).
3   Four simulation scenarios in total: HadGEM2-CO$_2$, HadGEM2-noCO$_2$, IPSL-CO$_2$ and IPSL-noCO$_2$.
4   Self-sufficiency in production is an indicator of import dependency, defined as the ratio of production to domestic consumption.

References

Abbott, P., and Borot de Battisti, A. (2011). Recent global food price shocks: Causes, consequences and lessons for African governments and donors. *Journal of African Economies*, *20*(suppl. 1), i12–i62.
Artavia, M., Blanco, M., Araujo-Enciso, S.R., Ramos, F., Van Doorslaer, B., Fumagalli, D., Niemeyer, S., Fernández, F.J., and M'Barek, R. (2014). Production and crop roots (causes?)

of volatility measures including partial stochastic simulations of yields and macroeconomic variables. Scientific Paper no. 2, ULYSSES project, EU 7th Framework Programme, Project 312182 KBBE.2012.1.4–05.

Baffes, J., and Haniotis, T. (2010). Placing the 2006/08 Commodity price boom into perspective. Washington, DC: The World Bank, Development Prospects Group.

Bondeau, A., Smith, P., Zaehle, S., Schaphoff, S., Lucht, W., Cramer, W., Gerten, D., Lotze-Campen, H., Müller, C., Reichstein, M., and Smith, B. (2007). Modelling the role of agriculture for the 20th century global terrestrial carbon balance. *Global Change Biology, 13*(3), 679–706.

Britz, W., and Witzke, H.P. (2014). *CAPRI model documentation.* Institute for Food and Resource Economics, University of Bonn. http://www.capri-model.org

Brümmer, B., Korn, O., Schüsser, K., and Jamali Jaghdani, T. (2013). Volatility analysis: Causation impacts in retrospect (2007–2011) and preparing for the future. Working Paper 6, ULYSSES project, EU 7th Framework Programme, Project 312182 KBBE.2012.1.4–05.

Burrell, A., and Nii-Naate, Z. (2013). Partial stochastic analysis with the European Commission's version of the AGLINK-COSIMO model. n.p.

Dufresne, J.L., Foujols, M.A., Denvil, S., Caubel, A., Marti, O., . . . and Vuichard, N. (2012). Climate change projections using the IPSL-CM5 Earth System Model: From CMIP3 to CMIP5. *Climate Dynamics, 40*(9–10), 2123–2165.

EC. (2012). Medium-term prospects for EU agricultural markets and income 2014–2024. n.p.

EC. (2013). Prospects for EU agricultural markets and income 2014–2024. n.p.

EC. (2014). Prospects for EU agricultural markets and income 2014–2024. n.p.

FAO. (2009). Declaration of the world summit on food security, WSFS 2009/2. n.p.

FAO. (2010). Price volatility in agricultural markets. n.p.

FAO et al. (2011). Price volatility in food and agricultural markets: Policy responses. n.p.

Fernández, Francisco J., and Blanco, Maria. (2014). Integration of biophysical and agro-economic models to assess the economic effects of climate change on agriculture: A review of global and EU regional approaches. Economics Discussion Papers, no. 2014-48, Kiel Institute for the World Economy. http://www.economics-ejournal.org/economics/discussionpapers/2014-48.

Gilbert, C.L. (2010). How to understand high food prices. *Journal of Agricultural Economics, 61*(2), 398–425.

Gohin, A., and Chantret, F. (2010). The long-run impact of energy prices on world agricultural markets: The role of macro-economic linkages. *Energy Policy, 38*(1), 333–339.

Headey, D., and Fan, S. (2008). Anatomy of a crisis: The causes and consequences of surging food prices. *Agricultural Economics, 39*, 375–391.

IPCC. (2014). Summary for policymakers. In C.B. Field, V.R. Barros, D.J. Dokken, K.J. Mach, M.D. Mastrandrea, T.E. Bilir, M. Chatterjee, K.L. Ebi, Y.O. Estrada, R.C. Genova, B. Girma, E.S. Kissel, A.N. Levy, S. MacCracken, P.R. Mastrandrea, and L.L. White (Eds.), *Climate change 2014: Impacts, adaptation, and vulnerability. Part A: Global and sectoral aspects. Contribution of Working Group II to the Fifth Assessment Report of the Intergovernmental Panel on Climate Change* (pp. 1–32). Cambridge, UK, and New York: Cambridge University Press.

Kriegler, E., O'Neill, B.C., Hallegatte, S., Kram, T., Lempert, R.J., Moss, R.H., and Wilbanks, T. (2012). The need for and use of socio-economic scenarios for climate change analysis: A new approach based on shared socio-economic pathways. *Global Environmental Change, 22*(4), 807–822.

Magrini, E., and Donmez, A. (2013). Agricultural commodity price volatility and its macroeconomic determinants: A GARCH-MIDAS approach. n.p.

Naylor, R.L., and Falcon, W.P. (2010). Food security in an era of economic volatility. *Population and Development Review, 36*(4), 693–723.

Nelson, G., Rosegrant, M.W., Koo, J., Robertson, R., Sulser, T., Zhu, T., Ringler, C., Msangi, S., Palazzo, A., Batka, M., Magalhaes, M., Valmonte-Santos, R., Ewing, M., and Lee, D. (2009). *Climate change: Impact on agriculture and costs of adaptation.* Washington, DC: DFPRI. doi: 10.2499/0896295354

OECD-FAO. (2013). OECD-FAO Agricultural Outlook 2013. n.p.

OECD-FAO. (2014). OECD-FAO Agricultural Outlook 2014. n.p.

Parry, M.L., Rosenzweig, C., Iglesias, A., Livermore, M., and Fischer, G. (2004). Effects of climate change on global food production under SRES emissions and socio-economic scenarios. *Global Environmental Change, 14*(1), 53–67.

Rosenzweig, C., Elliott, J., Deryng, D., Ruane, A.C., Müller, C., Arneth, A., Boote, K., Folberth, C., Glotter, M., Khabarov, N., Neumann, K., Piontek, F., Pugh, T.A.M., Schmid, E., Stehfest, E., Yang, H., and Jones, J.W. (2013). Assessing agricultural risks of climate change in the 21st century in a global gridded crop model intercomparison. *Proceedings of the National Academy of Sciences, 111*(9), 3268–3273.

Swinnen, J., and Squicciarini, P. (2012). Mixed messages on prices and food security. *Science, 335*(6067), 405–406.

Tangermann, S. (2011). Policy solutions to agricultural market volatility: A synthesis. n.p.

Trostle, R. (2008). *Global agricultural supply and demand: Factors contributing to the recent increase in food commodity prices* (Rev. ed.). Darby, PA: Diane Publishing.

Van Diepen, C.A., Wolf, J., Van Keulen, H., and Rappoldt, C. (1989). WOFOST: A simulation model of crop production. *Soil Use and Management, 5*, 16–24.

von Lampe, M., Willenbockel, D., Ahammad, H., Blanc, E., Cai, Y., Calvin, K., Fujimori, S., Hasegawa, T., Havlik, P., Heyhoe, E., Kyle, P., Lotze-Campen, H., d'Croz, D.M., Nelson, G., Sands, R.D., Schmitz, C., Tabeau, A., Valin, H., van der Mensbrugghe, D., and van Meijl, H. (2014). Why do global long-term scenarios for agriculture differ? An overview of the AgMIP global economic model intercomparison. *Agricultural Economics, 45*(1), 3–20.

Van Vuuren, D.P., Edmonds, J., Kainuma, M., Riahi, K., Thomson, A., Hibbard, K., Hurtt, G.C., Kram, T., Krey, V., Lamarque, J.F., Masui, T., Meinshusen, M., Nakicenovic, N., Smith, S.J., and Rose, S.K. (2011). The representative concentration pathways: An overview. *Climatic Change, 109*, 5–31.

5 Transparency of food pricing in the European Union

Steve McCorriston and Stephan von Cramon-Taubadel

1 Background: concern about the performance of the food supply chain

The so-called 'food price crisis' of 2007–2008 focused attention on the functioning and performance of the food supply chain around the world. In the European Union, the EU Commission began monitoring the situation in 2007 and published an interim report on *Food Prices in Europe* in 2008 (EU Commission, 2008). In 2009, the Commission communication *A Better Functioning Food Supply Chain in Europe* concluded that 'structural weaknesses' coupled with 'pervasive inequalities in the bargaining power between contracting parties' in the food supply chain were contributing to slow and sometimes asymmetric price transmissions that 'delay necessary adjustments', 'prolong market inefficiencies' and 'can exacerbate price volatility in agricultural commodity markets' (EU Commission, 2009, p. 4). Based on this diagnosis, the Commission identified three cross-cutting policy priorities:

1   promote sustainable and market-based relationships between stakeholders in the food supply chain;
2   increase transparency along the chain to encourage competition and improve its resilience to price volatility; and
3   foster the integration and competitiveness of the European food supply chain across Member States.

(EU Commission, 2009, p. 5)

The first of these priorities addresses the possible detrimental impact of unfair trading practices that can arise due to imbalances in the bargaining power of participants in the food supply chain, as well as issues arising from the ability of some participants to exercise market power and distort competition. The second priority addresses the need to improve the quantity, quality and availability of price and market information along the entire food supply chain in particular with a view to ensuring that derivative markets contribute to price discovery and risk management at the agricultural commodity end of the chain. Finally, the third priority is aimed at removing the remaining barriers that undermine the functioning of the Internal Market and thus reduce resilience to shocks in the food supply chain.

Against this background, the Transparency of Food Prices (TRANS-FOP)[1] project brought together researchers from 13 partner institutions in 10 EU Member States between 2011 and 2013 to analyse the transparency of food pricing with a multidisciplinary approach. The main objectives of TRANSFOP were:

1   to address the key aspects of the food supply chain that determine the transmission of price changes from farm to consumer levels, emphasising the role of competition in the intermediate and retails stages of the food supply chain and the regulatory environment in which firms compete;
2   to address how the variation in the structure of the food supply chain across EU Member States contributes to food price adjustment in different countries; and
3   to generate an Action Plan for improving food supply chain performance based on the results of the research.

Members of the TRANSFOP consortium expanded research on the food supply chain throughout the EU in a number of important directions: (a) focusing on comprehensive coverage of price transmission processes across EU Member States; (b) employing new and previously unexplored data sources to understand food price dynamics in the food chain and to assess the pressures underpinning the changing structure of the food supply chain throughout the EU; and (c) developing theoretical insights to assess price dynamics in the context of market frictions. Moreover, throughout the programme, there was close interaction with stakeholders and users of research to ensure that the research was being focused in a way that would have a meaningful impact on policy developments throughout the EU. The aim of this chapter is twofold: first, to outline the main findings of the TRANSFOP research programme in light of the main objectives noted above; and second, to highlight the main issues raised in the form of an 'Action Plan' for stakeholders and future research on how to promote more transparency in the food sector in the future. This Action Plan formed the basis of the recommendations from the TRANSFOP consortium which were delivered to the European Commission following the completion of the TRANSFOP project.

2 Main findings

In the course of our work on TRANSFOP, we confirmed that the nature of price transmission in the food supply chain is highly heterogeneous across Member States and individual branches (e.g. dairy, cereals, fruits and vegetables) within the EU.[2] Common methods of analysis and modelling can be applied to different branches and Member States, but the interpretation of their results is highly specific to the Member State and branch of the food chain that is being considered. In this context, the EU food supply chain is not a single entity. Instead, the functioning of food supply chains differs across Member States, even when the analysis is focused on the same commodity. These differences may reflect a variety of factors, from sector specific issues (for example, the structure of food supply chains in different Member States) to barriers to competition and macroeconomic factors (such as differences in exchange rate regimes).

One of point of departure for TRANSFOP was the observation that *experiences with food price inflation* as a result of the 2007–2008 and subsequent food price shocks differed considerably across Member States (Lloyd et al., 2015). Our results indicate that, in general, new Member States tended to have more volatile rates of food inflation than other Member States, but that no other grouping could be identified. For example, despite sharing a common currency, the Euro Zone countries did not share a common food inflation experience. Aside from the experience of new Member States, the food inflation experience differed, most notably for the United Kingdom. In addition, food inflation has been more volatile than nonfood inflation. These issues have an important macroeconomic dimension, since how monetary authorities deal with volatile food inflation can have important implications for inflation targeting, aside from the obvious direct impact on households of high and volatile food prices.

Our *analysis of price transmission* confirmed that the strength of price transmission varies considerably across products and Member States. 'One-to-one' price transmission in the food supply chain is, as predicted by theory, the exception and not the rule.[3] One-to-one transmission is only likely to arise in an ideal world of perfect competition and frictionless transactions between spatially separated markets for a homogeneous product. Vertical price transmission between different processing stages of the food chain will, as a rule, not be one-to-one, and even in the spatial context departures from the competitive, frictionless benchmark will likely result in imperfect price transmission (subject to other considerations). For example, assuming the demand conditions are not too stringent,[4] departures from the competitive benchmark will likely result in less than one-to-one price transmission. This has an important implication, since it implies that we should expect that upstream farm level prices would be more responsive to shocks than downstream retail level prices. However, this observation aside, other aspects of the price transmission process were also investigated.

Specifically, we did not find evidence that asymmetric price transmission is prevalent in the food supply chain (see Hassouneh et al., 2015). Furthermore, it was not possible to establish a robust empirical link between either the strength or the symmetry/asymmetry of price transmission and concentration in the branch being studied. However, this conclusion must be considered tentative as analysis was limited by data availability. Overall, there is evidence that farm prices adjust more strongly to shocks than prices at other stages of the food

supply chain. Theoretical analysis that extends existing models of price transmission to include the costs of vertical coordination, search, monitoring and
contract enforcement shows that under realistic conditions price transmission
in the food chain can be complex, displaying nonlinearity such as threshold
effects and price ranges over which no transmission takes place. This has implications for empirical work on price transmission in the food supply chain that
remain to be explored.

Analysis in TRANSFOP using highly disaggregated scanner data on retail
food prices generated insights into *retailers' pricing strategies*. Elements of the
research programme focused on retailers' use of sales (i.e. temporary price
reductions) which characterises the pricing practices of many retailers and is
an important dimension of how retailers compete. We found that sales make a
significant contribution to overall retail price variation. In the UK, only a small
proportion of the observed price variation is common across the major retailers, suggesting that cost shocks originating at the manufacturing level are not
one of the main sources of price variation (Lloyd et al., 2014).

We also found that once sales had been accounted for, retail prices can be
'sticky'. While this is consistent with the price transmission analysis reported
above, the sticky nature of food prices relates to the underlying pricing strategies of retailers. The results revealed substantial heterogeneity in retailer pricing
strategies, even for identical products. This is an important dimension of the
functioning of the food-retailing sector that had not been observed to date.

The penetration of private label products is an increasingly important feature
of the retail food sector, and several TRANSFOP consortium members analysed the price dynamics of private label versus nationally branded products.[5]
This perspective enables us to observe differences that relate to the structure
of the food supply chain, since private labels suggest some vertical control over
pricing as distinct from the manufacturer–retailer relationships that characterise
the pricing of branded products (Bonnet et al., 2015). Important differences in
the pricing of national brands compared with private labels were found. Cost
pass-through is different for private labels and national brands, and for some
national brands it can even exceed 100% (i.e. retailers sometimes amplify cost
variations to consumers). Sales are more relevant for national brands than for
private labels, and brand loyalty by consumers tends to reduce the magnitude
and the frequency of price promotions, especially for the strongest brands. We
find no evidence that stronger brands use asymmetric cost-price adjustments
to generate higher margins, but it appears that national brand prices tend to
increase with increasing private label shares. This may be evidence that retailers
use private labels to discriminate prices among different groups of consumers.[6]

Access to scanner data also highlighted some other features of the retailing
sector across the EU that had not been accounted for in research that exists to
date. Thus, while national data sources typically report a single price for a commodity aggregate (e.g. bread), we also note that prices and retailer strategies can
also vary according to retail outlet: our analysis for Germany and Italy where

TRANSFOP researchers had access to detailed data shows that price levels, price changes and the use of sales can vary according to whether the product is on sale at a hypermarket, supermarket or convenience store. This, in turn, also matters for addressing price transmission, which can therefore vary by outlet. In addition, and following some recent research in macroeconomics, scanner data can be used to derive more appropriate price indices to derive inflation measures which will therefore vary by outlet (and commodity chain) as well (see Castellari et al., 2015).

Regarding *concentration in the food supply chain* and its possible implications for price transmission, our analysis identified several, sometimes counteracting, effects. This issue is complex. Generally, increasing concentration can be expected to reduce price transmission. However, in the context of a vertically related food supply chain, concentration has both horizontal and vertical effects. As a result, there is no clear expectation as to how increasing concentration will affect price transmission. Furthermore, increased concentration may not be harmful for consumers if it affects bargaining power which, in turn, has an influence on upstream suppliers. This is an issue that requires further attention, both from the research communities and competition authorities.

In large part, the difficulty with concentration measures is that they may not be accurate means via which to gauge the intensity of competition in the food sector (or any other sector for that matter). As is well known in industrial organisation, it is behaviour rather than firm numbers that really matters for addressing competition. Thus, while the UK has a relatively concentrated retail food sector, a prolonged investigation by the UK Competition Commission did not find that the food retailing chains acted against the consumer interest. However, addressing competition issues is complex, with both horizontal and vertical dimensions noted above, and where the nature of the links between stages in the food supply chain may give rise to anticompetitive concerns that easily accessible concentration ratio data will not pick up. Understanding competition in the food chain and how it relates to price transparency across EU Member States will be an ongoing policy and research issue for many years to come.

How consolidation in the food sector occurs and what form it takes is another issue that was addressed in the TRANSFOP programme. The focus here was on distinguishing between horizontal and vertical mergers. These two alternative forms can have different implications for the price transmission process and there are offsetting influences on how price transmission will be affected. Specifically, increasing horizontal concentration due to mergers and acquisitions can allow enterprises to realise economies of scale which, in turn, can lead to offsetting increases in price transmission. Similarly, a vertical merger or acquisition that eliminates the problem of double marginalisation in a particular food supply chain can increase price transmission. Vertical mergers and acquisitions can also reduce vertical coordination cost and the risk of 'hold up'[7] and other market failures. To the extent that this is true, increasing vertical concentration need not lead to weaker price transmission in the food supply chain (Swinnen and Vandeplas, 2015). The food sector throughout the EU is characterised by both forms of consolidation, and future research should address this issue in greater detail. Importantly, to the extent that consolidation may improve the functioning of the supply chain, removing barriers to promoting an active market for corporate control is an important consideration for providing a more unified policy space throughout the EU.

TRANSFOP also identified a number of *important gaps in our current understanding* of processes in the food supply chain and issues that will require additional research in the future. One of these issues concerns the need to carefully disentangle static concerns, such as a low farm share in the food retail bill, from dynamic developments, such as technical change and growing consumer preferences for convenience and variety that lead to increasing value added in downstream stages of the food supply chain.

Another issue with potentially critical implications for the analysis of price transmission and food supply chain performance is the need to account for the multi-product nature of pricing behaviour, especially at the processing and retail levels; retail chains may have thousands of products on sale in a given outlet at any point in time. Hence, inter- and intra-substitutability between products is a further issue for the researcher to address. Price transmission analysis that follows individual components of the food supply chain (e.g. fluid milk from the farm gate to the retail store) fails to account for the fact that processors transform farm products into broad ranges of differentiated products and that retailers pursue pricing strategies that encompass groups or baskets of final products. This therefore has implications for studying price transmission and poses a wider range of challenges that do not appear in more traditional time series econometric approaches to the transmission process.

To the extent that aspects of the competition process underpin many of the issues associated with food price dynamics across the EU, further research into the complex nature of the competition process in food supply chains is also a prerequisite for more meaningful insights. In this regard, it is important to address not only horizontal competition issues in the food supply chain, but also vertical issues. These are not unrelated, since the horizontal dimension of competition interacts with the vertical dimension; i.e. reducing the number of firms or outlets at one stage also reduces the number of buyers or sellers at other stages. Similarly, vertical control also affects the intensity of horizontal competition. More specifically, addressing in detail competition between stages in the food supply chain is important in assessing the form and extent of potentially unfair business practices and gauging the extent of buyer power. It should be noted here that pioneering work by TRANSFOP researchers used a structural model employing scanner data to identify how alternative forms of contracts between retailers and food manufacturers affected the price transmission process, using data for the sugar and dairy sectors in France. From the policy end, some attention to these issues has already been alerted in the recent report by the High Level Forum for a Better Functioning Food Supply Chain (EU Commission, 2014). The increasing concerns associated with vertical relations in the food supply chain call for further focused research on these issues.

A final finding that emerged from TRANSFOP is that the *available data* do not permit us to address and answer many of the most pressing questions about food prices and the performance of the food supply chain in a consistent manner across commodity sectors and across EU Member States. Data are especially lacking at the intermediate stages of the food supply chain between the farm and consumer ends. It is precisely at these intermediate stages – for example, where large processors contract with large food distributors and retailers – that transparency is most lacking but critically necessary if research is to cast light on questions of concentration, competition and price transmission. But even at the farm gate and consumer levels, homogeneous data across a larger set of Member States and key food products are required to broaden the basis for robust results on the nature and patterns of price transmission. While price data are clearly of special importance in this regard, data on quantities transacted, market structures and contractual arrangements are required to link price transmission results to underlying structural causes and distributional implications.

3 Elements of an action plan

Drawing on the results outlined above, we drafted a four-part Action Plan. These actions should also be seen in connection with the recent *Report of the High Level Forum* on the functioning of the food supply chain (EU Commission, 2014).

1) *Maintain and strengthen the current commitment to monitor prices.* Instruments such as the European Food Prices Monitoring Tool[8] and the Commodity Price Dashboard[9] have made an important contribution to increasing the transparency of food pricing in the EU. However, the coverage that these instruments provide across Member States and food products is uneven. Many Member States established or scaled up national price monitoring instruments in the aftermath of the 2007–2008 and subsequent food price crises.[10] These national instruments often include more detail and analysis than can be found in the EU instruments, but they are very heterogeneous. As a first step, Member States could contribute to a meta-dataset that contains a comprehensive descriptive inventory of the data that are already available at the national level. Second, this inventory could be used to identify a series of steps to harmonise and extend national price monitoring instruments, beginning with relatively easy measures (e.g. publishing weekly data that are used to calculate the monthly averages that have been published to date) and progressing to more ambitious steps (e.g. persuading Member States to agree on a core set of products for which all will publish comparable price data).

To improve the empirical basis for analysis that can inform policies for the food supply chain, we also recommend that the coverage of prices at intermediate stages of the chain be enhanced. In addition, the temporal and spatial resolution of the data that are collected should be increased for a set of key products across all Member States. For the most part, EU price monitoring tools provide information on monthly national average prices. The aggregation (averaging) that takes place to produce these data can obscure underlying price transmission processes. This is especially the case in large Member States, where spatial averaging purges data of information about regional differences. Furthermore, research has demonstrated that temporal averaging (i.e. converting daily or weekly observations into monthly averages) systematically distorts the speed of price transmission that is estimated using price data. For this reason, we recommend that regionalised weekly price data be collected and monitored at initial, intermediate and terminal stages of the chain for a set of critical food products.

2) *Enhance monitoring of the structure and the functioning of the food supply chain* in different Member States and for critical food products. Information on prices in the supply chain is important but only part of a larger equation. Theory shows that food prices depend in a complex manner on other input prices and contractual arrangements, factors that are not static but rather subject to change over time. Information on these factors is needed to inform price transmission analysis, to interpret the results of this analysis and to derive robust conclusions for policy. For example, as reported above, we were not able to establish a clear link between either the speed or the symmetry/asymmetry of price transmission and concentration in different branches of the food supply chain. However, this result may be due to the fact that homogeneous information about concentration at various stages of the food chain for a representative set of products and Member States is not available. Hence, we were obliged to work with proxy measures of concentration that may have distorted the results; as we have noted above, these proxy measures do not necessarily reflect the nature or intensity of competition throughout the food supply chain.

We condition this call for improved monitoring with the caveat that transparency does not always have unambiguously beneficial effects on the performance of the food supply chain. Enterprises have a legitimate interest in protecting confidential information, and in some cases increased transparency might even foster collusion between actors in the food supply chain. It is therefore important to distinguish between public transparency, which may be constrained to limit such negative effects, and controlled access to more detailed, confidential information that can be analysed to support policymaking and regulatory efforts. Increased cooperation between research and competition authorities to permit an in-depth analysis of specific cases of conduct and performance in the food supply chain could prove extremely fruitful for both parties, and should therefore be developed and tested.

3) *Explore the potential of scanner data* to increase the transparency of food pricing in the EU. Scanner data can generate valuable insights into price transmission for private labels as opposed to national brands; they can help us understand the role of sales and promotions in retail price variability; and they can

cast light on food pricing behaviour in different types of retail outlets. Scanner data on prices and quantities sold can also be used to analyse the implications of food price volatility for consumer welfare.

However, there are also many challenges associated with the use of scanner data to analyse food price transmission and food chain performance. These challenges include the high cost of scanner data and the fact that they are collected by private enterprises that do not appear to have clear and consistent policies for making these data available for public or research use. Questions regarding the coverage provided by scanner data in different Member States and for different product groups, and whether and how these data can be used to generate representative insights into food pricing, need to be addressed. The sheer size of scanner datasets and the volume of data that would accumulate and require processing if scanner data from most or all Member States were collected systematically also give rise to questions. More research into the challenges and the potential uses of scanner data is required to provide a basis for informed decisions and productive use.

4) *Continue to improve the functioning of the food supply chain.* In its 2009 Communication, the Commission stated that 'significant imbalances in bargaining power between contracting parties are a common occurrence and . . . may lead to unfair trading practices, as larger and more powerful actors seem to impose contractual arrangements to their advantage' (European Commission, 2009, p. 5). However, as outlined in the *Report of the High Level Forum*, getting stakeholders to agree on precise definitions of what constitutes 'unfair trading practices' and on Principles of Good Practice that reflect a common understanding of fairness in business-to-business relations has proven difficult (EU Commission, 2014). Our results indicate that with appropriate safeguards in place, mergers and acquisitions that increase concentration in the food supply chain can also improve its functioning, for example by allowing firms to capture economies of scale or by reducing double marginalisation in the chain. Although there are exceptions in some Member States and branches of the food chain, in general it appears that food retailers have more market power than processors and wholesalers. Hence, there is a pronounced need to ensure appropriate monitoring and regulation of the food retail sector.

Some stakeholders and policy makers hope that allowing and encouraging producers of agricultural commodities to organise themselves could reduce imbalances in bargaining power vis-à-vis processors and thus make producers less susceptible to unfair trading practices. For historical reasons, producer organisations are, however, less prevalent in new than in old Member States, and it is unclear whether policies to encourage such organisations will succeed in the new Member States. More detailed research on the forms and impact of unfair trading practices and how they can be effectively monitored and appropriately regulated will require further research with strong collaboration between stakeholder and research communities.

Notes

1 FP7 Grant KBBE-265601–4.
2 Details of the analyses which we report on here can be found on the TRANSFOP web-site: www.transfop.eu. In addition, a summary of the issues pertinent to recent research on price dynamics across the EU food sector can be found in McCorriston (2015).
3 More specifically, recognising that raw agricultural commodities are only one input into the production of final retail food products, 'perfect' price transmission should reflect the share of the agricultural input in total cost of producing the final product.
4 Essentially, that the slope of the demand function is not 'too' convex'. See Lloyd et al. (2015) for a more detailed exposition of the theory of price transmission.
5 Private labels refer to the retailer distinguishing the product as being produced under the instruction of and marketed within its stores as the specific retailer's brand, while national brands relate to products produced by food manufacturers and sold nationally and, in most cases, in all retail chains. The growing penetration of private labels has been one of the main features of the food-retailing sector in recent years.
6 The role of brands in spatial and temporal pricing decisions is discussed in Loy and Glauben (2015).
7 The risk of hold-up is related to a bargaining power situation that arises from verbal or nonstandardized contracts.
8 See http://ec.europa.eu/enterprise/sectors/food/competitiveness/prices_monitoring_en.htm
9 See http://ec.europa.eu/agriculture/markets-and-prices/price-monitoring/index_en.htm
10 See, for example France's *Observatoire de la formation des prix et des marges des produits alimentaires* (https://observatoire-prixmarges.franceagrimer.fr/Pages/default.aspx); Bel-gium's *Prizenobservatorium* (http://economie.fgov.be/nl/fod/structuur/Observatoria/Prijzenobservatorium/#.Uu5sL7QSxAc); and Italy's *Osservatorio Prezzi e Tariffe* (http://osservaprezzi.sviluppoeconomico.gov.it/).

References

Bonnet, C., Corre, T., and Réquillart, V. (2015). Price transmission in food chains: The case of the dairy industry. In S. McCorriston (Ed.), *Food price dynamics and price adjustment in the EU*. Oxford University Press.

Castellari, E., Moro, D., Platoni, S., and Sckokai, P. (2015). The use of scanner data for meas-uring food inflation. In S. McCorriston (Ed.), *Food price dynamics and price adjustment in the EU*. Oxford University Press.

EU Commission. (2008). Communication from the Commission of the European Com-munities to the European Parliament, the Council, the European Economic and Social Committee and the Committee of the Regions – Food prices in Europe. COM (2008) 821 final, Brussels. Retrieved from http://eur-lex.europa.eu/LexUriServ/LexUriServ.do?uri=COM:2008:0821:FIN:EN:PDF

EU Commission. (2009). Communication from the Commission of the European Com-munities to the European Parliament, the Council, the European Economic and Social Committee and the Committee of the Regions – A better functioning food supply chain in Europe. COM (2009) 591 final, Brussels. Retrieved from http://eur-lex.europa.eu/legal-content/EN/TXT/HTML/?uri=CELEX:52009DC0591&from=en

EU Commission. (2014). Report of the High Level Forum for a Better Functioning Food Supply Chain. Ares(2014)3414151–15/10/2014, Brussels. Retrieved from http://ec.eu-ropa.eu/enterprise/newsroom/cf/itemdetail.cfm?item_id=7838

Hassouneh, I., Holst, C., Serra, T., von Cramon-Taubadel, S., and Gil, J.M. (2015). Overview of price transmission and reasons for different adjustment patterns across EU Member States. In S. McCorriston (Ed.), *Food price dynamics and price adjustment in the EU*. Oxford University Press.

Lloyd, T.A., McCorriston, S., and Morgan, C.W. (2015). Food inflation in the EU: Contrasting experience and recent insights. In S. McCorriston (Ed.), *Food price dynamics and price adjustment in the EU*. Oxford University Press.

Lloyd, T.A., McCorriston, S., Morgan, C.W., and Poen, E. (2014). Retail price dynamics and retailer heterogeneity: UK Evidence. *Economic Letters, 124*, 434–438.

Loy, J-P., and Glauben, T. (2015). Spatial and temporal retail pricing on the German beer market. In S. McCorriston (Ed.), *Food price dynamics and price adjustment in the EU*. Oxford University Press.

McCorriston, S. (Ed.) (2015). *Food price dynamics and price adjustment in the EU*. Oxford University Press.

Swinnen, J., and Vandeplas, A. (2015). Price transmission in modern agricultural value chains: Some conceptual issues. In S. McCorriston (Ed.), *Food price dynamics and price adjustment in the EU*. Oxford University Press.

6 A review of the effects of contextual factors on price volatility transmission in food supply chains

Tsion Taye Assefa, Miranda P. M. Meuwissen and Alfons G. J. M. Oude Lansink

1 Introduction

Global agricultural prices have experienced an increasing degree of volatility in the last decade (FAO et al., 2011). Prices rose sharply in 2006 and 2007, reaching peak levels in the second half of 2007 for some products and in the second half of 2008 for others, and then plummeted sharply in the second half of 2008 to rise sharply back in 2011 (FAO et al., 2011). Demand-increasing factors, such as economic growth, shifting dietary patterns in developing countries and growth of the biofuel industry, and factors related to the structure of agricultural markets, such as the weak transfer of market price signals to farmers, are attributed to the recent rise in food price volatility (Rabobank, 2011). While there is no generally accepted definition of price volatility (Serra and Zilberman, 2013), it is commonly agreed that price volatility is characterized by price changes that are unpredictable and unanticipated in nature (Piot-Lepetit, 2011; FAO et al., 2011; Serra and Zilberman, 2013; Rabobank, 2011). Price changes along a well-established trend reflecting market fundamentals and with known cyclical patterns are less a matter of concern (FAO et al., 2011) and are not defined as price volatility.

The impacts of price volatility extend to all actors in the food supply chain. Price volatility implies larger risks to farmers, who may react by reducing output supply and investments in productive inputs (Seal and Shonkwiler, 1987; Rezitis and Stavropoulos, 2009; Sckokai and Moro, 2009; Piot-Lepetit, 2011; Tangermann, 2011; Taya, 2012). Furthermore, agricultural input price volatility exposes the downstream sector of food supply chains to sourcing uncertainties, forcing food and agricultural companies to alter their sourcing strategies as a coping mechanism (Rabobank, 2011). On the other end of food supply chains, unexpected increases in prices pose food security risks, particularly to consumers who spend a large share of their income on food items (Hernandez et al., 2011). These chain-wide implications of food price volatility stress the importance of investigating the mechanism by which price volatility transmits along the chain.

Curbing price volatility transmissions in food chains requires an understanding of the factors that affect these transmissions. One point worth noting is the distinction between price transmissions and price volatility transmissions.

The transmission of prices in levels along the chain is necessary for a market to operate efficiently (Chavas and Mehta, 2004), for the maximization of producers' and consumers' welfares, and for an effective transmission of policy induced price measures (Meyer and von Cramon-Taubadel, 2004; Vavra and Goodwin, 2005; Ben-Kaabia and Gil, 2007). On the other hand, price volatility transmission entails the transmission of risks due to unpredictable price changes from one market to another (Apergis and Rezitis, 2003), and this transmission should be minimized. This highlights a potential conflict between market measures intended to improve price transmissions and those intended to reduce price volatility transmissions. In this regard, identification of the factors affecting each type of transmission can help design policy measures or risk management tools that can achieve higher price transmissions as well as lower volatility transmissions. This chapter gives an overview of the factors that affect price volatility transmissions and price transmissions in food supply chains. This is achieved through a review of the literature on price transmission and price volatility transmission.

This chapter proceeds in section 2 with a discussion of differences in the definition of price transmission and price volatility transmission. This is followed by a review of the factors affecting price volatility transmissions in section 3 and a review of those that affect price transmissions in section 4. Section 5 briefly compares the factors identified in sections 3 and 4 and concludes the chapter.

2 Price transmission and price volatility transmission: definitions

Price transmission and price volatility transmission are similar in that they both deal with price linkages along the chain. However, whereas price transmission refers to the linkages between the conditional mean prices, price volatility transmission refers to the linkages between the conditional variance of prices (Natcher and Weaver, 1999). Price transmission deals more generally with the relationship between the predictable "portions" of prices, whereas price volatility transmission deals with the relationship between the unpredictable portions of prices. Price volatility transmission is also defined as the degree to which price uncertainty in one market affects price uncertainty in other markets (Apergis and Rezitis, 2003).

If price volatilities are fully and instantaneously transmitted along the chain, one would expect a near to unity correlation between price volatilities at different market levels (Serra, 2011). It can be the case that the predictable portion of prices is perfectly transmitted, whereas the unpredictable portion is not. Figure 6.1 illustrates a situation that implies a perfect price transmission in levels and an imperfect price volatility transmission for a chain consisting of a farm and retail sector of an unprocessed agricultural food product (to allow direct comparison of the degree of price transmission). Farm and retail price predictions can be made based on market fundamentals such as past prices, the degree of market competition, and demand and supply conditions.

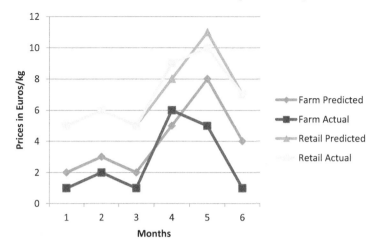

Figure 6.1 Price transmission and price volatility transmission: an illustration.

Figure 6.1 shows that the predictable portion or the conditional means of farm and retail prices follow each other both in the short and long run. This indicates that price transmission in levels is perfect. However, the graph on actual prices shows that farm prices deviate more often from the mean values than the retail prices do. This implies that farm prices are less predictable than retail prices, and that the farm price unpredictability does not translate into unpredictable retail prices. This implies imperfect price volatility transmission from farm to retail, even though causality cannot be directly inferred from the figure.

3 Factors affecting food price volatility transmission

Table 6.1 provides a summary of studies that investigated price volatility transmission in food supply chains. The data in Table 6.1 follows from the literature review by Assefa et al. (2013) and Assefa et al. (2015). The overview of studies shows that price volatility transmission is bidirectional. The factors that the authors suggested as having an effect on the degree of transmissions are reported in the last column of Table 6.1. No formal tests of such effects are conducted, however, in any of the reported studies. The suggested factors can be categorized as farm-level and retail-level factors. Each category is briefly discussed next.

3.1 Farm-level factors

The nature of farm production, inelastic farm-level demand, farm input cost share, and contracts fall into the category of farm-level factors. While the first two factors can explain the higher level of farm price volatility relative to the retail stage, the latter two factors can explain the level of volatility transmissions across these two chain stages. According to Apergis and Rezitis (2003) and

Table 6.1 Summary of the reviewed price volatility transmission literature

Authors (date)	Countries	Products	Chain stages	Sample period	Transmission of volatility detected	Direction of detected volatility transmission	Factors affecting volatility transmissions
Khan and Helmers (1997)	US	Feed (corn), beef, poultry, pork	Feed – farm – wholesale – retail	1970–1981	Yes	From feed to farm	Contracts
Natcher and Weaver (1999)	US	Beef	Feeder cattle – live cattle – wholesale – retail	1970–1983	Yes	Bidirectional across all chain stages	None
Buguk et al. (2003)	US	Catfish	Feed – farm – wholesale – retail	1980–2000	Yes	From feed to farm; From wholesale to farm; From farm to wholesale	Market power
Apergis and Rezitis (2003)	Greece	Agricultural products	Agricultural input – agricultural output – retail	1985–1999	Yes	From feed to farm; From consumer to farm	• Contracts • Nature of agricultural production • Inelastic farm-level demand
Rezitis (2012)	Greece	Lamb, beef, pork, poultry	Farm – retail	1988–2000	Yes	From farm to consumer; From consumer to farm	None
Chavas and Mehta (2004)	US	Butter	Wholesale – retail	1980–2011	Yes	N/A[1]	None
Zheng et al. (2008)	US	45 retail food items	Retail	1980–2004	Yes	From farm to retail	• Market power • Farm input cost share
Mehta and Chavas (2008)	Brazil–US	Coffee	Farm (Brazil) – wholesale (US) – retail (US)	1975–2002	Yes	N/A	None

Study	Country	Commodity	Relationship	Period		From farm to retail	Driver
Uchezuba et al. (2010)	South Africa	Boiler	Farm – retail	2000–2008	Yes	N/A	Market power
Serra (2011)	Spain	Beef	Farm – retail	1996–2005	Mixed	N/A	Market power
Alexandri (2011)	Romania	Agricultural price indices	Farm – retail	2006–2010	Yes	N/A	• Retail marketing strategy • Inelastic farm-level demand
Rezitis and Stravapoulaus (2011)	Greece	Broiler	Farm – retail	1993–2009	No	N/A	Market power
Rezitis (2012)	Greece	Beef, lamb, pork, poultry	Farm – retail	1993–2008	Yes	N/A	None
Khiyavi et al. (2012)	Iran	Poultry	Feed – farm – retail	1997–2010	Yes	From feed to farm; From retail to farm	• Contracts • Nature of agricultural production • Inelastic farm-level demand

[1]Not applicable

Khiyavi et al. (2012), farmers cannot quickly respond to market price signals due to time lags in farm production. This in turn leads to farm prices being more volatile than wholesale and retail prices. The other factor causing a mismatch between farm and downstream stage price volatility is the inelasticity of farm-level demand compared to consumer demand. This implies that an oversupply at the farm level is not proportionately matched by an increase in retail demand, causing farm prices to drop further.

Contracts are argued by Khan and Helmers (1997), Apergis and Rezitis (2003), and Khiyavi et al. (2012) to reduce volatility transmissions in the chain. According to Khan and Helmers (1997), contract production helped to reduce the transmission of corn price volatility to beef and poultry prices. On the other hand, Apergis and Rezitis (2003) argue that, although farmers have a contract for their inputs, their output prices can be affected by price shocks coming from output markets if they do not enter into price-fixing contracts for their outputs. Khiyavi et al. (2012) argue that the sensitivity of agricultural outputs to agricultural input and retail price volatilities would be reduced if farmers had used contracts for their inputs and outputs. Finally, the low share of farm inputs in retail prices is argued to be responsible for the low responsiveness of retail prices to the volatility of farm prices (Zheng et al., 2008).

3.2 Retail-level factors

A commonly mentioned reason for the low transmission of price volatility through the supply chain is actors' market power, and retail market power in particular (Buguk et al., 2003; Zheng et al., 2008; Uchezuba et al., 2010; Serra, 2011; Rezitis and Stavropoulos, 2011). Retail market concentration is argued to cause consumer prices to be irresponsive to the volatility of farm prices. According to Serra (2011), retailers use their market power to transmit farm price volatility in calmer periods (periods with limited news on bovine spongiform encephalopathy [BSE] crisis), but do not transmit in turbulent times (when news of BSE cases is widespread). Marketing strategies of retailers also reduce the transmission of farm price volatility to consumers (Alexandri, 2011). According to Alexandri, retailers keep consumer prices rigid due to consumers' sensitivity to frequent price changes. Buguk et al. (2003) argues on the other hand that even farmer market power can reduce volatility transmissions in the chain. They argue that farmers organized in cooperatives can use their market power to asymmetrically transmit input price shocks to the next stage.

4 Factors affecting food price transmission

Table 6.2 summarizes the main factors affecting price transmission (in levels). It should be noted that although the list of the reviewed studies is not exhaustive, it provides the key factors affecting price transmission. In contrast to the price volatility transmission literature, the price transmission literature has

Table 6.2 Summary of factors affecting price transmissions

Author (Date)	Country	Product	Chain stages	Sample period	Asymmetry detected?	Factors affecting price transmission
Reagan and Weitzman (1982)[1]	—				Yes	Adjustment costs
Mankiw (1985)[1]	—				Yes	Adjustment costs
Shonkwiler and Taylor (1988)	US	Orange juice	Processing – retail	1976–1985	No	Adjustment costs
Weaver et al. (1989)	US	Meat, poultry, eggs, fish, cereals	Farm – retail	1969–1981	Asymmetry not studied	Market concentration
Schroeter and Azzam (1991)	US	Pork	Farm – wholesale	1972–1988	Asymmetry not studied	Market power
McCorriston and Sheldon (1996)	EU	Banana	Wholesale – retail	N/A[2]	Yes	Number of stages in the chain and market power
Bernard and Willet (1996)	US	Broiler	Farm – wholesale – retail	1983–1992	Yes	Market power
Levy et al. (1997)	US	Various retail food products	Retail[3]	1991–1992	Yes	Adjustment costs
Azzam (1999)[1]	—	—			Yes	Market power and adjustment costs
Bettendorf and Verboven (2000)	Netherlands	Coffee	Farm – retail	1992–1996	Asymmetry not studied	Cost share of farm input and market power
Mc Corriston et al. (2001)[1]	—	—			Asymmetry not studied	Market power and processing technology in food industry
Miller and Hayenga (2001)	US	Pork	Farm – wholesale – retail	1981–1995	Yes	Adjustment costs and market power

[1]Indicates theoretical paper
[2]Not applicable. Simulations are made.
[3]Studies focusing on the retail stage study retail price rigidity using scanner data

theoretically and/or empirically tested for the effects of the factors mentioned in the table on the level of price transmission. Another distinction between these two streams of literature is that a focus of the price transmission literature has been the detection of asymmetries in price transmissions. Table 6.2 also indicates whether the reviewed studies detected transmission asymmetries. The commonly mentioned factors affecting price transmissions are briefly discussed next.

4.1 Market power

As Table 6.2 indicates, market power is an important factor determining the degree of price transmission. Market power often results in asymmetric price transmission, whereby actors transmit input price increases more than price decreases. Market power also results in output price rigidity, in which the output price does not react to both input price increases and decreases. Such abuse of market power is mainly reported in downstream stages of the food supply chain (wholesaler and retail), which are more concentrated than the farm sector. Besides their large number and the homogeneous nature of their products, the inability of farmers to easily control supply weakens their bargaining position vis-à-vis the buyers. According to Acharya et al. (2011), retailers exercise more market power during periods with excess farm production than when supply is in shortage. Market power also helps the downstream sector secure a constant or a higher margin in times of market crises. For instance, Lloyd et al. (2006) show that the BSE crisis had a differential impact on producer and retail prices, and therefore on farm–retail margins. In the absence of market power, the crisis would have had the same impact on the two prices and therefore should not have had an impact on the farm–retail margin.

Some authors, on the other hand, argue that market power does not always reduce price transmission through the chain. By considering the case of retailers that compete with competitors within their vicinity, Azzam (1999) suggests that retail prices are more flexible when retailers have market power than when they are in vigorous competition. He also shows that positive asymmetric price transmission occurs whether firms have market power or not. Weaver et al. (1989) support the view that market power as measured by concentration increases the transmission of upstream price changes. They assert that increased concentration increases the efficiency of firms and reduces the need for firms to postpone the transmission of upstream price decreases. As put by Azzam (1999, p. 997), "the temptation to secure such cost savings may have overwhelmed the incentives for oligopolistic output restrictions".

4.2 Adjustment costs

Price adjustment cost at the retail stage is the second commonly mentioned factor affecting price transmission in the chain. Adjustment costs are also labelled as repricing costs or menu costs, and they refer to any costs incurred in repricing decisions. According to Miller and Hayenga (2001), retailers do not respond to high-frequency/temporary price changes because of the high cost of adjusting inventories and other costs involved in changing prices. According to Azzam (1999), retailers change prices only when the extra profit from repricing is greater than the cost incurred to reprice. These costs include the time of relabelling products and the goodwill lost because of frequent repricing. Adjustment costs not only cause rigidity in output prices but also result in asymmetric price transmission. For instance, Reagan and Weitzman (1982) argue that firms prefer to increase inventory in times of low prices instead of lowering their output prices. In times of high market prices, on the other hand, firms respond by increasing their prices. This is because the cost of increasing inventory at times of decreasing prices is less than the cost of producing new inventory at times of increasing prices.

4.3 Other factors

Other factors affecting price transmission are the number of stages in the chain, the cost share of farm input in final output, the food processing technology, psychological pricing, government regulations, the perishability of the product, and inflation. The effect of farm input cost share on the degree of price transmission was formally shown by Bettendorf and Verboven (2000). They show that the low share of the costs of farm outputs in marginal costs reduced more farm price transmissions than did the degree of retail market power. Government policies that influence food prices also have their own effects on price transmission. Romain et al. (2002) show, for instance, that policies that open local markets for competition and those that put ceilings on retail prices lead to a symmetric transmission of farm price changes to the retail stage. Government policies can also have the effect of reducing farm price transmissions. For instance, Kinnucan and Forker (1987) attribute the asymmetric price transmission by retailers to government regulation that support the prices received by farmers. They argue that middlemen may view farm price increases as permanent, whereas they view farm price decreases as temporary expecting the government to interveve to raise back farm prices. This is turn results in a less complete transmission of farm price decreases. Psychological pricing consists of setting prices just below some particular pricing points. These pricing points contribute to price rigidity because consumers are believed to react easily if prices go beyond those pricing points (Herrmann and Moeser, 2006). The perishability of a product also determines the degree of price transmission. Kim and Ward (2013) find that falling farm prices are transmitted far faster than rising farm prices because the rise in the prices of highly perishable goods can reduce the volume of sales. Finally, inflation is shown by Acharya et al. (2011) to have an asymmetric effect on the transmission of farm price to consumers. This is because retailers are reluctant to reduce prices in times of inflation while they transmit price increases.

5 Factors affecting food price volatility transmission and food price transmission: implications

A comparison of factors affecting price volatility transmission and food price transmission reveals that actors' market power is an important factor that reduces both types of transmissions (see Chapter 5, McCorriston and von Cramon-Taubadel). Factors such as adjustment costs and various pricing strategies of actors downstream to the farm sector also relate to actors' exercise of market power. While a lower price volatility transmission benefits chain actors, a lower price transmission could be economically costly. The retail sector is often alleged to use market power to keep consumer prices rigid or to transmit only farm price increases to the consumers. A competitive retail market implies a higher transmission of farm price decreases to the consumers while it also implies a transmission of farm price volatilities. Alternatively, while a competitive retail sector implies a higher transmission of consumer price increases to the farmers, it also implies an increased transmission of consumer price drops caused by sudden drop in demand (due to, for instance, consumer panics resulting from news on an animal health scare). This indicates that market measures intended to improve price transmissions can have the undesired effect of increasing price volatility transmission.

Contracts are the second most important factor mentioned in the price volatility transmission literature. Contracts are however not indicated as an important factor within the price transmission literature. The use of contracts among competitive chain actors can reduce price volatility transmission while enhancing the transmission of the predictable portion of price changes. Although one can hypothesize that the factors reducing price transmission also reduce the transmission of price volatility, one should still conduct empirical research to verify this. Such empirical studies are currently lacking and are an interesting avenue for future research.

This review showed that since both price transmission and price volatility transmission deal with price linkages in the chain, both types of transmissions can be affected by similar factors. While such factors can have desirable effects on one type of transmission, they may have the opposite effect on the other type of transmission. This indicates that different market measures that complement each other apply for the two types of transmissions. An example is the encouragement of market competitions to enhance price transmissions while at the same time encouraging contractual relations among chain actors.

References

Acharya, R.N., Kinnucan, H.W., and Caudill, S.B. (2011). Asymmetric farm–retail price transmission and market power: A new test. *Applied Economics, 43*(30), 4759–4768.

Alexandri, C. (2011). Analysis of price transmission along the agri-food chains in Romania. *Agricultural Economics and Rural Development, 8*(2), 171–189.

Apergis, N., and Rezitis, A. (2003). Agricultural price volatility spillover effects: The case of Greece. *European Review of Agricultural Economics, 30*(3), 389–406.

Assefa, T.T., Meuwissen, M.P.M., and Oude Lansink, A.G.J.M. (2013). Literature review on price volatility transmission in food supply chains, the role of contextual factors, and the CAP's market measures. Retrieved from http://www.fp7-ulysses.eu/publications/ULYS SES%20Working%20Paper%204_Price%20volatility%20transmission%20in%20food%20 supply%20chains.pdf

Assefa, T.T., Meuwissen, M.P.M., and Oude Lansink, A.G.J.M. (2015). Price volatility transmission in food supply chains: A literature review. *Agribusiness, 31*(1), 3–13.

Azzam, A.M. (1999). Asymmetry and rigidity in farm-retail price transmission. *American Journal of Agricultural Economics, 81*(3), 525–533.

Ben-Kaabia, M., and Gil, J.M. (2007). Asymmetric price transmission in the Spanish lamb sector. *European Review of Agricultural Economics, 34*(1), 53–80.

Bernard, J.C., and Willett, L.S. (1996). Asymmetric price relationships in the US broiler industry. *Journal of Agricultural and Applied Economics, 28*(2), 279–289.

Bettendorf, L., and Verboven, F. (2000). Incomplete transmission of coffee bean prices: Evidence from The Netherlands. *European Review of Agricultural Economics, 27*(1), 1–16.

Buguk, C., Hudson, D., and Hanson, D. (2003). Price volatility in agricultural markets: An examination of U.S. catfish markets. *Journal of Agricultural and Resource Economics, 28*(1), 86–99.

Chavas, J.P., and Mehta, A. (2004). Price dynamics in a vertical sector: The case of butter. *American Journal of Agricultural Economics, 86*(4), 1078–1093.

FAO, IFAD, IMF, OECD, UNCTAD, WFP, the World Bank, the WTO, IFPRI, and the UN HLTF. (2011). Price volatility in food and agricultural markets: Policy responses. Retrieved from http://www.oecd.org/dataoecd/40/34/48152638.pdf

Hernandez, M., Ibarra, R., and Trupkin, D. (2011). How far do shocks move across borders? Examining volatility transmission in major agricultural futures markets. Retrieved from http://www.um.edu.uy/docs/working_paper_um_cee_2011_09.pdf

Herrmann, R., and Moeser, A. (2006). Do psychological prices contribute to price rigidity? Evidence from German scanner data on food brands. *Agribusiness, 22*(1), 51–67.

Khan, M.A., and Helmers, G.A. (1997). Causality, input price variability and structural changes in the U.S. livestock-meat industry. Paper submitted to Western agricultural economics association meeting, Reno, Nevada.

Khiyavi, P.K., Moghaddasi, R., Eskandarpur, B., and Mousavi, N. (2012). Spillover effects of agricultural products price volatilities in Iran. *Journal of Basic and Applied Scientific Research, 2*(8), 7906–7914.

Kim, H., and Ward, R.W. (2013). Price transmission across the U.S. food distribution system. *Food Policy, 41*, 226–236.

Kinnucan, H.W., and Forker, O.D. (1987). Asymmetry in farm-retail price transmission for major dairy products. *American Journal of Agricultural Economics, 69*(2), 285–292.

Levy, D., Dutta, S., Bergen, M., and Venable, R. (1997). The magnitude of menu costs: Direct evidence from large U.S. supermarket chains. *The Quarterly Journal of Economics, 112*(3), 791–825.

Lloyd, T.T., McCorriston, S., Morgan, C.W., and Rayner, A.J. (2006). Food scares, market power and price transmission: The UK BSE crisis. *European Review of Agricultural Economics, 33*(2), 119–147.

Mankiw, N.G. (1985). Small menu costs and large business cycles: A macroeconomic model of monopoly. *The Quarterly Journal of Economics, 100*(2), 529–537.

McCorriston, S., Morgan, C.W., and Rayner, A.J. (2001). Price transmission: The interaction between market power and returns to scale. *European Review of Agricultural Economics, 28*(2), 143–159.

McCorriston, S., and Sheldon, I.M. (1996). The effect of vertical markets on trade policy reform. *Oxford Economic Papers, 48*(4), 664–672.

Mehta, A., and Chavas, J.P. (2008). Responding to the coffee crisis: What can we can we learn from price dynamics? *Journal of Development Economics, 85*(2), 282–311.

Meyer, J., and von Cramon-Taubadel, S. (2004). Asymmetric price transmission: A survey. *Journal of Agricultural Economics, 55*(3), 581–611.

Miller, D.J., and Hayenga, M.L. (2001). Price cycles and asymmetric price transmission in the U.S. market. *American Journal of Agricultural Economics, 83*(3), 551–562.

Natcher, W.C., and Weaver, R. (1999). The transmission of price volatility in the beef market: A multivariate approach. Paper selected for presentation at the American Agricultural Economics Association annual meeting, Nashville, Tennessee.

Piot-Lepetit, I. (2011). Price volatility and price leadership in the EU beef and pork meat market. In I. Piot-Lepetit and R. M'Barek (Eds.), *Methods to analyse agricultural commodity price volatility* (pp. 85–106). New York: Springer Science + Business Media.

Rabobank. (2011). Rethinking the food and agribusiness supply chain; impact of agricultural price volatility on sourcing strategies. Retrieved from http://hugin. info/133178/R/1549493/476482.pdf

Reagan, P.B., and Weitzman, M.L. (1982). Asymmetries in price and quantity adjustments by the competitive firm. *Journal of Economic Theory, 27*(2), 410–420.

Rezitis, A.N. (2012). Modelling and decomposing price volatility in the Greek meat market. *International Journal of Computational Economics and Econometrics, 2*(3), 197–222.

Rezitis, A.N., and Stavropoulos, K.S. (2009). Modelling pork supply response and price volatility: The case of Greece. *Journal of Agricultural and Applied Economics, 41*(1), 145–162.

Rezitis, A.N., and Stavropoulos, K.S. (2011). Price transmission and volatility in the Greek broiler sector: A threshold cointegration analysis. *Journal of Agricultural and Industrial Organization, 9*(1), 1–35.

Romain, R., Doyon, M., and Frigon, M. (2002). Effects of state regulations on marketing margins and price transmission asymmetry: Evidence from the New York City and Upstate New York Fluid milk markets. *Agribusiness, 18*(3), 301–315.

Schroeter, J.R., and Azzam, A.M. (1991). Marketing margins, market power, and price uncertainty. *American Journal of Agricultural Economics, 73*(4), 990–999.

Sckokai, P., and Moro, D. (2009). Modelling the impact of the CAP single farm payment on farm investment and output. *European Review of Agricultural Economics, 36*(3), 395–423.

Seal, J., and Shonkwiler, J. (1987). Rationality, price risk, and response. *Southern Journal of Agricultural Economics, 19*(1), 111–118.

Serra, T. (2011). Food scares and price volatility: The case of the BSE in Spain. *Food Policy, 36*(2), 179–185.

Serra, T., and Zilberman, D. (2013). Biofuel-related price transmission literature: A review. *Energy Economics, 37*, 141–151.

Shonkwiler, J.S., and Taylor, T.G. (1988). Food processor price behaviour: Firm level evidence of sticky prices. *Agricultural and Applied Economics, 70*(2), 239–244.

Tangermann, S. (2011). Risk management in agriculture and the future of the EU's Common Agricultural Policy. Retrieved from http://ictsd.org/downloads/2011/12/riskmanagement-in-agriculture-and-the-future-of-the-eus-common-agricultural-policy.pdf

Taya, S. (2012). Stochastic model development and price volatility analysis. OECD Food, Agriculture and Fisheries Working Papers, No. 57, OECD Publishing. Retrieved from http://dx.doi.org/10.1787/5k95tmlz3522-en

Uchezuba, I.D., Jooste, A., and Willemse, J. (2010). Measuring asymmetric price and volatility spillover in the South African broiler market. Retrieved from http://ageconsearch. umn.edu/bitstream/96434/2/179briol.pdf

Vavra, P., and Goodwin, B.K. (2005). Analysis of price transmission along the food chain. OECD Food, Agriculture and Fisheries Working Papers, No. 3, OECD Publishing. doi:10.1787/752335872456

Weaver, R.D., Chatting, P., and Banerjee, A. (1989). Market structure and the dynamics of retail food prices. *North Eastern Journal of Agricultural and Resource Economics, 18*(2), 160–170.

Zheng, Y., Kinnucan, H.W., and Thompson, H. (2008). News and volatility of food prices. *Applied Economics, 40*(13), 1629–1635.

7 Impacts of increased food prices and volatility on households' welfare

Sol García-Germán, Cristian Morales-Opazo, Alberto Garrido, Emiliano Magrini, Jean Balié and Isabel Bardají

1 Introduction

There have been major changes in the world food economy over the past decade: price volatility has increased (with two major cereal price spikes, one in 2007–2008 and one in 2010–2012, see Chapter 2 and section 2 in this chapter); oil prices grew to a maximum of US$140 per barrel in 2008, dropped in 2009 to US$45 and ran below US$60 by the end of 2014; world food demand increased; the industrialised world underwent serious economic crises; exchange rates became more volatile; and productivity gains in agriculture slowed down with respect to the previous decades. And yet, the prices of maize, wheat, soybeans and rice entered 2015 at much lower levels than in January 2012 and 2013; milk prices in the EU are declining in response to the end of milk quota (see Chapter 15). Altogether these new developments seem to put on hold the future trends of higher food prices the world would enter after 2012, as predicted by researchers and institutions (Dawe et al., 2015). Many economies began 2015 with very low inflation – some even bordering on the risk of deflation.

High food price levels and volatility have drawn the attention of governments and international organizations around the world. In addition to the short run impacts that high food prices can cause on poor consumers, food price volatility is also undesirable from a long-run economic viewpoint. Unexpected commodity price fluctuations reduce consumer and investor confidence in all countries (Anderson, 2012). Jha and Rhee (2012) estimated that food price increases in 2012 could have cut economic growth in Asian countries by 0.06 to 0.61 percentage points. The rise of agricultural commodity prices does not necessarily translate into immediate rises of food prices at the domestic level, but in open economies it is difficult to isolate domestic prices from international markets' instability (Flachsbarth and Garrido, 2014). For low-income countries, the prospect of facing high food prices raises a policy dilemma between price insulation or focusing on safety nets (see Chavas et al., 2014).

Increased food prices affect consumers not only in developing countries, but also among the poorest and most vulnerable households in developed countries (Dewbre et al., 2008; Gilbert and Morgan, 2010; Lloyd et al., 2011;

Huang and Wu Huang, 2012). Between 2005 and 2011, food price inflation was higher than nonfood inflation in OECD countries (McCorriston, 2014), a development rarely seen in the previous two decades. As food price levels rise, the expenditure of households devoted to other necessities, like health or education, falls, hurting the poorest households and increasing their vulnerability (Cockx et al., 2015). This chapter reviews the literature on impacts of high and volatile food prices, differentiating between high-income countries' and low- and middle-income countries' consumers and households.

The chapter is organized as follows. In the second section, we synthesise and comment on recent consumer price trends and movements. In the third section, we review the literature about possible impacts on both consumers and households. The last and fourth section draws some policy conclusions.

2 Food price levels and volatility

2.1 Price level and volatility of food prices in high-income countries

Consumer food prices grew significantly during the food crisis. Table 7.1 reports the percentage of months in which the ratio of the index of Consumers' All Food Prices and the index of Consumers' Unprocessed Food Prices ran above the Harmonised Index of General Consumer Prices (HICP) between January 2000 and November 2014 in 28 Member States (MS) of the European Union. The ratios have been calculated for the entire period and also for the first half (2000M1–2006M12) and for the second half (2007M1–2014M11).

Looking at the entire period (2000–2014) only in Ireland, Greece, Spain, Portugal and Romania, the percentage of months with the index All Food Prices being above the HICP was below 50%. In the other 23 MS, the index of All Food Prices ran above HICP more than half of the months between 2000 and 2014. The index of Unprocessed Food Prices ran below 50% of the months in Bulgaria, Czech Republic, Ireland, Greece, Spain, Croatia, Luxembourg, Portugal and Romania.

The shaded areas represent the countries whose percentage of months with food prices running above the HICP diminished in the second period (2007M1–2014M11) with respect to the first (2000M1–2006M12). With some exceptions, in the majority of MS, the percentage of months with All Food Prices running above HICP increased in the second period (only in eight this was not the case). But, in 12 MS the percentage of months with Unprocessed Food Price Indices running above HICP diminished in the second period.

Table 7.2 reports the monthly volatility (past) of the same food price indices shown in Table 7.1, also splitting the period into two halves, with 2006M12 being the final month of the first period. In the third and sixth columns, we report the ratio of the monthly volatility of the food price indices between the second and the first period. If this ratio is above 100%, it means that monthly volatility increased in the second period (2007M1–2014M11) with respect to the

Table 7.1 Percentage of months with Food Price Indices being greater than HICP General Consumer Prices during 2000M1–2014M11, 2000M1–2006M12 and 2007M1–2014M11 for All Food Prices and for Unprocessed Food Prices

Member State	All Food Prices			Unprocessed Food Prices		
	2000M1–2014M11	2000M1–2006M12	2007M1–2014M11	2000M1–2014M11	2000M1–2006M12	2007M1–2014M11
Belgium	82.1%	61.9%	100.0%	62.0%	58.3%	65.3%
Bulgaria	84.4%	71.4%	95.8%	31.8%	55.9%	10.5%
Czech R.	64.2%	64.3%	64.2%	44.7%	67.9%	24.2%
Denmark	92.7%	84.5%	100.0%	64.2%	85.7%	45.3%
Germany	89.9%	84.5%	94.7%	86.6%	85.7%	87.4%
Estonia	79.3%	59.5%	96.8%	78.2%	89.3%	68.4%
Ireland	48.0%	77.4%	22.1%	38.0%	77.4%	3.2%
Greece	44.7%	72.6%	20.0%	40.2%	70.2%	13.7%
Spain	36.9%	23.8%	48.4%	35.7%	27.4%	43.2%
France	64.8%	67.9%	62.1%	84.4%	69.0%	97.9%
Croatia	80.8%	44.0%	90.5%	25.0%	44.0%	20.0%
Italy	81.6%	67.9%	93.7%	60.3%	58.3%	62.1%
Cyprus	65.4%	26.2%	100.0%	70.4%	36.9%	100.0%
Latvia	63.1%	21.4%	100.0%	58.7%	36.9%	77.9%
Lithuania	73.2%	42.9%	100.0%	82.7%	63.1%	100.0%
Luxembourg	75.4%	71.4%	78.9%	47.5%	69.0%	28.4%
Hungary	94.0%	86.3%	100.0%	86.3%	68.5%	100.0%
Malta	84.9%	71.43%	96.8%	81.0%	66.7%	93.7%
Netherlands	81.6%	85.7%	77.9%	93.8%	91.7%	95.8%
Austria	84.9%	67.9%	100.0%	81.0%	63.1%	96.8%
Poland	74.3%	47.6%	97.9%	64.2%	50.0%	76.8%
Portugal	49.2%	83.3%	18.9%	46.4%	88.1%	9.5%
Romania	31.5%	72.6%	0%	28.0%	64.4%	0%
Slovenia	91.6%	82.1%	100.0%	90.5%	82.1%	97.9%
Slovakia	73.2%	80.9%	66.3%	58.1%	79.8%	38.9%
Finland	69.8%	50.0%	87.4%	72.1%	54.8%	87.4%
Sweden	85.5%	77.4%	92.6%	82.7%	66.7%	96.8%
United Kingdom	78.1%	53.6%	100.0%	83.1%	64.3%	100.0%

Source: Eurostat (2015). Data for Croatia only available from 2004M12 onwards. Data for Hungary and Romania only available from 2000M12 onwards. All Food Prices only available from 2000M12 onwards. All Food Prices Index includes bread and cereals, meat, fish and seafood, milk, cheese and eggs, oils and fats, fruit, vegetables, sugar, jam, honey, chocolate and confectionery, food stuffs not elsewhere classified. Unprocessed Food Price Index includes meat, fish and seafood, fruit and vegetables.

	All Food Price Indices			Unprocessed Food Price Indices		
	Volatility	Volatility		Volatility	Volatility	
Member State	2000M1–2006M12 (1)	2007M1–2014M11 (2)	(3)=(2)/(1) (%)	2000M1–2006M12 (4)	2007M1–2014M11 (5)	(6)=(5)/(4) (%)
Belgium	0.012	0.016	138.8	0.022	0.030	135.4
Bulgaria	0.035	0.013	120.6	0.068	0.070	103.5
Czech Republic	0.015	0.008	173.1	0.028	0.051	185.2
Denmark	0.009	0.006	122.4	0.018	0.018	103.3
Germany	0.012	0.013	83.5	0.023	0.019	82.4
Estonia	0.014	0.007	124.1	0.023	0.026	111.5
Ireland	0.007	0.008	135.9	0.011	0.014	132.9
Greece	0.022	0.020	62.1	0.041	0.029	70.4
Spain	0.007	0.013	126.6	0.010	0.016	155.1
France	0.010	0.006	98.6	0.017	0.017	100.3
Croatia	0.009	0.007	160.7	0.016	0.025	155.6
Italy	0.005	0.015	109.6	0.008	0.011	131.8
Cyprus	0.026	0.015	107.4	0.049	0.051	105.7
Latvia	0.021	0.011	100.2	0.039	0.033	86.5
Lithuania	0.014	0.008	114.7	0.024	0.022	88.4
Luxembourg	0.005	0.010	113.5	0.007	0.009	128.0
Hungary	0.021	0.009	109.8	0.040	0.045	112.2
Malta	0.020	0.019	157.4	0.038	0.058	151.4
Netherlands	0.012	0.011	73.6	0.023	0.013	58.8
Austria	0.012	0.007	134.1	0.023	0.030	130.1
Poland	0.018	0.008	99.5	0.035	0.031	88.3
Portugal	0.010	0.008	140.0	0.014	0.023	159.3
Romania	0.020	0.009	100.9	0.027	0.022	81.2
Slovenia	0.016	0.009	101.9	0.030	0.035	116.6
Slovakia	0.016	0.005	98.8	0.026	0.027	106.3
Finland	0.013	0.006	139.0	0.025	0.028	112.7
Sweden	0.011	0.006	104.0	0.022	0.021	99.1
United Kingdom	0.010	0.008	115.2	0.019	0.017	89.9

Source: Eurostat (2015). Data for Croatia only available from 2004M12 onwards. Data for Hungary and Romania only available from 2000M12 onwards.

first (2000M1–2006M12). Except for the shaded cells, in most MS consumer food prices became more volatile in the second period (2007M1–2014M11) than in the first period (2000M1–2006M12).

Both Tables 7.1 and 7.2 show that in most MS, consumer food prices grew more rapidly than the general consumer price index (HICP) between 2000 and 2014, and that food price monthly volatility increased during the second half of the period (from 2007M1 to 2014M11). However, there are significant differences across MS in terms of both increased food prices and volatility. Furthermore, it seems that All Food Prices became more volatile and grew more rapidly than Unprocessed Food Prices. The reasons for this different behaviour of the two EU food price indices have not been established in the literature in depth (see Chapters 5 and 6, which review the literature on price transmission over the value chain).

García-Germán et al. (2015a) showed that there is a long-run relationship between world agricultural commodity prices and consumer food prices in over half of the Member States, depending on the world agricultural commodity price index used. This, and the fact that food prices behaved quite differently in the 28 MS, indicates the complexity and diversity that characterise the food markets even in small neighboring countries using the same currency and integrated in common markets (see also Chapter 5).

2.2 Price level and volatility of staple food prices in low-income countries

Large differences in food prices can be found across low-income countries (LICs). While the level of domestic market prices in 2013 was generally higher than it was before the world price shocks (2007), this has not been true in all countries – indeed, the variability across countries is striking (see Pierre et al., 2014; Demeke et al., 2014; Dawe et al., 2015). This implies that improved incentives for farmers are less than it would be indicated by the behaviour of world prices, but also that consumers are less negatively affected.

Dawe et al. (2015) show that across 103 case studies for rice, wheat and maize, 28% had lower real prices in 2013 than in the first half of 2007; this percentage is roughly similar across crops. Thus, while domestic prices have broadly trended upward since 2007, there are many exceptions, highlighting the importance of a country-specific analysis (e.g. Abdulai, 2000; Balcombe et al., 2007; Baquedano et al., 2011; Burke and Myers, 2014; Cudjoe et al., 2010; de Janvry and Sadoulet, 2010).

For example, in Bangladesh, real domestic rice prices in 2013 were 8% lower than in the first half of 2007. This is similar to the change in world prices in real local currency terms, as Bangladesh has a relatively open rice trade policy that allows the private sector to arbitrage price differentials with external markets (Dorosh, 2009). But in China and the Philippines, despite the decline in world rice prices measured in real local currency terms, domestic prices have increased substantially due to rising costs of production and various support policies (see Gale, 2013, for China; and Briones and Galang, 2014, for the Philippines), as well as the fact that the countries have not sourced cheaper supplies from world markets.

This diversity of the behaviour of staple food prices (see FAO, 2014) shows that the general increase in real domestic food prices in many countries is not necessarily due to higher world market prices. A more open trading system would have led to lower domestic prices, but it also depends on other factors such as trade and domestic policies.

In Indonesia and the Philippines, for example, import restrictions in recent years have pushed domestic rice prices up, even while world rice prices were falling. This is just one of many examples where drivers other than world prices have effects on domestic prices. In a broader sense, however, the world food price crisis created the political response to impose such import restrictions.

There are many other examples as well. In Mozambique, import tariffs on cereals were reduced substantially in 2008 and have subsequently been maintained at the new lower levels. Temporary policies also affect domestic prices, e.g. export bans (for maize in Tanzania in 2011) and public stock releases (of maize in Ghana for 2011). Foreign exchange policy can also play a role, especially where these markets are thin, as in Ethiopia where the central bank reduced allocations of US dollars to wheat and maize importers in 2008, aggravating the effect of the world price shock on domestic markets (Durevall et al., 2013).

In terms of price volatility, Demeke et al. (2014) show that if we compare world price volatility across rice, wheat and maize, the measures are similar for all three crops, even if the world rice market is supposed to be more volatile because it is 'thinner', meaning that only a relatively small percentage of total production enters international trade. This suggests that the role played by the world market and its influence on price volatility are not clear.

These findings are consistent with those of Dawe et al. (2015), FAO et al. (2011) and Pierre et al. (2014), who found that domestic rice and wheat prices in African countries were more stable than maize prices (as well as being more stable than prices of other staples such as cassava, sorghum and millet). Greater price volatility for domestic maize prices may be due to the fact that a lesser proportion of global maize production is irrigated (20%, compared with 62% for rice and 31% for wheat; Portmann et al., 2010), which makes maize supply more unstable than rice's.

Another reason why domestic maize prices may be more prone to volatility (relative to rice and wheat) because of the very thin international market for white maize, which is the maize that dominates human consumption. This might explain the weak connection between domestic and international markets, which lessens the potential for international maize markets to play a stabilising role in domestic price formation. However, Dawe et al. (2015) explain that since white and yellow maize are substitutes (for farmers, if less so for consumers), the yellow maize international market might still be able to provide some stability to domestic prices in the event of domestic production shocks. The fact that large quantities of maize are used for biofuels might be another possible reason for greater domestic maize price volatility, although if this were a key driver one might expect that the mechanism would work through more volatile world market maize prices and their linkages with oil prices. But, world market maize prices are no more volatile than world market rice or wheat prices – the key difference is domestic price volatility (see Pierre et al., 2014). Thus, the reasons behind domestic maize price volatility need more investigation.

3 How have increased food prices and price volatility affected consumers and households?

3.1 Evaluations for high-income countries

Wealthier consumers respond to higher prices, spending more to buy what they would have purchased anyway. The European Commission (2008) claimed that the effect of higher expenditure devoted to food on the purchasing power and standard of living of consumers in the EU is small because of the relatively low share of food in total household expenditure. Recent work carried out by García-Germán et al. (2015b) shows that the percentage of households in the EU suffering some kind of food deprivation[1] is nonnegligible in some Member States (Figure 7.1). These authors showed that the percentage of households, belonging to the lowest income quintile who declare being food deprived between 2004 and 2011 is explained by changes both of the consumer food prices and the deviations of food price inflation over general inflation (see Table 7.1).

However, there are large differences in the share of income spent on food across EU Member States and even across income classes within each MS (Figure 7.1). Food demand and consumption are not only functions of income, but also of income distribution (Cirera and Masset, 2010). The share of food expenditure in the budget of poorer households is higher. As food prices rise, the expenditure devoted to other necessities, such as health or education, falls, hurting poor households. In this way, the share of food in households' total budgets can be considered as an indicator of vulnerability to unexpected price changes (Schnepf, 2012; García-Verdú et al., 2012; Cockx et al., 2015).

Huang and Wu Huang (2012) find that an increase in food and energy prices in the United States would give rise to substantial consumer welfare loss, especially for low-income households. In the case of a 10% (25%) rise in both food and energy prices, consumer welfare loss would represent 7.15% (17.40%) of their income in the households belonging to the lowest income quintile.

Gregory and Coleman-Jensen (2013) find that the household participants of the Supplemental Assistance Program (SNAP, formerly Food Stamps) in the US are more sensitive to food prices, while the effect on the food security

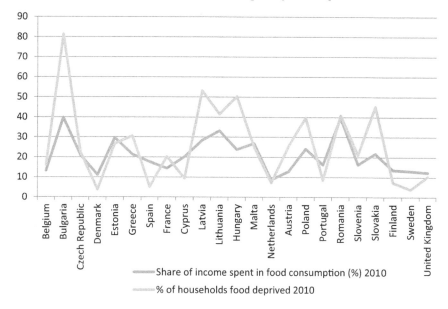

Figure 7.1 Percentages of food consumption expenditure and food deprivation among households in EU belonging to the lowest income quintile based on MS income distribution.

Source: Data from EU-SILC. 'This publication is based on data from European Commission, Eurostat, EU Statistics on Income and Living Conditions [EUSILC LONGITUDINAL UDB 2005 – version 2005–1 from 15–09–07; EUSILC LONGITUDINAL UDB 2006 – version 2006–2 from 01–03–2009; EUSILC LONGITUDINAL UDB 2007 – version 2007–5 from 01–08–2011; EUSILC LONGITUDINAL UDB 2008 – version 2008–4 from 01–03–2012; EUSILC LONGITUDINAL UDB 2009 – version 2009–4 from 01–03–2013; EUSILC LONGITUDINAL UDB 2010 – version 2010–4 from 01–03–2014; EUSILC LONGITUDINAL UDB 2011 – version 2011–2 from 01–03–2014]. EUROSTAT has no responsibility for the results and conclusions. The responsibility for all conclusions drawn from the data lies entirely with the author(s).' Weighted shares according to the household cross-sectional weight included in the survey's longitudinal files and EUROSTAT. Household Budget Surveys – Structure of consumption expenditure amongst households of the lowest income quintile (COICOP level 2). Data for Italy (2010) and Luxembourg (2010) not available. Methodologies used by the countries for data collection are not totally harmonised.

status of nonparticipants is zero. They found that an increase of $10 in the food index (less than one standard deviation) results in increases of the prevalence of food insecurity of 5%, 5.1% and 12.4%, respectively, for household, adult and child. SNAP reduces the probability of households' food insecurity by 17.4%, which represents a reduction of 33.7% of prevalence.

Similar results were obtained by Grethe et al. (2012) assessing the distributional effects on domestic household income in Israel. As a result of high world food prices, total household income declines and hence consumption and welfare decline. Income effects are progressive as higher income households suffer higher income declines as they receive a lower share of transfer income from the government. However, the regressive effect on the expenditure resulting from high expenditure share in low-income households overcompensates the income effect. As a result, low-income households are more affected and the increase of food price skews the income distribution in Israel.

Therefore, when looking at the impacts of food price rise and increased volatility, it is useful to consider the role of food expenditure in the average budget and the overall purchasing power of an average household. Figure 7.1 shows the food consumption expenditure in the lowest income quintile in the MS in the EU and the percentage of households that declared not being able to afford a meal with meat, chicken, fish (or vegetarian equivalent) every second day. Looking at the figure, two important observations should be made. First, there are significant differences within MS in the EU, ranging from less than 10% of overall consumption expenditure devoted to food in Luxembourg, to nearly 40% in Romania and Bulgaria. And second, there is positive correlation between the percentages of households suffering food deprivation and of income expended in food consumption, though the correlation is low. Some of the recently acceded countries have a greater percentage of households being food deprived than the share of income (Bulgaria, Hungary, Latvia, Poland and Slovenia). Southern countries (Greece, Spain, Portugal and Cyprus) have a proportionally smaller percentage of food deprived households than the recently acceded countries, in comparison with the share of income spent in food. In the US, the share of the highest (lowest) income quintile spent 11.6% (16.1%) of disposable income on food in 2011 (Schnepf, 2012).

One final comment relates to potential health effects of increased food prices. Jones et al. (2014) show that in the UK in 2012, the price of less healthy items was £2.50 per 1000 kcal, whereas more healthy items were priced at £7.49. Antentas and Vivas (2014) documented that Spanish consumers confronting higher food prices reduce their expenditures more on other goods (−3.2%) than on food (−0.2%). These authors also report significant changes in the composition of diets, with a notable increase of legumes, fruits and vegetables, food consumed at home and low-quality food items. Whether or not expensive food may result in worse diets or eating habits (Jones et al., 2014, and Antentas and Vivas, 2014, provide conflicting evidence), it can potentially affect other components of households' material well-being. Antentas and Vivas (2014) report that the economic crisis (2008–2013) made 41.2% of households reduce food expenditures, and almost 70% reduced the consumption of gas, 64.2% in clothes, 69.9% in leisure and 66.1% in holidays. Investigating both spheres of the households' well-being is complex, because consumer food price indices do not provide an accurate view of the actual cost of food items paid by consumers and because the indirect effect of increasing food prices is not easy to measure.

3.2 Evaluations for low-income countries

The impacts of higher and volatile food prices on poverty are likely to be very diverse, depending upon the reasons for the price change and on the structure of the economy (Ivanic and Martin, 2008). This includes the macroeconomic conditions, the country's net international trade position and the food production and consumption patterns of different households groups at the subnational level (see Anríquez et al., 2013; Hertel and Winters, 2006; Ravallion and Lokshin, 2005). A great deal depends on the distribution of net buyers and net sellers of food among low-income households (Aksoy and Isik-Dikmelik, 2008).

Aksoy and Isik-Dikmelik (2008) claimed that in order to understand the importance of higher food prices for welfare, poverty and food security, it is important to distinguish between net food sellers and net food purchasers. A net food seller is someone for whom total sales of food to the market exceed total purchases of food from the market, whereas for a net food purchaser the reverse is true. Net food consumers will generally be hurt by higher food prices, while net food producers will benefit. It is also true that whether a given household is a net food producer or consumer depends on market prices (see Zezza et al., 2008 and Anríquez et al., 2013). Higher prices will discourage consumption, encourage more production and possibly convert some households from net purchasers to net sellers. Lower prices could do the opposite.

Although nearly all urban dwellers are net food consumers, not all rural dwellers are net food producers (see Timmer, 1991). In fact, small farmers and agricultural labourers are often net consumers of food, as they do not own enough land to meet the entire household's food needs. These landless rural households are often the poorest of the poor. Although some of these labourers work on farms and are occasionally paid in food, they typically do not earn enough food to sell a surplus on the market (see Timmer, 1993, and Gulati and Dutta, 2010). Instead, they need to purchase food in markets and are likely to benefit from lower prices.

It has been argued that higher food prices will substantially hurt poor net food consumers because food is typically a large share of expenditure for the poor (Compton et al., 2010). Since many farmers are poor, higher prices could help to alleviate poverty and improve food security. However, these authors concluded that 'most poverty impact came from increasing depth of poverty in the already-poor, rather than increased "poverty headcount"' (p. ii).

In addition, concluded Hertel et al. (2004) that incomes of farm households, frequently one of the poorest groups in low-income countries, may be increased by higher commodity prices. However, according to de Janvry and Sadoulet (2010), the benefits of higher food prices to poor farm households may be less than they might at first appear, since these benefits depend not on what they produce, but on their net sales of these goods. For example, many farm households may not be able to shift into commercial crop production and sales as a response to trade reform even if it is a much more profitable activity, because (small-scale) farmers face high transaction costs in marketing their products or receiving modern inputs (Key et al., 2000). Cadot et al. (2005) showed that in the case of Madagascar's subsistence farmers, these transaction costs could be equivalent to one to two years of the value of their marketable production.

Ivanic and Martin (2014) find strikingly different impacts on poverty of price increases of wheat, rice and maize in the short term and in the long term. In general, short-term impacts are poverty increasing, but in the long term these authors find reversed effects in reducing poverty. Long-term effects are favoured because supply elasticity is greater than demand elasticity, so poverty reversals can be important for maize, wheat and rice producers.

Robles and Torero (2010) found that higher prices increased poverty in Guatemala, Honduras, Nicaragua and Peru. Dawe and Slayton (2010) summarised a large number of studies on rice, and again found that the poorest quintile of the population is nearly always a net purchaser of rice. Verpoorten et al. (2013) suggest that heterogeneous effects in self-reported food security are consistent with economic predictions, as they are correlated with economic growth and net food consumption (both at the household and country level). Specifically, in the face of rising food prices, self-reported food security improved on average in rural households, while it worsened among urban households, a finding that holds when using global prices or domestic food prices.

Using the estimated expenditure and price elasticities, Magrini et al. (2015) calculated the effects of a price change on welfare, measured as the proportion of total consumption expenditure needed to make the household indifferent between the old and the new prices in five countries; households' consumption expenditures on food in five LICs are reported in Table 7.3. Not surprisingly, the most important food category is cereals – mainly composed of maize, rice, wheat, sorghum and millet – which cover from 30% of the total food expenditure in Tanzania to 47% in Ethiopia.

In particular, Magrini et al. (2015) analysed the impact of the 35% price increase observed in the FAO cereal price index between 2010 and 2011.

Table 7.3 Budget shares for food

	Ethiopia	Tanzania	Niger	Malawi	Bangladesh
Food Expenditure Share	78.78%	70.60%	71.58%	78.11%	56.13%
Budget Shares					
Cereals	47.15%	30.03%	46.32%	32.21%	40.15%
Livestock and Liv. Products	14.16%	19.78%	19.84%	20.34%	24.30%
Fruits and Vegetables	3.64%	13.48%	4.59%	13.88%	15.38%
Tubers and Plantains	4.71%	9.22%	7.32%	5.76%	3.17%
Pulses and Oils	10.57%	9.92%	8.68%	10.44%	7.91%
Other Foods	19.76%	17.57%	13.25%	17.36%	9.09%
Number of Households	3969	3924	3968	3247	4423
Reference Year	2011/12	2010/11	2010/11	2011	2011/12
Survey Provider	WB	WB	WB	WB	IFPRI

Source: Magrini et al. (2015).

Note: WB = World Bank; IFPRI = International Food Policy Research Institute

Table 7.4 Welfare effects of a 35% increase in the cereal price (positive changes indicates a welfare loss)

	Ethiopia	*Tanzania*	*Niger*	*Malawi*	*Bangladesh*
Total	5.75%	6.16%	12.76%	3.81%	7.86%
Urban	9.50%	7.30%	10.39%	3.20%	8.61%
Rural	5.21%	5.61%	14.26%	5.50%	7.41%
1st Quintile	5.03%	4.86%	14.62%	4.35%	12.14%
2nd Quintile	4.84%	5.75%	14.19%	3.22%	8.89%
3rd Quintile	5.54%	6.73%	13.67%	3.64%	7.61%
4th Quintile	5.94%	7.20%	12.36%	3.87%	5.58%
5th Quintile	7.38%	6.24%	8.94%	4.00%	5.09%
Net Buyer	13.77%	9.35%	13.45%	8.22%	12.24%
Net Seller	−1.44%	−2.52%	−0.69%	−1.23%	−4.20%

Source: Magrini et al. (2015).

Table 7.4 reports the results of the simulation. A positive change indicates a welfare loss while a negative change corresponds to a welfare gain.

As it can be seen in Table 7.4, the results vary significantly across countries. Several reasons can be invoked in order to explain this heterogeneous response to the same price shock for economies with similar structures in terms of food expenditure. First, countries with higher budget shares devoted to cereals tend to suffer more. However, two additional key factors explain the results, including (a) the differences in the substitution effect, which allows households to better switch from cereals to other cheaper food groups, and (b) the differences in the share of net food sellers, which partially offset the welfare losses experienced by net food buyers.

Magrini et al. (2015) also investigated the distributional effects of the price change using the per capita consumption expenditure quintiles. For Ethiopia and Tanzania, the lower quintiles would experience lower welfare losses with respect to the better-off households. However, the magnitude of the difference between quintiles is limited and almost null for Malawi. Moreover, the same shock has very different consequences for Niger and Bangladesh, where an increase in the cereal price would result in much higher welfare losses for the poorest quintile than the richer ones.

Finally, they compared the welfare effects of the price change, looking at the net position of the households. As expected, cereal net buyers experience significant welfare losses while net sellers report welfare gains. However, the magnitude of the effects for each group relative to the total average impact matters. For example, in Ethiopia the welfare losses for net buyers would be more than double (13.77%) the national average (5.75%), which includes net sellers and self-sufficient households.

This difference raises two important considerations. Firstly, cereal producers in Ethiopia are able to reduce the negative impact of the price shock because a substantial part of the domestic production is marketed. Secondly, it is likely that a subgroup of the population (e.g. net buyers) will be heavily affected by the price change, even if the aggregate results may suggest otherwise. This last point is particularly important for policymakers interested in setting up national policies to control prices and support food security. The other countries show approximately the same pattern, except for Niger where the impact on net buyers corresponds to the total average, because the production effect is very limited and cereals are mainly bought on the market.

Finally, while the literature on the impact of price changes on household welfare in developing countries is quite extensive, very few works try to capture the consequences of price volatility. Recent work by Bellemare et al. (2013) shows that for Ethiopian households, the welfare gain for eliminating price volatility is actually increasing in income, contradicting the common beliefs that food price stabilisation policies would be more beneficial for the poorest households. This conclusion is supported by Magrini et al. (2015), who concluded that policies that limit price increases would benefit the poorest households more than attempts to reduce price volatility or untargeted support programmes.

4 Final remarks

In this chapter, we have reviewed the most recent literature on increasing consumer food price levels and variability and the impacts on consumers and households, both in high- and low-income countries. The behaviour of consumer food prices before, during and after the food crisis varies significantly across HICs and LICs. Even in the Euro Zone, a closely integrated common market system with a common currency, price indices behaved quite differently both in levels and volatility across Member States. Similarly, large differences can be found across LICs. Neither in HICs nor in LICs has the volatility of world food markets translated into similarly large price movements in domestic consumer food prices. Price transmission is a very complex process, in which a wide range of factors, notably public policies, explains large differences of transmission elasticities (see Chapters 5 and 6).

A number of empirical, theoretical and data issues underlie the difficulties in assessing the impacts of higher food prices on consumers, including the collection of prices and the composition of indices. Adding more complexity to the assessments is the fact that consumers adapt both their purchasing and eating habits in ways that are not easy to identify clearly. Also, retailers (supermarket chains) in urban areas around the world pursue very dynamic marketing and pricing strategies, as new research is now showing (see Chapter 5).[2] A policy implication is that correctly measuring food price indices, beyond food price inflation, will help governments to develop efficient and equitable food assistance policies. Another one is the importance of keeping track of the people's share of food expenditure as an indicator of households' exposure to increasing food prices. Obviously, the greater the share of food expenditure, the greater the exposure in LICs but also in HICs. However, equally important are the competitive regimes in different stages of the value chain.

At the policy level, there are numerous entry points which would deserve further elaboration and research. First, especially in developing countries, the macroeconomic aspects of food prices are relevant and far from being fully understood. Second, while the question of slow and gradual domestic food price adjustment to, or insulation from, international price surges has been given some attention, no clear guidelines emerge from this literature. There is some consensus about insulation benefits for poor consumers, not so much about the best way to do it. For instance, it is not clear which are the indirect effects on the producing sector and the timing of gradual price adjustments, or even whether they can be implemented effectively in all contexts.

The macroeconomic management of the price adjustment process is crucial in countries where food has a significant weight within indices of inflation. In high-income countries, wages, salaries, pensions and many government programmes are linked to inflation through adjustment clauses to maintain purchasing power of consumers. In general, food price inflation is more volatile than 'all-items' or 'core' inflations. But as poor consumers' shares of food expenditure are higher than the median consumers' in all economies, the impact of increased food prices has both a larger direct and indirect effect on their material well-being and welfare. Furthermore, in most industrialised countries, food prices grew more rapidly than nonfood prices for most of the months between 2000 and 2014, especially in the second half of the period. This, added to the fact that healthier food items are significantly more expensive than less healthy ones (Jones et al., 2014), may have long-term health impacts amongst the most vulnerable households.

Lastly, in low-income countries, the welfare programmes (income and food support; cash transfer, safety nets) clearly help poor households to cope with food price increases. There is general recognition that such programmes need to be targeted and well administered. However, scaling up food and income support is much easier than scaling it down, and the administrative burden to reach the most vulnerable is nonnegligible and perhaps beyond the capacity of many LICs. It is hoped that governments will recognize that policy preparedness and reliance on Early Warning Systems are essential elements to anticipate and effectively respond to price shocks.

Notes

1   EU statistics on income and living conditions (EU-SILC) is the EU reference study for comparative statistics on income distribution and living conditions in the EU. The study covers a wide range of indicators of material deprivation. One question included in the survey is 'Can your household afford a meal with meat, chicken, fish (or vegetarian equivalent) every second day?' The survey is administered annually in all EU MS and was started in 2003.
2   EU Project TRANSFOP (http://www.transfop.eu/) has developed path-breaking methods and uses massive databases of food prices in Europe. Chapter 5 in this book, by McCorriston and von Cramon-Taubadel, summarises the main conclusions of TRANSFOP.

References

Abdulai, A. (2000). Spatial price transmission and asymmetry in the Ghanaian maize market. *Journal of Development Economics, 63*, 327–349.

Aksoy, A.M., and Isik-Dikmelik, A. (2008). Are low food prices pro-poor? Net food buyers and sellers in low income countries. Policy Research Working Paper Series 4642. World Bank, Washington, DC.

Anderson, K. (2012). Distortions to agricultural versus non-agricultural producer incentives. *Annual Review of Resource Economics, 1*, 55–74.

Anríquez, G., Daidone, S., and Mane, E. (2013). Rising food prices and undernourishment: A cross-country inquiry. *Food Policy, 38*, 190–202.

Antentas, J.M., and Vivas, E. (2014) Impacto de la crisis en el derecho a una alimentación sana y saludable. Informe SESPAS 2014. *Gaceta Sanitaria, 28*(S1), 58–61.

Balcombe, K., Bailey, A., and Brooks, J. (2007). Threshold effects in price transmission: The case of Brazilian wheat, maize, and soya prices. *Journal of Agricultural Economics, 89*(2), 308–323.

Baquedano, F.G., Liefert, W., and Shapouri, S. (2011). World market integration for export and food crops in developing countries: A case study for Mali and Nicaragua. *Agricultural Economics, 42*, 619–630.

Bellemare, M.F., Barrett, C.B., and Just, D.R. (2013). The welfare impacts of commodity price volatility: Evidence from rural Ethiopia. *American Journal of Agricultural Economics 95*(4), 877–899.

Briones, R., and Galang, I. (2014). The continuing saga of rice self-sufficiency in the Philippines. Philippine Institute for Development Studies Policy Notes No. 2014–08.

Burke, W.J., and Myers, R.J. (2014). Spatial equilibrium and price transmission between Southern African maize markets connected by informal trade. *Food Policy, 49*, 59–70.

Cadot, O., Dutoit, L., and Olarreaga, M. (2005). How costly is it for poor farmers to lift themselves out of subsistence? CEPR Discussion Papers 5392, C.E.P.R. Discussion Papers.

Chavas, J.P., Hummels, D., and Wright, B.D. (Eds.). (2014). *The economics of food price volatility.* Chicago: The University of Chicago Press.

Cirera, X., and Masset, E. (2010). Income distribution trends and future food demand. *Philosophical Transactions of the Royal Society B, 365*, 2821–2834.

Cockx, L., Francken, N., and Pieters, H. (2015). Food and nutrition security in the European Union: Overview and case studies. FOODSECURE Working paper no. 31. Retrieved from http://www.foodsecure.eu/PublicationDetail.aspx?id=77 [Accessed in May 16 2015]

Compton, J., Wiggins, S., and Sharada, K. (2010). *Impact of the global food crisis on the poor: What is the evidence?* London: Overseas Development Institute.

Cudjoe, G., Breisinger, C., and Diao, X. (2010). Local impacts of a global crisis: Food price transmission, consumer welfare and poverty in Ghana. *Food Policy, 35*, 294–302.

Dawe, D., Morales Opazo, C., Balie, J., and Pierre, G. (2015). How much have domestic food prices increased in the new era of higher food prices? *Global Food Security. Volume 5.*

Dawe, D., and Slayton, T. (2010). The world rice market crisis of 2007–08. In D. Dawe (Ed.), *The rice crisis.* London: Earthscan.

de Janvry, A., and Sadoulet, E. (2010). The global food crisis and Guatemala: What crisis and for whom? *World Development, 38*(9), 1328–1339.

Demeke, M., Morales-Opazo, C., and Doroudian, A. (2014). Staple food prices in sub-Saharan Africa the context of a crisis: Challenges and policy options. Scientific Paper 7B, ULYSSES project, EU 7th Framework Programme, Project 312182 KBBE.2012.1.4–05. Retrieved from http://www.fp7-ulysses.eu/

Dewbre, J., Giner, C., Thompson, W., and Von Lampe, M. (2008). High food commodity prices: Will they stay? Who will pay? *Agricultural Economics, 39*(supplement s1), 393–403.

Dorosh, P. (2009). Price stabilization, international trade and national cereal stocks: World price shocks and policy response in South Asia. *Food Security, 1*, 137–149.

Durevall, D., Loening, J.L., and Birru, Y.A. (2013). Inflation dynamics and food prices in Ethiopia. *Journal of Development Economics, 104*, 89–106.

European Commission. (2008). Subject: Update on recent price developments in EU-27 agriculture and retail prices. Note for the file, Brussels, Belgium, August 4.

Eurostat (2015). Statistics on price indices. Brussels. Retrieved from http://appsso.eurostat. ec.europa.eu/nui/show.do

FAO. (2014). *State of food insecurity in the world.* Rome: FAO.

FAO, WFP, and IFAD. (2011). *State of food insecurity in the world.* Rome: FAO.

Flachsbarth, I., and Garrido, A. (2014). The effects of agricultural trade openness on food price transmission in Latin American countries. *Spanish Journal of Agricultural Research, 12*(4).

Gale, F. (2013). Growth and evolution in China's agricultural support policies. Economic Research Report Number 153. United States Department of Agriculture Economic Research Service.

García-Germán, S., Bardají, I., and Garrido, A. (2015a). Evaluating transmission prices between global agricultural markets and consumers' food price indices in the EU. *Agricultural Economics*, under revision.

García-Germán, S., Bardají, I., and Garrido, A. (2015b). Analysis of material deprivation in the EU under food price volatility and rise. Scientific paper 10, ULYSSES project, EU 7th Framework Programme, Project 312182 KBBE.2012.1.4–05. Retrieved from http:// www.fp7-ulysses.eu/

García-Verdú, R., Selassie, A., and Thomas, A. (2012). Inclusive growth in the sub-Saharan Africa: Evidence from six countries during the recent high-growth period. In R. Arezki, C. Pattillo, M. Quintyn, and M. Zhu (Eds.), *Commodity price volatility and inclusive growth in low-income countries* (pp. 245–295). Washington, DC: International Monetary Fund.

Gilbert, C.L., and Morgan, C.W. (2010). Food price volatility. *Philosophical Transactions of the Royal Society B, 365*, 3023–3034

Gregory, C.A., and Coleman-Jensen, A. (2013). Do high food prices increase food insecurity in the United States? *Applied Economic Perspectives and Policy, 35*(4), 679–707.

Grethe, H., Siddig, K., Götz, L., and Ihle, R. (2012). How do world agricultural commodity price spikes affect the income distribution in Israel? Paper at the GEWISOLA 2012, Hohenheim, Germany, September 26–28.

Gulati, A., and Dutta, M. (2010). Rice policies in India in the context of the global rice spike. In D. Dawe (Ed.), *The rice crisis: Markets, policies and food security.* London: FAO and Earthscan.

Hertel, T.W., and Winters, L.A. (Eds.). (2006). *Poverty and the WTO.* New York: Palgrave Macmillan and The World Bank.

Hertel, T.W., Ivanic, M., Preckel, P., and Cranfield, J. (2004). The earnings effects of multilateral trade liberalization: Implications for poverty. *The World Bank Economic Review, 18*(2), 205–236.

Huang, K.S., and Wu Huang, S. (2012). Consumer welfare effects of increased food and energy prices. *Applied Economics, 44*, 2527–2536.

Ivanic, M., and Martin, W. (2008). Implications of higher global food prices for poverty in low-income countries. *Agricultural Economics, 39*, 405–416.

Ivanic, M., and Martin, W. (2014). Short- and long-run impacts of food price changes on poverty. Policy Research Working Paper 7011. World Bank Group, Washington, DC.

Jha, S., and Rhee, C. (2012). Distributional consequences and policy responses to food price inflation in developing Asia. In R. Arezki, C. Pattillo, M. Quintyn, and M. Zhu (Eds.), *Commodity price volatility and inclusive growth in low-income countries* (pp. 225–244). Washington, DC: International Monetary Fund.

Jones, N.R.V., Conklin, A.I., Suhrcke, M., and Monsivais, P. (2014). The growing price gap between more and less healthy foods: Analysis of a novel longitudinal UK dataset. *PLoS ONE, 9*(10), 1–7.

Key, N., Sadoulet, E., and de Janvry, A. (2000). Transactions costs and agricultural household supply response. *American Journal of Agricultural Economics, 82*(2), 245–259.

Lloyd, T.A., Morgan, C.W., Davidson, J., Halunga, A., and McCorriston, S. (2011). Retail food price inflation modelling project final report. University of Nottingham, University of Exeter.

Magrini, E., Morales Opazo, C., and Balié, J. (2015). Price shocks, volatility and household welfare: A cross-country inquiry. ULYSSES Policy Brief No.5. April. Retrieved from http://www.fp7-ulysses.eu/publications.html [Accessed on May 5, 2015]

McCorriston, S. (2014). Competition in the food chain. Retrieved from http://www.transfop.eu/media/universityofexeter/businessschool/documents/centres/transfop/Competition_in_the_Food_Chain.pdf [Accessed on Aug 4, 2014]

Pierre, G., Morales-Opazo, C., and Demeke, M. (2014). Analysis and determinants of retail and wholesale staple food price volatility in developing countries. Scientific Paper No. 3, ULYSSES project, EU 7th Framework Programme, Project 312182 KBBE.2012.1.4–05. Retrieved from http://www.fp7-ulysses.eu/publications.html

Portmann, F.T., Siebert S., and Döll, P. (2010). MIRCA2000—Global monthly irrigated and rainfed crop areas around the year 2000: A new high-resolution data set for agricultural and hydrological modeling, *Global Biogeochemical Cycles, 24*, GB1011, doi:10.1029/2008 GB003435

Ravallion, M., and Lokshin, M. (2005). Testing poverty lines. *Review of Income and Wealth, 52*(3), 399–421.

Robles, M., and Torero, M. (2010). Understanding the impact of high food prices in Latin America. *Economia, 10*, 117–164.

Schnepf, R. (2012). Consumers and food price inflation. Congressional Research Service. September. Washington, DC. Retrieved from http://www.fas.org/sgp/crs/misc/R40545.pdf [Accessed on Jan 2, 2015]

Timmer, P. (1991). Food price stabilization: Rationale, design, and implementation. In Dwight H. Perkins and Michael Roemer (Eds.), *Reforming economic systems* (pp. 219–248 and 456–459). Cambridge, MA: Harvard University Press.

Timmer, P. (1993). Food price stabilization: The relevance of the Asian experience to Africa. In Nathan C. Russell and Christopher R. Dowswell (Eds.), *Policy options for agricultural development in Sub Saharan Africa* (pp. 107–127). Geneva: Centre for Applied Studies in International Negotiations.

Verpoorten, M., Arora, A., Stoop, N., and Swinnen, J. (2013). Self-reported food insecurity in Africa during the food price crisis. *Food Policy, 39*, 51–63.

Zezza, A., Davis, B., Azzarri, C., and Covarrubias, K. (2008). *The impact of rising food prices on the poor.* Rome: Food and Agriculture Organization.

Part 2

The views of some stakeholders

8 Are derivatives introducing distortions in agricultural markets?

Adamo Uboldi

1 Introduction

Volatility in agricultural commodities markets has been in the spotlight for a while. Considered as a threat to global food security, it has been analyzed by experts, debated by policymakers, and often misinterpreted by the press. Indeed, price level changes are often misunderstood and classified as volatility phenomena.

Agricultural prices decreased (in real terms) for a long period, and only recently was there a reversing signal, suggesting a possible increase in the future. It must be acknowledged that fertilizers and energy mainly contributed to the wide price spikes during the two crises in 2008 and 2012.

Contrary to the common perspective, with an annual large grid and long observations interval, volatility decreased. Figure 8.1 sums up this double behavior: prices rose while volatility lowered significantly. It should be noted that the choice of pivotal years (2009 in particular) is crucial and that 2014 data are partial. The landscape is completely different when considering the short-term horizon and data based on higher frequency: this fact makes questionable even the definition of "highly volatile markets".

While the effects and implications are clearer, a lot of papers have been published without reaching a consensus on the causes of agricultural commodities volatility. The ULYSSES project's works are an important contribution to the process.

Overall, the stream of literature has been inconclusive up to now. Inputs cost has been indicated as a trigger of price explosion, as has co-movement among commodities following oil prices. Financialization is among the most-quoted candidate causes, even if there is not an agreement on what financialization means!

2 Financialization

On one hand, financialization is represented by the massive flow of capital into agricultural futures markets and other activities, such as index contracts or agricultural exchange trade products (ETP). The sudden move of capital from

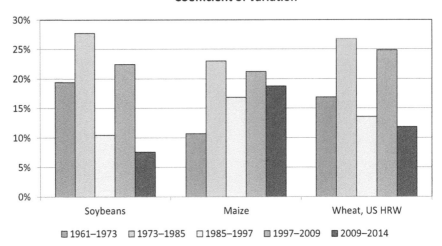

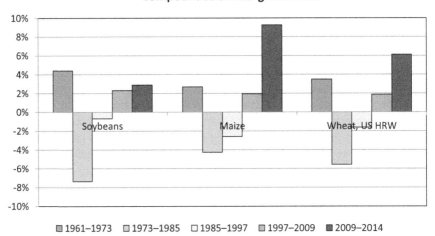

Figure 8.1 Coefficient of variation (top) and compounded annual growth rate (bottom) of soybeans, maize, and wheat (US HRW).
Source: Elaboration of World Bank data.

one suffering financial sector (credit default swap, securitization, government bonds, etc.) to another clearly caused serious issues to financial stability. When hedge funds started to pump up capital into agricultural contracts, several bells began ringing.

Some years later, we can draw some lessons: as expected, more capital made the markets more liquid and hence more resilient and efficient. The main fear was the consequent upward pressure to prices, caused by a significant increase of long positions. Some increases were registered, but at the same time, hedging has become easier, which is a massive gain. Concurrently, long positions contributed to stabilizing the markets and to decreasing risk premiums, so there's growing consensus on a mildly positive impact of index funds' activity.

On the other hand, I am more interested in describing the increase of financial engineering in agricultural markets and discussing how and why investment banks "invaded the field".

Box 8.1 Options and derivatives

In finance, a derivative is a type of contract that takes its value from the performance of an underlying entity: the underlying entity can be an asset, index, interest rate, etc., and it is often simply called the "underlying". Derivatives are used for many purposes, such as insuring against price movements (hedging), increasing exposure to price movements for speculation, or getting access to otherwise hard-to-trade assets or markets. It should be remarked that futures are derivatives, the simplest case of forward contract.

Among all derivatives, I shall focus on options since they are the most relevant, interesting, and standardized class.

An **option** is a type of financial contract which gives the buyer ("owner") the **right**, but not the obligation, to buy or sell an underlying instrument: the purchase, if the option is exercised, happens at a specified strike price (K) on (or before) a specified maturity date (T). Important asymmetry: the seller of the option has the corresponding **obligation** to fulfil the transaction (to sell or buy) if the buyer exercises the option. On the negotiation day (t), the buyer pays upfront a premium, the price of the option, to the seller in order to have this right. An option that conveys to the owner the right to buy at a specific price is referred to as a call (C), while an option that conveys the right of the owner to sell at a specific price is called a put (P).

The main link among options and an underlying asset is the so called **put–call parity formula**:

$$C(t) - P(t) = S(t) - K \cdot B(t,T)$$

where:
C(t) is the value of the call at time t (negotiation time),
P(t) is the value of the put of the same expiration date T,
S(t) is the spot price of the underlying asset,
K is the strike price, and
B(t,T) is the present (t) value of a zero-coupon bond that matures to 1€ at maturity time T.

In other words, K·B(t,T) is the current, at time t, value of K€ at time T.

At the beginning of the 2000s, derivatives were less than marginal in the agricultural sector, while they already gained dominance in other sectors. Options on stock exchange indexes such as the S&P500 already had trading volumes that were ten times higher than the underlying basket of shares. The landscape was completely different in the agricultural finance sector; in fact, options represented a small corner of the trading platform. In 2009, options written on the MATIF wheat contract (probably the most important European agricultural future contract) were still less than 1% of the market; three years later, they represented 20% of the cake. The values were much higher in the US, since options were introduced before.

2.1 Why such an increase?

First of all, a significant change of players took place; traditional actors were probably reluctant to introduce new, more complicated instruments whose price was, and still is, difficult to link to the underlying commodity value. Sophisticated mathematics is required together with market knowledge, so small cooperatives and small traders had to rely on financial expertise provided by other actors, who at a certain point decided to step into agricultural commodities markets on their own.

This triggered a new factor, the increase in financial engineering involved in commodities trading. Just as an example, I recently found a "double barrier knock-out Bermudan" option in the basket offered to customers by a bank specializing in agricultural hedging: how can a farmer correctly evaluate the offer?

Last but not least, derivatives are particularly appealing to the so called "speculators" class for two reasons: delivery is not necessarily physical, often just netting of position, and they also allow a massive use of financial leverage. Indeed, margins are also required to trade futures, but the ratio among upfront payment and final cash flow is particularly low, making derivatives a perfect tool to "enter the market" with a small amount of cash, even while taking relevant positions. That is why all of a sudden aggressive investment banks started to deal with maize and wheat.

3 Policy issue

The financial crisis triggered, with a significant delay, a massive amount of legislation on both sides of the Atlantic: namely, Dodd-Frank in the US and the EU package MIFID-MAR-EMIR.[1] Agricultural commodities markets have been influenced by the new regulations in many ways – position limits, obligation to register contracts, and so on. A wide amount of scientific literature and policy papers have been published on many related subjects, disclosing widely positive and rarely negative effects of the new regulations. From my point of view, there still is at least one open question.

Futures markets were already rather well regulated, and the surveillance/monitoring has been overall very efficient through years; indeed, futures markets are still alive after more than two centuries and several crises. On the contrary, options had been left into the over-the-counter market (OTC) for many years: by definition, it is a market of purely bilateral transaction among customers who found an agreement on their own. It seems nothing too serious, except that the amount of OTC contracts (all sectors included) is actually 700 trillion dollars, yes, *trillion*, prudently estimated by the International Swap and Derivatives Association (ISDA). It is true that there is some double counting and that some compression and netting could significantly reduce this huge amount, but still it's ten times the world GDP! More interesting, it's 15 to 20 times the amount of regulated finance.

Dodd-Frank and the EU financial directives push at least standardized options ("plain vanilla" European and American type) into the stock exchange framework and hence under the supervision umbrella; this is very good. At the same time, for many other contracts there is only the obligation to report or register activity in specified trade repositories, while for few other contracts and few other players there are no constraints.

My question is: **can volatility coming from the synthetic derivatives world affect futures markets and consequently spot markets?** The answer is not trivial, of course.

Spot markets and futures markets are strictly connected: convergence at delivery date is a standard check, and every time it fails to happen, severe investigations start both from supervisory authorities and by market makers on their own.

Slightly more complicated is to judge the relation among futures and options. Analytical tools are really different: futures market volatility analysis is generally based on historical/realized volatility, while for options the main variables are implicit volatility and risk neutral probability, both forward-looking measures.

As already described in the Box 8.1, the put–call parity formula is the main chain among the derivatives market and the underlying assets market.

In reality, the parity is systematically violated, because friction costs, margins, and brokerage fees unbalance the delicate abstract equilibrium given by the formula. To be clearer: the put–call parity formula is already not obeyed in highly liquid and efficient markets, so there is no hope that it works with agricultural commodities.

Do agricultural markets need a different treatment? More specifically, are position limits and circuit breakers enough to make the markets properly functioning? At a larger scale, these points lead to concerns which bring to the forefront the debate about food security, a hot policy item within the G20 initiative.

4 Ongoing work

In a recent paper (Sanfelici and Uboldi, 2014), a rather similar situation was analyzed, aiming at understanding whether high-frequency data machinery for the underlying asset was compatible with a risk-free measure approach to perform option pricing. Indeed, many volatility estimators are now available: they are all historical/realized measures, while option pricing techniques are based on the forward-looking risk-free measure. The old style Black–Scholes approach (volatility is the only input, price is the output) is now not only abandoned, but even reversed: implied volatility is obtained backwards from options prices. The analysis was performed on the S&P500, probably the most liquid contract worldwide, and the output should be read as follows:

Provided that the "right" high frequency volatility estimator and the "right" jump filtering technique are applied with an ad-hoc stochastic volatility model, it is possible to have high-quality option pricing. In other, hopefully simpler, words: **the two markets (underlying asset and derivatives) are blended and there is a bridge properly functioning that allows viable hedging strategies.**

Ongoing research is developed to understand whether the same results apply to agricultural commodities and corresponding derivatives.

In fact, several variables are really different in synthetic and agricultural markets: the ratios among open interest and volumes are not comparable, option quotas in the markets are completely different, even trading frequencies are different, and so on. Clearly, the possibility to implement robust and reliable hedging strategies is at stake.

5 Conclusion

Price volatility is a serious threat to market stability, to a properly functioning food chain, and to overall food security. In the last years, many financial products were introduced into the agricultural commodities markets, making hedging strategies more technical, even if easily available through financial intermediaries. This contributed to facilitating the migration of capital together with financial players into agricultural markets. The so-called speculators are crucial to market viability: if a player would like to get rid of a type of risk, there should be somewhere another one willing to bear it, when adequately compensated.

At the same time, derivatives introduce new and relevant policy issues, and the supervisors should investigate whether distortions from the synthetic derivatives market can negatively affect the spot market.

This does not happen with solid, robust, and highly liquid markets, but the question is still on the table for young, least-developed, and sometimes illiquid agricultural commodities markets.

More precisely: relatively recent agricultural derivatives markets are developing, following the way paved by stock/equity markets. Positive features are welcome; higher liquidity, lower friction costs, efficient hedging, and transparent risk transfer would be beneficial. On the contrary, the increased technicality and enhanced financial engineering introduce threats to market stability and could generate serious problems, such as the so called "Flash Crash" in 2010. Are circuit breakers sufficient to curb high-frequency speculation and algorithmic trading?

Further research is needed.

Note

1   Markets in Financial Instruments Directive (MIFID), Market Abuse Regulation (MAR), European Market Infrastructure Regulation (EMIR).

Reference

Sanfelici, S., and Uboldi, A. (2014) Assessing the quality of volatility estimators via option pricing. *Studies in Nonlinear Dynamics & Econometrics, 18*(2), 103–124.

9 The view of farmers
German pig producers

Torsten Staack

1 Introduction: the interest group of pig farmers in Germany (ISN)[1]

The ISN represents the economic and political interests of German pig farmers. The objective of our organization, which has about 11,000 members in Germany, is to strengthen the competitiveness of German pig farmers. Hence, market conditions and public relations play a central role in our work. Besides that, we execute project work in order to provide effective and economically viable solutions to crucial questions, especially those concerning the animal welfare discussion. This also includes forward-looking issues and current societal debates. The ISN has extensive experience in the field of public relations, as well as in teaching the context and reality of pig farming.

2 Pig farming in Germany – still a story of success?

Pig farming has written a phenomenal success story over the last ten years in Germany. The German pork sector shifted from being a net-importing country with a self-sufficiency degree of 80 percent to a powerful exporter with a self-sufficiency degree of 115 percent within the last decade. Pig meat is in demand all over the world, but German products are best known for high quality. This is because of strict production standards comprising hygienic and quality regulations throughout the whole supply chain.

In 2014, approximately 42 million piglets were produced in Germany. Moreover, we import about 11 million piglets, predominantly from Denmark and The Netherlands. Hence, about 53 million fattening pigs were merchandised in 2014 from German farmers to domestic slaughterers. In addition to the living imports of fattening pigs, 58 million pigs were slaughtered in 2014.

Considering the last 25 years, the number of pig farmers in Germany has decreased by 90 percent. At the same time, the amount of pigs has increased by about 8 percent. This means that in 1999, 141,000 pig farmers kept approximately 26 million pigs; today, in 2014, only 27,000 pig farmers manage a population of 28 million pigs. In relation to this, the average number of pigs per farm has increased from 185 pigs to 1,000 pigs.

Nevertheless, in some regions of intense processing of animals, one can identify the development during the last years of a particular farm structure. For instance, the region known as Oldenburger Münsterland (in northern Germany, federal state of Lower Saxony) has the largest density of livestock in Germany. In most cases, an enlargement of a typical family farm in this region has been marked by a gradual construction of new stables with a size between 1,000–2,000 finishing pig places during the last 10 or 20 years. Until today, the majority of farms increased to an average livestock of more than 5,000 pigs. Against the background of economic assumptions at the same time, such a development is extremely remarkable. In 2013, the fluctuation of the average pig price varied from 1.3 to 1.45 euro per kg carcass weight.

The fact that a typical family farm took the step forward to increase the farm structure is a clear indication of the adaptation capacity of pig farmers to volatile prices. In addition, the concentration of the up- and downstream sector (for instance, animal feed companies or food-processing companies) contributes significantly to the prosperity of livestock farms in this region. Furthermore, policymakers too have paid heed to an agricultural development in dialogue with the business community.

3 Great adaptability of the pig farmers concerning price volatility

Discussing the critical topic of price volatility in the pig market by view of the national association for pig producers, it should be emphasized that a large proportion of pig farmers can cope very well with price fluctuations. The current pig market is characterized by a very dignified system of commercialization opportunities. Thus, ISN's point of view is that the success of the pig farmers highly depends on their trading skills. It leads to the fact that both piglet producers as well as fattening farmers deal continuously with the optimal conditions to sell their animals.

The price for piglets, as well as the price for the slaughtered pigs, complies with weekly price announcements of more than 30 producer associations within Germany. A uniform price mask provides a fixed weekly rate that applies to all members. It is even estimated that this basis price applies to more than 80 percent of the weekly marketed quantity of meat. The differences between the farms are caused by some allowances and deductions to the weekly basis price according to the corridor of the price mask of each slaughterhouse (e.g., slaughter weight, indications of liver, pneumonia). Assuming a gross margin of 25 euro per fattening pig, a rise of 2 cents per kg improves the profitability by almost 10 percent.

4 The key to success – free market without any political subsidies

During the last few years, the pork industry has barely received any political subsidies. Furthermore, there are no quotas or similar listing regulations that affect price supports. An instrument to mitigate price volatility would be the hedge of purchase and sale on the commodity exchange. An exchange board for pigs and piglets exists in Germany. The so-called EUREX has a registered office in Frankfurt on the Main. Farmers can ensure their marginal returns when they house the animal. However, the acceptance is very low on both the sellers and buyers for various reasons. Predominantly, the market position of the big slaughter companies plays a great role. The oligopolistic structure (the largest four slaughterers hold 60 percent of the market share) does not incentivize the slaughterhouse firm to hedge purchase prices.

In order to eliminate any impacts of volatile prices, most pig farmers pursue a strategy of risk anticipation. In particular, animal feed, as one of the major expense factors, is predominantly being hedged or purchased together with larger associations to cope with the price. Similarly, fixed contracts between the piglet producers and takers are commonly used. In this way, a fixed link to the fattening farm can be managed.

5 Period of structural change due to social expectations

Currently, German pig farmers undergo a period of consolidation. Particularly in the region with a great livestock density, the **competition for land** is disproportionally high. Livestock farmers have to pay extreme lease prices in order to handle their manure corresponding to sustainable agriculture and husbandry. In addition, the new building legislation clearly complicates the creation of larger stables, because this is only possible with the consent of the local community. Especially in regions where the population of livestock has reached a critical status, the development of farms is almost impossible.

The **pressures of society in relation to animal welfare** have also increased. Many people have become detached from agriculture and rural life and no longer know about the modes of production. This leads to excessive and unrealistic expectations for farmers, which they cannot satisfy anymore. The political answer to this social development leads mostly into legal regulations. For instance, every stable with more than 1,500 pigs or, respectively, 560 sows needs to have a filter. The investment for a filter is projected to an average of 5 euro per fattening pig. Moreover, the time period for the transport of the animals should be limited. Consequently, the amount of different political restrictions hinders the structural change of farms. Bureaucracy is a major driver forcing smaller farms to give up production. Low production numbers just cannot compensate the cost for the administrative effort every farmer has to make, be it in accounting or audits for quality assurance (e.g., a new database for the consumption of antibiotics). Regardless of the size of the farm, there are costs that have to be compensated.

6 Conclusion and requests

In the ISN's opinion, the pig market can consequently regulate itself best – therefore ISN makes the following requests of European agricultural policy:

1 **Free market** without any trade barriers: In the EU, this is the key to success for European pig farmers. Politics should distance itself from any market interventions (e.g., quotas, export subsidies). ISN regrets that the EU's Commissioner of Agriculture Mr. Hogan has deviated from his original opinion of refusing the storage of pig meat. Public stock keeping is counterproductive and will lead to greater problems in the future.

2 When transposing a European law, it must be ensured that **legal bills are transferred equally and chronologically in national law** in all Member States, in order to avoid competitive disadvantages for certain farmers within Europe. For instance, by means of the regulation of group housing for sows, we have experienced a dramatic distortion of competition of sow farms in Germany. Whereas almost 99 percent of the sows in Germany were kept in the group, this figure was 80 percent in Spain as of 1 January 2014.

3 The ISN asks policymakers to **exploit new export markets**. Germany became a net exporter of pig meat in 2007 and depends on international trade. There are about 2,500 different products made from pigs, but there surely is no market for every specialty everywhere due to the various habits in nutrition. The European Union traditionally exports trotters or tails to Asia, but Europeans consume the finer parts themselves, a successful complete exploitation of the whole carcass. Especially with the current problems of marketing in goods to regions with political issues such as Russia, it is essential that the European Union move negotiations forward with potential markets (e.g., South Asia, Indonesia, Taiwan, Mexico).

4 **Access for third country markets**: For many meat products, the EU has a great competiveness in global markets (high quality and food safety, labor and cost efficiency, structure in modern farms, access to global feed markets, modern slaughter capacities).

5 **Protection of high EU standards**: The requirements for keeping pigs in the EU are described as significantly higher than in most other regions in the world. In particular, the requirements of the local population have led to these standards. Thus, policymakers have to take care to demand the same standards for imports (especially trade agreements). This includes, for example, the ban on the import of meat from animals treated with growth hormones.

6 The **transparency of the market** should be a priority. Where fewer and growing companies influence or even determine the market, the distribution channels disappear. That has a negative effect on competition. Market transparency is the key factor for active participation of pig farmers in market activities.

7   Not only is price volatility one of the dominant issues that farmers have to cope with, but also the **absence of planning reliability concerning political decisions**. ISN requests policies that support farmers with as little intervention as possible and as much as necessary. The ISN stands against any political interventions such as export refund or subsidized private storage. Due to the short-term orientation of the pork industry, the quantity will remain in the market. Some political interventions are important, though, to solve animal welfare issues, such as the prohibition of castration and tail docking. The pork industry itself makes great efforts to achieve a better level of animal welfare. Sustainability and animal welfare should be gatekeepers to the market in the future. However, this development needs to be driven very carefully and from a scientific point of view. The economic aspects have to be considered as well.

Note

1   Interessengemeinschaft der Schweinehalter Deutschlands e.V. https://www.schweine.net/

10 Mitigating the effects of agricultural price volatility

A European cereal grower's point of view

Nicolas Ferenczi

1 Overview

As elsewhere in the world, European cereal growers strive to earn their living from sales once all costs have been paid. In this search for competitiveness, since the common agricultural policy (CAP) was implemented in 1962, the growers used to focus on yields and the cost of production. This was due to the fact that the European Union cereal market was protected by tariffs, export subsidies and public storage, leading to high and stable prices for farm products. However, the recent CAP reforms have opened the EU market, leading to price instability. Facing global volatile prices as of the 2000s, EU farmers have been forced to adapt and mitigate the impact of market volatility.

Focusing on the example of French cereal growers, this chapter provides an empirical analysis of three categories of instruments farmers can use to manage their price risks and cope with volatility: price hedging, farm insurance and reserve schemes. Finally such tools are put in perspective and possible lines of thought are addressed on how these could be used as policy instruments in the future CAP.

Price hedging is a service traditionally offered by grain collectors, these being cooperatives or merchants, through various grain-marketing schemes. These range from 'pool pricing', in which the collector bears the full price responsibility, to increasingly popular 'fixed price' contracts, which allow growers to decide on the day and price of the deal. Selling can be disconnected from physical storage and delivery. Surging price volatility in Europe has also led to a growing use by farmers of price hedging contracts, which are generally backed on futures markets.

Farm insurance is not very well developed in Europe; this is for several reasons, including a relatively stable climate (and formerly, prices) and the fact that EU subsidies are focused on direct income support. However besides nonsubsidized hail and other single-hazard insurance which is widespread in grain production across Europe, subsidized multi-hazard climatic insurance has developed to cover over 70% of Spanish cereals supported by national subsidies, as well as 35% of French cereals as a result of the introduction of EU subsidies.

In the case of France, insurance penetration growth is likely to level off due to public budget limitations.

Deposit schemes are national policy instruments that are widely used in Canada and Australia and to a limited extent in France. Farmers are incentivized, either through delayed taxation or through direct subsidization, to deposit cash in a dedicated savings account in good years and withdraw funds in lean years.

The above instruments, which are ineffective against consistently low prices, display different time scopes (seasonal vs. interannual volatility) and types of risk addressed (price vs. climate, minor vs. major amplitude). Due to their counter-cyclical natures, subsidized farm insurance as well as savings accounts may be seen as promising policy instruments in the volatile, long-term future. However, in the framework of the CAP post 2020, these raise new legal, institutional, and political challenges in Europe: national competence hence potential competitive distortions, budget variability, lower price signals, 'moral hazard', efficacy/cost ratio, or compatibility with decoupled farm payments.

2 The new context and the menu of options

2.1 The emergence of cereal price volatility

In the three decades following its launch in 1962, the CAP was based on the so-called *préférence communautaire*, protecting the European market for farm products by the combined effects of variable import duties, variable export subsidies and a minimum, domestic 'intervention price' enforced through public storage. This provided relatively high and stable prices to European producers of cereals and other products. Such incentives to production allowed Europe to gain food self-sufficiency as intended. However, in the 1970s, this led to an exportable surplus in grains, which increased the costs of operating the CAP and eventually triggered major policy changes. From 1992 to 1996, successive CAP reforms gradually decreased import duties and intervention prices, introducing direct farm subsidies designed to compensate for lower prices. Cereal prices dropped dramatically, as in the example of milling wheat (Figure 10.1), where the minimum price almost halved from €194 to €100 per tonne, a level consistently below international prices, hence no longer effective as a floor price.

As of 2001, actual EU prices have been on par with world prices. Since the mid 2000s, global cereal price volatility has also been much higher than the previous decades. As a result, a cereal price risk has emerged and surged in the 2000s, forcing European farmers, as do others in the world, to manage their price risk.

2.2 Grain-marketing schemes and price hedging

In France and in many EU countries, cereal growers generally do not sell their products directly to users. Agricultural collectors, these being cooperatives or private merchants, are market operators who purchase cereals from (and often

Figure 10.1 Evolution of global and EU cash market prices for milling wheat.
Source: Data compiled by *Association Générale des Producteurs de Blé et autres céréales* (AGPB).

sell farm inputs to) farmers. Collectors store the grains in their silos and resell them to processors and exporters.

The traditional marketing scheme in France is referred to as 'pool pricing', whereby the collector takes the grain at harvest against a front payment, stores it, resells it and pays a balance to farmers at the end of the marketing season based on the average selling price (Table 10.1). The management of the price risk is transferred to collectors, who generally split their sales (e.g. committing one tenth every month) and/or hedge their price commitments using futures and derivatives markets. Through pool pricing, collectors smooth out farm prices, acting as shields for farmers against seasonal price volatility. Farmers delegate marketing (and often storage) and, for a given quality and logistics, are all paid the same price.

As price volatility rose, however, producers increasingly turned to alternative marketing schemes, primarily 'fixed' price contracts. These include spot price contracts and fixed price forwards, both widely offered by collectors besides pool pricing. The price is fixed at the contracting date, allowing farmers to decide upon their selling date and price. Unlike pool pricing, such contracts imply a commitment by farmers to deliver a given volume of a specific quality at a given date, the price being either based on the cash market price of the day for immediate delivery or based on the futures market price for future delivery (including pre-harvest selling). This allows for disconnecting selling (chosen day) from physical delivery, storage being either on a farm or a service specifically charged for by collectors (Table 10.1).

In the particular case of pre-harvest selling, fixed price forwards are price hedging tools that give farmers the opportunity to set their price and crop acreage accordingly, based on the futures prices of the various crops as listed at sowing time for delivery at (or after) harvest.

Table 10.1 Main types of grain marketing contracts available to farmers in France

Types of marketing contracts	Principle for price determination	Contracting date	Price	Delivery date	Payment date	Storage	Volume commitment	Other specifications	Complements
Pool price contract	Season average collector selling price Season average cash market price Season average collector fixed price	Before or at harvest	Set by collector at end of season	Harvest (generally) or set dates	Account at delivery, balance at season end	Generally Collector	No		Price hedging option
Spot price contract	Daily price as proposed by collector, cash market based Daily price as proposed by collector, with reference to futures markets	Mainly after harvest	Fixed in contract	Before or at price fixing	Often account at delivery	Farmer or collector	Yes	Quality Settlement month	Price hedging; Collector storage
Forward contract	Fixed price determined at contract time, often according to futures markets Price determination defined in contract according to futures/ a specific formula	Mainly before harvest	Fixed in contract Defined in contract	Set in contract	Full at delivery	Farmer or collector	Yes	Quality	Price hedging; Collector storage
Specific outlet contract	Determined in contract, either fixed or with reference to futures markets	Before harvest	Defined in contract	Set in contract	Full at delivery	Farmer or collector	Yes	Variety, quality	

Source: AGPB.

Under fixed pricing, unlike pool pricing, producers manage their own price risk. Once a fixed price contract has been signed, the price risk *stricto sensu* has disappeared. However, other risks still remain, including a risk on the quantities and qualities to be actually harvested (in the case of pre-harvest selling), a margin risk (when the cost of production is not fully known), as well as a risk of foregone income (if prices are to rise thereafter).

In the last few years, French grain growers have been increasingly using hedging tools in combination with physical sale contracts, and cooperatives and private merchants have developed a growing range of such contracts. This is the case with those forward contracts in which the price is not fixed but to be determined at delivery time with reference to financial markets. For example a forward sale contract associated with 'call' options allows farmers to participate in the eventual price increase between selling and delivery, so that only the risk of price decrease is eliminated (see Box 10.1). To a lesser extent, some farmers also buy derivatives offered by financial institutions, including futures and options listed on regulated markets, and 'over-the-counter' (OTC), unregulated contracts mimicking the former that are often used for crops not listed on futures markets. All these services aim at transferring a price risk from a farmer to a counterpart against fees plus, in the case of listed derivatives, deposits and margin calls.

Box 10.1 Simple hedging strategies using call or put option contracts

Suppose you are a farmer. You have two ways of setting your price early, say at sowing time (say November 2014), fixing your price as the futures price for harvest delivery (say August 2015) as quoted in November 2014, while benefitting from an eventual price increase between November 2014 and August 2015. In simple terms, and disregarding the otherwise relevant transaction and basis costs, the options would be:

1   Either you 'sell forward' now (November 2014) at a fixed price, i.e. the current (November 2014) price of the August 2015 futures contract. The forward contract specifies that the price is firm and delivery takes place only later (at harvest). In parallel, you buy now an August 2015 **call** (i.e. a buying option). When August 2015 comes, if the futures price has decreased, you benefit from the higher, November 2014 price and do not exercise your **call**. If the futures price has increased, you exercise your **call**, i.e. you use the call to buy an August 2015 futures contract at the initially agreed (lower) price, and you immediately resell it at the (higher) August 2015 price.

(Continued)

Box 10.1 Continued

2   Or you do not want to sell now (November 2014) and decide to wait and see until August 15. However, you now (November 2014) hedge your price on the futures market by buying an August 2015 **put** (selling option). When August 2015 comes, you sell your grain at the spot or nearby futures price. If the futures price has increased, you benefit from the price increase and do not exercise your **put**. If the futures price has decreased, you have sold your grain at a lower price but you exercise your **put**, i.e. you buy an August 2015 futures contract at the current (lower) price, and you immediately resell it under the **put** at the initially agreed (higher) price.

Note that this is all disconnected from storage and physical delivery. If this is harvest time and you have to make a decision, then in both strategies you have either to store on farm or to buy storage capacity from your collector. Otherwise you are forced to deliver and sell now, and either you sell at harvest at spot (often low) or pool price, or you sign some OTC contract from your collector, whereby he will buy and store now, the price being either fixed now or set later.

The psychological aspects of marketing strategies and price hedging are noteworthy, although rarely addressed in the literature. Farmers opting for schemes other than pool pricing are often looking for a better price than the pool price or their fellow producers', this either by selling early when they expect the market to fall or delaying sales when they see an upward trend. Interestingly, results from a survey by *Coop de France Métiers du grain* suggest producers are more sensitive to the latter. During periods of rising prices, such as 2006–2007 and 2009–2010, French wheat producers have turned to significantly less pool pricing and more fixed price marketing than in the previous seasons, possibly with the idea of delaying sales to get better than pool prices (Figure 10.2). However, in the absence of reliable data from statistics or surveys, many market players and experts express doubts about whether, based on the average over several years, farmers in fixed price contracts consistently succeed in 'beating' pool prices.

Finally, while mitigating the effects of cereal price volatility to farmers, price hedging instruments display limitations linked to the financial markets on which they are backed. Some of these are:

- No protection against low prices: even though it can buffer price volatility over one or a few seasons, price hedging has no effect against consistently low prices over a long-term period;
- Their cost, typically €5 to €20 per tonne of cereals for options, is the price to pay to financial intermediates and counterparts to whom the price risk is transferred;

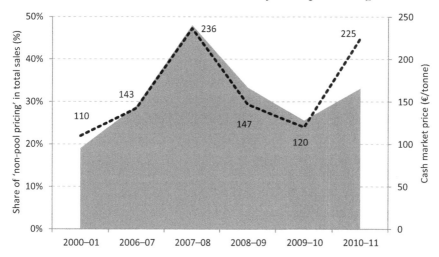

Figure 10.2 Marketing of common wheat in France: share of the marketing schemes other than pool pricing in total farmer sales vs. market price. Area (left axis): Percentage share of the schemes other than pool pricing (spot price, forwards, specific outlet) in total annual sales of the farmers; dotted line (right axis): cash market price in €/tonne, delivered Rouen, annual average 1 July–30 June.
Source: Survey of grain collecting co-ops (representing 44% of French grain deliveries), Coop de France Métiers du grain, 2010.

- The limited scope of futures markets for grains, both in terms of products and geography. For example, Euronext Paris derivatives for milling wheat and rapeseed provide French and other north European growers with representative quotations and delivery points (respectively Rouen/Dunkerque and Moselle/Mittellandkanal/Wurzburg/Ghent). This is not the case for other grains where European futures markets do not exist or lack liquidity, and hence representativeness; nor is this the case in many European areas located far away from listed delivery places. In these cases, the 'basis risk' can be excessive, i.e. the difference between the reference futures market and the actual cash market (including transport cost and eventually price deviation between the target crop and the listed, reference crop).

Given these limits, it is important in the future that EU authorities allow financial markets to develop in agricultural commodities, maintain their integrity and convergence and expand their product range. EU financial regulations should also avoid measures that limit market liquidity and generate bureaucratic burdens on farmers and other commercial players.

2.3 Farm insurance

Unlike other regions, farm insurance is poorly developed in Europe due to the continent's relatively favourable and stable climate (and formerly prices), but also to limitations in public subsidies as a result of the CAP, whose support mechanisms are concentrated on direct payments to farmers.

Until the CAP reform of 2009 (the 'health check'), no CAP funds were available to fund farmer insurance, and only single hazard insurance, primarily hail (but also drought, frost, etc.), was significantly developed in Europe, this either with (Italy, Poland, Greece, Austria) or without premium subsidies from national budgets. The only noticeable exception was Spain, where about 70% of the grain crop acreage was covered with multi-hazard yield insurance involving an approximately 50% national subsidy.

Since 2010, EU member states were given the possibility to use CAP funds to subsidize premiums for crop (as well as animal) insurance policies, covering adverse climatic events, plant disease and pest infestation. As a result, multi-hazard climatic insurance has significantly developed in four member states beside Spain: France, Italy, Austria and Poland. Moreover, CAP-funded climatic insurance schemes have also been launched in the Netherlands and Hungary (Figure 10.3). Multi-hazard climatic insurance in France has grown from 25% of the arable crop area in 2005 to 32% in 2013, when 43% had hail insurance only and 25% had no insurance.

However, insurance development in arable crops is likely to level off in France for several reasons: financial losses for insurance companies due to adverse weather events in 2011 and 2013, limitations of EU funds to be channeled to insurance and political willingness to share subsidies among all agricultural productions, implying lower indemnity rate for production losses.

Gross margin risk coverage has been introduced in the CAP legislation as of 2015 in the form of public subsidies to mutual funds providing for an 'income stabilization tool'. However, this, as well as farm insurance providing

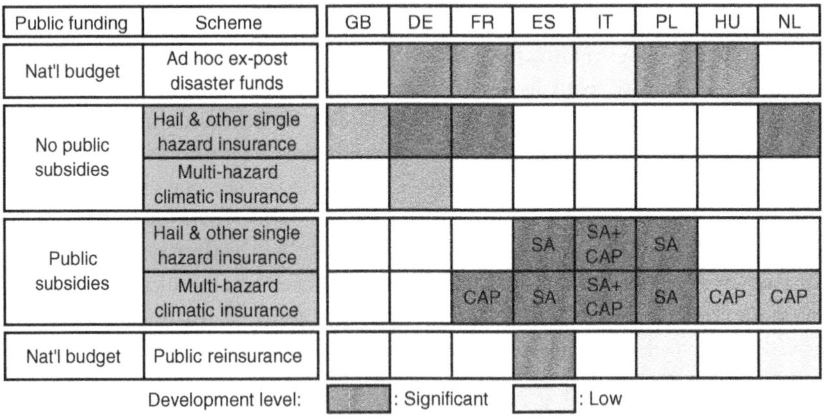

Public funding	Scheme	GB	DE	FR	ES	IT	PL	HU	NL
Nat'l budget	Ad hoc ex-post disaster funds								
No public subsidies	Hail & other single hazard insurance								
	Multi-hazard climatic insurance								
Public subsidies	Hail & other single hazard insurance				SA	SA+ CAP	SA		
	Multi-hazard climatic insurance			CAP	SA	SA+ CAP	SA	CAP	CAP
Nat'l budget	Public reinsurance								

Development level: ▓ : Significant   ☐ : Low

Figure 10.3 Crop insurance development in EU member states.
CAP = CAP subsidies (2010–2014: Articles 68d and 70 of EU Regulation 73/2009); SA = State aid
Source: AGPB.

price risk coverage (revenue, gross margin or income) will most probably not emerge in Europe until the end of the current CAP in 2020. Private insurance companies are not eligible for subsidized premiums and are reluctant, due to the systemic risk involved (price risk) and the absence of public reinsurance in most countries.

More generally, the CAP design, based on fixed, decoupled supports (which can also be seen as a buffer against farm income volatility), is clearly not appropriate for the development of (subsidized) farm insurance, being either climatic or even more so with price risk coverage: inflexible budgets, insufficient amounts funded by tapping into direct payments and a strict application of WTO rules (loss above 30% of five year average, and, for revenue/income insurance, maximum coverage 70% of loss).

However, farm insurance may have a future in the longer term as a major instrument in Europe's farm policy, following the examples of the United States and Canada.

2.4 Farm savings accounts

Another principle, as old as humankind, for farmers to cope with price volatility is the building of reserves whenever they are thriving to be used in years of low returns. The modern version uses money instead of food, and the first step is avoiding farm income taxation, usually based on the profit made the year before, which jeopardizes the business in a lean, high tax year following a high profit year. Unlike agricultural policy, farm taxation is of national competence in Europe and therefore widely varies among member states. Income averaging schemes, which even out farm taxes over several years, exist in a number of European countries, including France, the Netherlands and the UK.

Another step is providing incentives for farmers to set aside money in high income years to build up a cash reserve to draw upon in years of low income, enhancing farmers' self-reliance. Public support can be either through direct subsidies, as in the Canadian case, or as deferred income tax in the example of Australia.

Under the AgriInvest scheme in force since 1991, Canadian producers can establish savings accounts for risk management (Agriculture and Agri-Food Canada, undated). Annual deposits are taxed the same year and are subsidized with matching government contributions that are taxed upon withdrawal and are limited to 1% of net annual sales and C$15,000 per year. The account balance is capped at 25% of the average net annual sales in the last three years. Such schemes involving direct subsidization do not exist in Europe.

Australia's Farm Management Deposits scheme (FMD), launched in 1999, allows farmers to set aside income tax–deductible savings, which are later taxed when the funds are withdrawn from the dedicated savings account (Department of Agriculture, undated). The only conditions are the maximum amount on deposit (A$300,000) and an off-farm annual income that should not exceed A$100,000.

Even though such tools are under consideration in several countries (Germany, UK, US, etc.), France seems to be the only EU member state operating a scheme similar to Australia's FMD, named *Déduction Pour Aléas* (DPA). Annual savings are limited to €27,000 per year for a seven-year maximum, and balance amounts are capped at €150,000. The French DPA is not a success so far, as strict, cumbersome justifications of actual climatic or economic hazards are required if savings are to be withdrawn without paying a penalty fee.

The use of savings accounts, which can be supported either by deferred taxation or by direct, matching subsidies, is clearly a powerful 'self-insurance' tool for farmers to mitigate their interannual risk of price as well as adverse climatic conditions. In terms of farm management and public policy, they display obvious limits (e.g. they need several years of good income to become effective) while their advantages are as follows:

- Farm-specific timing and magnitude for risk management;
- Optimized farm expenditures by avoiding poorly timed investments and input purchases (as often the case in high income years for taxation purposes);
- Lower moral hazard and higher efficiency/cost ratio for public money than subsidized farm insurance;
- Modest cost for public budgets as exemplified in Canada and Australia.

3 Policy implications

From a policy viewpoint, limiting farm price volatility itself should be logically considered before supporting farmers in managing the consequences of volatility.

Agricultural market volatility is primarily about fundamentals, namely supply, demand and stocks. Volatility is a consequence of relative changes between these indicators, which themselves result from climate and human factors. As a traditional trader's saying puts it, 'high prices are the best measure against high prices'. In other words, in a well-functioning market where price changes are transmitted all the way to farmers and farmers are allowed to adapt, volatility is the best tool to limit volatility, as farmers will react to price fluctuations and adjust production accordingly.

Therefore key drivers to limit volatility include market functioning and transparency allowing fair price signals, low or no barriers allowing price signal transmission from global market to farm gate, and an agricultural environment enabling producers to respond. This includes input availability, sufficient grain storage capacity and regulations providing flexible land management and input rates. In the long-term context of increasing food demand as expected until 2050 with a largely stable global cropped area, agronomic progress (plant genetics, irrigation, precision farming, etc.) resulting in further yield growth is also a must in order to avoid tight markets and low stock levels that boost price levels and volatility.

Agricultural market volatility is useful, allowing for cash and financial markets to function smoothly. According to most political and economic analysts, agricultural market volatility is here to stay globally and in Europe. Therefore, price risk management is and will continue to be needed. On the downside, one should mention that this is time consuming, diverting farmers from what would be their sole focus in absence of volatility: agricultural production. The respective risks addressed and time scopes for various instruments to cope with market volatility are summarized in Figure 10.4.

Historically, the CAP was based on high, stable prices decoupled from the global market. Even though this offered clear advantages (production focus, technical progress), heading back to such a system seems unrealistic considering its high cost for European consumers and taxpayers, negative impacts on external markets, Europe's WTO commitments and the general trend for market globalization.

The current CAP involves a poorly protected internal market (low external barriers and public intervention), the bulk of public resources being devoted to stable, per hectare direct payments to farmers. Even though fixed supports are not risk management tools per se (Cordier, 2014), this economically sensible policy both allows price volatility to reach farmers and helps farmers to cope with it. Indeed, fixed payments can be channeled by producers to fund instruments such as price hedging, insurance and savings accounts. Government-supported savings accounts and climatic insurance can be seen as making fixed farm payments more flexible and turning them to countercyclical resources available whenever they are most needed.

As discussed above, there is room to develop such schemes in Europe in the years to come. However, given that they act as buffers of price variations over one or a few years, these can address only short- and medium-term volatility.

On the other hand, there is no effective instrument in the current CAP to limit or cope with long-term price volatility and in particular the risk of

	Seasonal price volatility	Interannual weather volatility	Interannual price volatility	Long-term price volatility
Marketing schemes/Price hedging	▓			
Yield insurance		▓		
Revenue/income insurance		▓	▓	
Savings accounts		▓	▓	
Direct countercyclical supports			▓	▓

Figure 10.4 Summary of tools to mitigate price volatility at farm level.
Source: AGPB.

consistently low prices. Countercyclical support measures are not available in the CAP. And even though the principle of price safety nets exists in the legislation, the actual floor prices are too far below the costs of production to be effective.

In the longer run, i.e. as of 2021, the next CAP reform may be a major one, given three current challenges:

1   Budget size: total public spending is set to be reduced;
2   Renationalization: current farm payments are diverging between sectors and regions across member states as a result of their national allocation largely at member state discretion as of 2015. Such farm policy is difficult to 'read' and will generate competitive distortions within Europe;
3   Legitimacy: citizens are aware of market volatility and have doubts about why farm payments are stable when needs for economic support vary greatly from year to year. This sets the trend of having payments more and more dependent upon what citizens can see, e.g. public goods, and particularly benefits delivered to the environment, as partly implemented through CAP 'greening' as of 2015.

What could the future CAP look like? In order to give food for thought, an interesting approach is considering how price volatility may be addressed in the future. As represented in Figure 10.5, tools to mitigate volatility suggest two possible avenues for the next CAP.

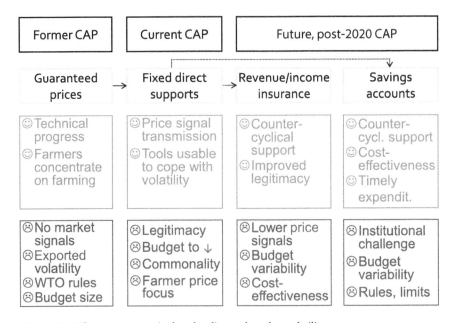

Figure 10.5 The common agricultural policy and market volatility.
Source: AGPB.

Shifting significant CAP resources to subsidizing farm revenue/income insurance would open the possibility of de facto countercyclical public support, hence increased public legitimacy. However, there are downsides and questions that are under debate with reference to the United States, where such evolution has taken place in the last decade: variable funding requirements challenging current EU budgetary rules; compatibility with significant fixed farm supports within tight budgets; efficiency/cost ratio of public money given the administrative cost of insurance companies and the need for public reinsurance; possible competitive distortions depending on allocations of funds between regions and productions; blurring of market signals that can enhance and export volatility; and the risk of moral hazard, given an effective farm insurance policy can lead farmers to change behaviours such as crop choice and cultivation practices.

Another option could be complementing fixed payments with incentives to channel supports and other resources into savings accounts. This could involve either deposit matching subsidies, as in Canada, or tax incentives, as in Australia. In turning direct supports into tools for market risk management, this would improve their efficiency as well as legitimacy. As experienced in Australia, benefits would also be found in overall farm management (timeliness of farm expenditures). However, this would also raise a number of difficulties regarding adoption by farmers as well as EU governance: budget variability, competence on fiscal policy, commonality. Work would be needed to test, evaluate and define rules, including eventual limits to yearly amounts set aside, account balances and origin of the funds; how to deal with the entry point when farmers cannot afford to build up savings; and how to treat deposits when producers retire or sell their businesses.

4 Conclusion

Even though not addressing the long-term low-price risk, subsidized farm insurance as well as savings accounts are instruments to cope with market volatility that are worth further investigation and debate. Given their countercyclical natures, these, alone or in combination, could play an increasing role in Europe's farm policy in the volatile, long-term future. However, in the framework of the CAP post 2020, these tools raise novel challenges in the legal, institutional and political fields: national competence leading to potential competitive distortions, budget variability, blurring of price signals and, in the case of insurance, moral hazard, efficacy/cost ratio and compatibility with decoupled farm payments.

References

Agriculture and Agri-Food Canada. (undated). AgriInvest. Ottawa, ON. Retrieved from http://www.agr.gc.ca/eng/?id=1291828779399

Coop de France Métiers du grain. (undated). Résultats de l'enquête 2010 auprès des coopératives sur l'évolution des modalités d'achat des grains, Paris, p. 7.

Cordier, J. (2014). Comparative analysis of risk management tools supported by the 2014 Farm Bill and the CAP 2014–2020. European Parliament, Brussels, p. 89. Retrieved from http://www.europarl.europa.eu/RegData/etudes/STUD/2014/540343/IPOL_STU%282014%29540343_EN.pdf

Department of Agriculture. (undated). Farm management deposits, Canberra City ACT, Australia. Retrieved from http://www.agriculture.gov.au/ag-farm-food/drought/assistance/fmd

11 Milk and dairy products' price volatility

EU dairy cooperatives attitude towards volatility

Wim Kloosterboer

1 Introduction

For a number of years now, price volatility has been on the political agenda. The reason is that in general a more stable price environment is judged as beneficial to most actors in the chain. The primary sector in particular is generally seen as a victim of the currently perceived excessive price volatility because farmers' incomes are immediately affected. Regular buyers and sellers of agricultural products or processed products should also favour a stable environment in which the partners can prepare budgets for the period to come.

There is a lot of discussion on volatility without exactly knowing what is meant by the term. Accordingly, much more attention is paid to price volatility in years with poor market circumstances than in the years with high prices. Volatility is then wrongly seen as a synonym for low prices. Some governments also adopt measures aiming to reduce volatility, without considering the negative effects this could have on their own economy or economies of other countries.

Therefore, measures that aim to reduce volatility should be taken with some care. Governments should try to understand the price-forming mechanisms, which can lead to volatility. This is one of the aims of a project like ULYSSES: it can be of assistance and improve transparency concerning the major underlying market mechanisms.

2 Some historical background

To prevent the negative consequences of price volatility, or at least to mitigate them, governments have tried to put a specific set of measures in place. Broadly speaking, a division can be made between ex-ante and ex-post measures in relation to price volatility: efforts being made to prevent volatility (ex ante) or to offset most of its negative consequences once it has occurred (ex post).

A clear example of an ex-ante policy was the EU market regulatory framework. Since the 1960s, the EU dairy sector was well protected against volatility by the measures of the EU common market policy. The floor price was determined by the intervention price of two base products: butter and skimmed milk powder. The intervention price guaranteed a level of prices that was very close to the actual market prices.

In support of the market price level, a whole variety of market support measures were possible, such as the feed programs for calf feed, butter support programs, and casein support. Exports were only possible by means of export restitutions. This resulted in a situation with limited price volatility for dairy products inside the EU. In fact, (some) volatility was by means of export refunds transmitted to foreign markets. The back side of this artificial price setting was that production surged enormously and enforced the introduction of a dairy production quota in 1983. In the 1980s, during the Uruguay round trade negotiations, export support mechanisms, and hence the refunds of the EU, were at the midst of the discussions. They resulted in an agreement by which export refunds were very much limited. The negotiations showed the vulnerability of the market regulatory system of the EU in terms of trade policy.

3 New market policy of the EU

Internal and external pressures paved the way for more reforms in the EU. In short, the following major changes characterized the EU market regulatory framework following the Luxemburg Agreements in 2003:

- The abandoning of the quota system on April 1, 2015
- Increase of dairy quota in 2006, 2007, and 2008 ("soft landing")
- Intervention price reductions in the years 2004–2007:
  o   Price reductions of butter: three years each with 7% and one year 4%
  o   Price reduction of skimmed milk powder: three years with 5%
- Together with the price reduction, the EU introduced milk premiums (€3.55/ 100 kg) as a compensation for the reform.

In 2008, the Health Check of the CAP introduced a policy of annual quota increases with the aim of having a soft landing towards the end of the quota regime in 2015.

3.1 Dairy package

After the large fluctuations of dairy market prices, the EU Commission came up with the so-called "dairy package" proposals, which were concluded in 2012. The package's major aim was to improve the contractual relations in the sector. In the dairy sector, producer organizations (POs) and interbranch organizations (IBOs) can be created. The key role a PO should play is in improving the bargaining power of the dairy producers. In most parts of the dairy sector, keeping in mind the prominent position of dairy cooperatives, this phenomenon is not likely to have a major impact. In fact, due to the unique relation between the owners of the cooperative who deliver the milk and the cooperative as a processor, there is no need for a PO.

Also, the milk package provides the Member State the possibility to make contracts between milk producers and dairies obligatory. A contract should specify price, volume, and duration. A contract should give the dairy farmer more certainty regarding the price to be expected and, hence, reduce the risks of price volatility. However, at this point, it is too soon to judge the overall consequences of the milk package.

3.2 Development of dairy prices in the EU since 2000

As stated earlier, EU intervention prices were reduced in three stages. In theory, in a situation of ongoing intervention, this would be equal to a milk price reduction of 20%. When we calculate the proceeds of milk based on the assumption that the total quantity of milk delivered is processed into butter and skimmed milk powder, a calculated milk price can be derived thereof. When the milk is processed into these two products and sold into intervention, we call this intervention equivalent the base price.

Figure 11.1 gives a clear indication of the variation between the two. At the beginning of this century, the market price closely followed the intervention equivalent. Later on, a gap developed between the two. Next to the increasing gap, one can clearly notice the increasing volatility of prices. The lower intervention level coincided clearly with an increase of the spread, not only at the downside, but also in upward price movements.

In the present EU market regulatory framework, a clear exception has been made for crisis situations with real market disturbances. Exceptionally, the European Commission might intervene in those cases. It is clear that, unlike

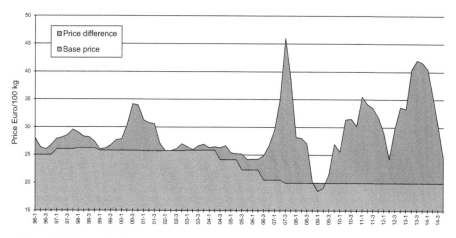

Figure 11.1 Base price (intervention) development and market price.
Source: Photocopied graph, based on Zuivel.nl.

what some expected, the market took its own direction despite the 20% reduction in calculated milk price.

Figures 11.2 and 11.3 illustrate the long-term development of the quotations for the intervention products in the EU. It seems that the much lower intervention levels ("safety net") increased price volatility in the EU of butter and skim milk powder (SMP). It is clear that initial reductions of the intervention price also drove market prices down. In 2007, a sharp surge in butter

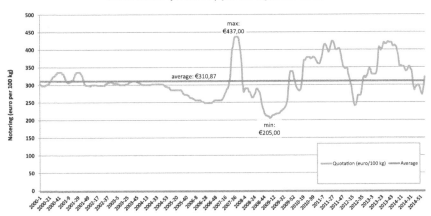

Figure 11.2 Dutch butter quotation: 2000 until now.
Source: Zuivel.nl.

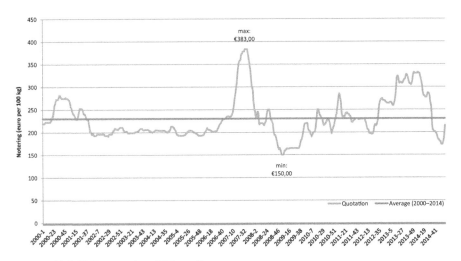

Figure 11.3 SMP quotation: 2000 until now.
Source: Zuivel.nl.

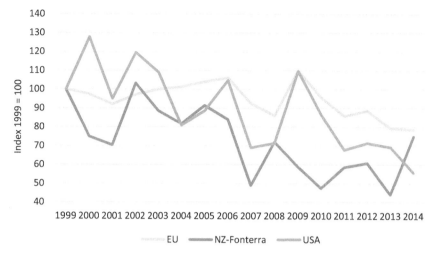

Figure 11.4 Comparison between EU average milk prices in € per 100 kg standard milk with New Zealand (Fonterra NZD/milk solids price) and US Class III price.
Source: Zuivel.nl.

prices to unprecedented levels was followed by a period of market turmoil. After that, we saw in general a price level above historical levels but with much higher spikes and lows.

When we compare volatility in the EU with respect to dairy prices paid in dairy regions around the world, we see in general that fluctuations in New Zealand and the United States were already existent before 2007–2008. But, EU fluctuations have not (yet) reached the level of the former two.

4 Possible policy measures

4.1 Ex-ante measures and dairy markets outlook

Recent years have shown that the possibilities for applying interventionist market measures (ex ante) are diminished. In this respect, it is even more important to understand the price development through the whole chain. EU working groups have been established to improve the understanding of the underlying mechanisms. It is a difficult task on which the work in the ULYSSES project also can be of help.

Further reforms and the growing international dependency effectively mean that possibilities for applying a set of national measures to set prices (ex-ante measures) are even more limited. This is also of major importance for the EU dairy industry, which is becoming increasingly active in international markets. To illustrate this, it is important to note that about 10% of the EU milk production is exported in the form of various products and it is likely to grow towards 2020. The export performance can be achieved thanks to the growing appetite worldwide for dairy products. For instance, OECD/FAO expects world import demand of butter (+17.2%), cheese (+20.1%), skimmed milk powder (20.9%), and whole milk powder (11.3%) to increase significantly in the years 2013–2022.

Governmental measures in this sense should contribute to these ambitions and not hurt the position of the dairy sector. Therefore, a return to supply management, the old EU quota system, as some advocate, is rejected by the EU dairy industry. The EDA (European Dairy Association) said in a recent statement[1] the following: "European Union policy for the dairy sector has been moving towards greater market orientation and this will culminate in the end of the public milk volume management in 2015. The abolition of quotas will allow the sector to realise its competitive potential and participate fully in the growth in world demand for dairy. The EU dairy sector, the milk producers and their milk processing companies, has been planning and investing on the basis of the abolition of quotas for the last few years. The process of reform that started in 2003 must not be put into reverse."

4.2 Need to differentiate between normal price spikes and extreme volatility: ex-post measures

As was expressed several times, the aim is to mitigate the consequences of extreme volatility. What should be interpreted as extreme? What is normal and part of the agricultural production cycle? Furthermore, which part of price movements is connected to currency variations and which to other commodities that sometimes form inputs to the dairy sector?

For farmers in the EU to become more resilient, ex-post measures will become more important for preventing the negative consequences of "normal" volatility. In the US, a lot of experience has been gained with alternatives for the market-based price support.

These measures include:

- Voluntary insurance schemes (often subsidized)
- Fiscal measures in order to build reserves
- Risk management schemes such as futures/options

Other forms of proposed policies are to protect margins instead of prices. At first sight, this seems interesting. But, at the EU level these measures will be difficult to execute, acknowledging the large differences in cost prices. In the US, the new Farm Bill introduced a dairy margin protection program. But, in the agricultural area, the US is much more uniform than the EU, and given the administrative burden, it is questionable whether this will provide a feasible instrument for the EU dairy sector.

Still, governments apply measures without clearly considering the adverse negative trade consequences. An important example of these measures is the export restrictions by applying taxes. Also, other trade policy measures have contributed to volatility, such as sanitary restrictions or even export food bans. In this respect, scientific support and advice is needed to prevent creating measures with adverse economic effects.

5 Answer of the industry on how to deal with the changing environment

There is no single answer for the whole dairy industry as such. The EU dairy industry is luckily very diversified, and this is also part of its power. In the northern part of the EU, large cooperatives determine the landscape; in the southern part, the picture is more diversified.

Some dairy processors have a long-standing position in catering to growing markets; others focus on niches at home or specialize in regional specialities.

Speaking for the dairy processing industry as a whole, I can say there is a huge trust in the products produced. The markets are there and, also for the far future, the EU dairy industry should have the ambition to fulfil growing needs for nutritional dairy products inside the EU, but increasingly outside the EU as well. This regional diversification might also prove to be one of the best measures to offset the effects of price volatility. Others might opt for a route of specialization of products, which are less dependent on the price spikes of commodities.

Looking at the input side, there are increasing efforts to make a more proper estimation of the milk we can expect and which has to be processed and eventually sold into the market. Unlike the cereal sector, the dairy sector in general was not until recently confronted with much price volatility. Additionally, the experience with instruments, which hedge those risks (futures), is limited. Despite some initiatives, at the moment there is no massive usage of futures markets in the EU as a means to offset the negative effects of extreme price volatility. Inevitably, there will be a learning curve, and in comparison with a country like the US, the EU is in a stage of infancy. Another reason for the lack of success until now might be that timely official statistics are lacking. On top of that, it is likely that the characteristics of dairy products, even the ones sometimes considered as "commodities", are much more diversified than the general staple products markets. In combination with the options mentioned, this might also be part of the answer for the EU dairy industry.

A particular phenomenon of the EU dairy sector is the strong presence of cooperatives. In France, about 50% of the milk is processed by cooperatives; in Germany it is more than 60%; in countries like Austria, Ireland, and the Netherlands it is more than 80%. FrieslandCampina, based in the Netherlands, is one the largest cooperatives in the world and will continue to build on the strength of the cooperative and use the strength of the chain. Milk production is not seen merely as providing input for processing, but should be an integral part of the chain. Through this connection within the chain, the partners in the chain are deemed to be less sensitive to general market volatility.

We expect a regulatory and economic environment in which we, as an industry, and to the benefit of our members, employees, consumers, and society, can prosper. FrieslandCampina is an example of a global operating dairy company which wishes to provide people with essential nutrients from dairy products during all phases of their lives. We nourish millions of people every day with a diversified set of products in European countries, but also in Asia and Africa. This diversification also makes the company somewhat less vulnerable to sudden price shocks. Normal volatility in markets and prices will be part of the game as already explained. This does not exclude that for particular emergency situations a sort of safety net, as already foreseen in the new set of rules of the common agricultural policy, can provide a floor for farmers' income.

Note

1   "EDA policy recommendations for the EU dairy market and its management", Brussels, January 2015.

12 Coping with food price volatility
The contribution of local food reserves

Gabriel Pons Cortès and Itzíar Gómez Carrasco

1 Introduction: contextual factors for local food reserves in low-income countries

Food price volatility (FPV) is a multidimensional issue. This necessarily implies that solutions must also be multiple and must be adopted at different levels, from local to global. Partial solutions can only achieve a limited degree of success and can neither prevent nor address the problem as a whole. Since the role of states in reducing, managing and coping with volatility is addressed in several chapters in this book, we will focus on the relationship that should exist between state initiatives related to food reserves and local initiatives promoted by NGOs.

Food reserves held by public agencies are controversial because managing them can have unintended effects on the markets where they intervene. But even if they are a matter of intense debate, food reserves or at least interventions in the grain markets are part of the reality: 23 countries in sub-Saharan Africa have made some kind of intervention in grain markets, most of them subsidizing food (FAO, 2009). Food reserves are required because markets are never perfect; regardless of their shortcomings, attaining food security and guaranteeing the right to food are important questions that require effective policies and interventions. Hence, the policy response cannot be to ignore these interventions, because we know they can harm the market and hinder efforts to improve food security. We, as practitioners and scholars, have spent years discussing this issue, given that the urgent need to intervene when people are suffering the effects of hunger is not easily compatible with avoiding harm to markets.

Governments have to act when there are sudden price spikes and falls, because they affect a large percentage of the population in countries where people spend high percentages of their income on food. Even in rural areas, most grain producers are net buyers of food (Barrett, 2008). In these circumstances, targeted social protection is crucial, even in the absence of price spikes. But is it possible to think, plan and execute targeted responses when a price spike affects millions of people? It is often said that state interventions cannot beat the market. But doing nothing to tackle price spikes is not an option; political needs (i.e. avoiding riots in the cities) will also have priority over economic orthodoxy.

Food reserves' efficacy is well proven. Indonesia, India and China, for instance, have been able to safeguard their populations from volatility by managing their food reserves and grain imports (Dawe and Timmer, 2012). But this does not mean that secondary effects are absent. Their crowding-out effect can harm temporal and spatial arbitrage and this affects not only grain traders. Farmers' initiatives aimed precisely at coping with FPV and trying to take advantage of price cycles to obtain a higher percentage of margins in the value chain are also impaired.

As a result of farmers' need for cash after harvest (to pay credit, school fees and so on) and poor storage capacity, farmers tend to sell off their production (see Figure 12.1, points 1 to 3). They then become net buyers and often

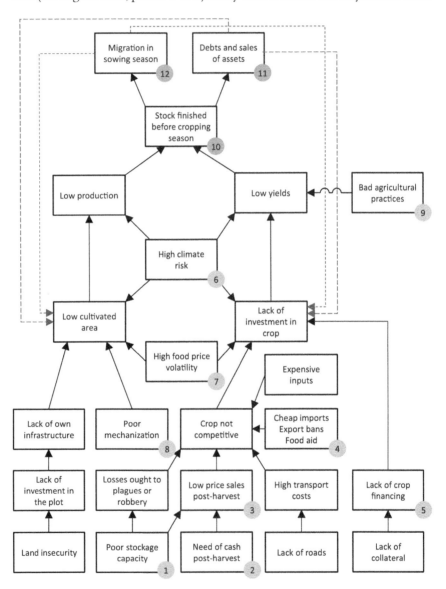

Figure 12.1 Causes of food insecurity for poor agricultural producers.
Source: Pons Cortès and Gómez (2012).

have to pay much higher prices for the 'same grain' when food becomes scarce (just before the next harvest; point 10). In order to solve this old and well-known problem, farmers organise themselves around cereal banks or other similar initiatives (generically, local food reserves, or LFR). Even though many in the development cooperation industry think that this is a failed solution buried by history, a mapping exercise of cereal bank federations carried out by Oxfam[1] shows that local food reserves are quite alive and showing good outcomes more often than might be expected. Some of their modalities, e.g. warehouse receipt systems (WRS), are being promoted all across Africa.

Local food reserves (particularly those that seek to increase food availability) can protect rural households from annual price spikes by stocking enough reserves to lower the price during the sowing season, when prices are usually higher. This can be done only to a certain extent: LFR are procyclical, just like national reserves, which implies that they are better stocked when the needs are less likely, and vice versa. Nevertheless, they are able to provide better prices to their members and/or users even in bad years.

Not all LFR sell at lower prices during the lean season. There are commercial LFR that aim to increase farmers' income by selling their stocks at higher prices, thereby overcoming their need to sell off just after the harvest. Sometimes both objectives coexist in the same LFR, managing both kinds of stocks.

2 Local food reserves can bring about other beneficial effects

LFR can strengthen other food security strategies because many activities take place around them. For instance, many organisations take advantage of the LFR to promote mechanization, credit and the improvement of agricultural practices (points 5, 8 and 9 in Figure 12.1). The latter is, according to Coulter (2006), the most revolutionary change that LFR can bring.

LFR carry out social protection initiatives in those places where state safety nets do not suffice or are non-existent. This is far from an ideal scenario, since it involves poor people taking care of others who are even poorer. LFR can protect livelihoods, to the extent that they allow people to continue with their economic activities during the lean season by avoiding migration and the selling of assets.

LFR also help to overcome the negative effects that isolation has on food security, since having local reserves in remote areas during the lean season can save transport costs to the nearest town to buy grain. Stability also implies that prices before the harvest should not be lower than after the harvest.

Finally, LFR empower populations, making them capable of undertaking new economic activities, decreasing dependence on middlemen and promoting social cohesion. This is especially the case for women.

3 Sources of vulnerability of local food reserves

There are three main reasons why LFR are vulnerable:

- Vulnerability to climate. Many LFR are in drought-prone areas and grains are produced mostly in rain-fed regimes. Drought often results in credit default. Moreover, turnover in drought years is lower, so LFR's incomes decrease.
- Bad promotion, planning or design as well as bad management.
- Price cycle inversions (i.e. paying higher prices when building stocks than the prices obtained in return when drawing them down).

3.1 Vulnerability to climate

Climate vulnerability can be tackled using **index insurance**. Index insurance is not new. But combining index insurance with social protection is new. Oxfam has developed an 'insurance for work' scheme in Ethiopia, the R4 programme,[2] in collaboration with the World Food Programme (WFP) and the government of Ethiopia: people work in WFP programmes and obtain in return an index insurance policy for cereal production.

Insurance can also be seen as a tool to improve targeting and avoid moral hazard: in the areas insured by farmers' organisations, those people who had voluntarily insured their production should have an advantage, for instance seeing their debt with the organisation cancelled.

Insurance is expensive and not sustainable before it reaches a critical mass. It is widely subsidized in rich countries and the same should be done in poor ones, especially when trying to offer insurance to the poorest people.

3.2 Needs of training and support

Design and management problems need training and support. Training is particularly necessary at local government levels and for farmers' organisations to improve management of these initiatives, which are often present in the least developed areas with high levels of illiteracy. Support must come from federations of local reserves: only when LFR link up do they have the capacity to share resources. In the mapping carried out by Oxfam, we saw that the LFR that survived were those linked to a federation.

3.3 What is needed: creating and linking information systems at different levels

Any form of coordination requires energy and information as fundamental inputs. Some years ago, it would have been utopic to think of an information system capable of keeping accurate data on stock levels and their specific location. Mobile technology, massive SMS sending, web mapping and GPS make information management easier.

Nowadays it is possible to know **when, where and for whom** to intervene. The more accurate the information is, the more possible it is to avoid harm during interventions. Cereal banks must be included in information provision for the national early warning systems in order to: (a) add information about food security using their own performance indicators as a proxy, and (b) provide information about the areas where government interventions must be channelled through farmers' organisations, in order to avoid harming them. An example of how this can be done can be consulted here: http://foodreserves. org/privat/.

3.4 Price cycle inversions are a more complex matter

No matter how well governments plan their interventions to lower a price spike, the market (local traders and farmers' organisations included) can be affected.

Price risk, from the perspective of local food reserves, is defined as the probability of purchasing grain at a price above its selling price. Price risk is not the same as price variation. The latter is necessary in order to cover related costs (such as maintenance, storage and transport). If the price is not higher at the end of the season than at the beginning, no trader will be willing to store. Price variation between seasons is also necessary in order to give signals to farmers to invest more or less in a crop, according to its abundance or scarcity in the market.

Two consecutive years with this problem can push LFR to bankruptcy. It is needless to recall that we do not only want stable and 'enclosed' price cycles, but also cycles that are wide enough to allow for temporal and spatial arbitrage.

According to a research analysing grain prices in Niger and Mali (CREDA-UPC-IRTA, 2013), cycle inversions can happen as often as one out of three years in some markets. Volatility is high and there is no easily identifiable pattern. In some cases, two good harvests in a row can be the cause, but in many occasions these inversions are due to government interventions in grain markets.

Food aid interventions can harm in different ways:

- They lower prices in markets when WRS or cereal banks have to sell. For instance, in research carried out in Niger during 2014, we asked the management committees if subsidized food interventions from government were causing losses, and 42% of them answered positively.[3]
- They destroy the credit culture. Many cereal banks give credit in grain during the hunger gap. If there is an intervention that does not take this mechanism into account, people do not repay their credits, arguing that aid interventions were part of a donation.

Avoiding these problems is not easy and the options have not been widely tested. Two sets of clear actions arise:

1   Avoid harmful interventions should be the rule in rural areas.
   - Coordinating national food reserves and local initiatives is the way to do it. For instance, contacting managers of local food reserves before selling at subsidized prices in the villages and channelling food aid through LFR in exchange for a little commission. A common political problem is that governments often prefer to channel food aid through the political authorities in the villages. Cereal banks can be seen as politically independent, which is not good if elections are looming.
   - Finding better ways to compensate the side effects of government interventions in markets. Use special funds to compensate the cereal banks, warehouse receipt systems and commercialisation cooperatives for the losses caused by food aid interventions.
2   Supporting local reserves through structured demand.

Another way of offsetting the side effects of national reserves on LFR is to link them through structured demand: part of the grain distributed through social protection programmes, like school feeding, can be provided by poor farmers who need to sell part of their production.

Good examples of this are the programme Purchase for Progress (P4P),[4] from WFP, which aims to integrate marketing commercialisation cooperatives and informal groups as providers of grain for food aid programmes, and the Procurement Governance for Home Grown School feeding project, from the Netherlands Development Organisation (SNV).

3.5 Better social protection and food aid targeting through the involvement of LFR

Community-based information systems can improve the accuracy of information about the state of food security before an intervention is launched. Including LFR in the management of government responses to FPV can improve targeting and will decrease corruption or mismanagement. Many LFR manage their own social protection schemes, reserving a part of their stocks to attend the emergencies of their associates. Their lists of the most vulnerable people are accurate and available. A combination of these lists with the information system can be a powerful tool to improve food aid interventions.

4 Conclusion

Governments should not be responsible for doing everything. Farmers' organisations are able to develop multiple strategies that can help them to cope with FPV at local level. Even though they are not able to cope with covariate risk, they can cope with minor shocks and help provide the information needed to improve targeting in government responses.

We need to develop instruments that are able to avoid or compensate the harm that government interventions cause farmers' organisations. This need is detected, but the right instruments are still to be developed. Future research should provide concrete solutions on how to make this much-needed coexistence between farmer's organisations and the unavoidable government responses to food insecurity a working reality.

Notes

1   See http://foodreserves.org/cartes-stocks/index.php
2   See http://www.oxfamamerica.org/explore/stories/r4-the-rural-resilience-initiative/
3   Mooriben, Fédération des Unions de Groupements Paysans du Niger, is a peasant organisation working in various sectors which takes into account the diversity of family-run farms. It has 63,000 members, of whom 62% are women. See http://www.sosfaim.org/lu/en/our-actions/niger-2/mooriben-federation-des-unions-de-groupements-paysans-du-niger/
4   See http://www.wfp.org/purchase-progress

References

Barrett, C.B. (2008). Smallholder market participation: Concepts and evidence from eastern and southern Africa. *Food Policy, 33*(4), 299–317.

Coulter, J. (2006). Review of cereal banks in western Kenya, draft final report. Consultancy Report for the Rockefeller Foundation, Nairobi, Kenya.

CREDA-UPC-IRTA. (2013). Managing price risk in local food reserves. OXFAM research reports.

Dawe, D., and Timmer, P.C. (2012). Why stable food prices are a good thing: Lessons from stabilizing rice prices in Asia. *Global Food Security, 1*(2), 127–133.

FAO. (2009). The state of agricultural commodity markets. Retrieved from FAO.org

Pons Cortès, G., and Gómez, I. (2012, October 23). First line of defence: Assessing the potential of local food reserves in the Sahel. Oxfam Research Reports. Retrieved from http://www.oxfam.org/en/grow/policy/first-line-defence-sahel

Part 3

Policy discussion and conclusions

13 Assessment of national policies in developing countries to combat and mitigate the effects of agricultural markets' excessive price volatility

Mulat Demeke and Jean Balié

1 Introduction

Market risks in agriculture are related to volatility of input and output prices, availability of inputs or credit, availability of markets for farm products, and variations in income derived from farming operations. Output price volatility is of particular concern to farmers, traders, processors, and agricultural finance providers. Nominal prices of agricultural commodities are generally more volatile than those of nonagricultural commodities, mainly because of disruptions in production due to natural factors such as climate variability and pest attacks, as well as inelastic supply and demand for agricultural products in the short run. It should, however, be noted that not all price variations are problematic. Price movements will not be a problem if they move along a smooth and well-established trend and reflect a typical and well-known seasonal pattern. Price variations become a problem when they are large and cannot be predicted, leading to uncertainty and increased risks for producers, consumers, and operators along the value chain (FAO et al., 2011).

Many factors contribute to output price variability. On the demand side, an increase or decrease in income and population growth, energy prices, and biofuel production may contribute to sudden price changes. On the supply side, overinvestment or underinvestment in agricultural production could lead to fluctuations in production and prices. Price and production risks are highly interrelated, as variability in production can result in high food price instability and vice versa.

Volatile and unpredictable prices reduce the quantity and quality of investment not only by farmers but also by traders, processors, and distributors. Unstable prices prevent farmers from making adequate investments in inputs, accessing credits, and accelerating their supply responses (Poulton et al., 2006; Dawe, 2001; Timmer, 1989). If significant, food price shocks can cause major macroeconomic instability and serious development challenges. Inflationary pressures, balance of payment, and public deficits may increase with significant rise in food prices, resulting in further negative consequences for poverty and food security (Díaz-Bonilla, 2008). When faced with the challenges of inefficient international markets and highly volatile food prices during the high food price crisis of 2007–2008, governments responded with a number of policy measures to manage excessive price risks. Policies associated with managing food price volatility can be divided into two major categories:

1　Price stabilizing strategy: policy instruments designed to reduce price volatility; and
2　Strategy for coping with price volatility: policy interventions intended to reduce the effects of price volatility on producers, consumers, processors, traders, and other value chain operators.

Table 13.1 summarizes the different types of policies that governments can adopt as part of their price stabilization or coping strategy. In practice, the merits of each policy need to be assessed from different perspectives before being applied. Governments need to know the effectiveness, implementation modalities, and time dimensions of the various policies in managing price volatility. Policies designed to stabilize prices are largely implemented in advance of the occurrence of excess volatility (ex-ante) while coping strategies are implemented right before (ex-ante) or after (ex-post) the price shock. As part of the coping strategies, government policies may encourage agents to retain and manage the risks by themselves (risk retention) or transfer them to a third-party entity (risk transfer).

Table 13.1 Policy responses in managing price volatility in developing countries

	Objective of the policy	
	Stabilize prices	*Cope with price instability*
Long term	Develop infrastructure and logistics*** • Transport and communication • Storage and post-harvest technology Improve market institutions*** • Warehouse receipt systems • Commodity exchanges • Market information Support sustainable production and productivity growth*** • R&D, irrigation • Risk management for producers Facilitate trade** • Regional trade • Bilateral and international trade agreements	Develop risk-transfer mechanisms*** • Forward contracts and futures markets • Insurance schemes including weather-based index insurance Support sustainable social protection programs** • Pensions, unemployment benefits, medical care, etc. • School feeding programs Promote sustainable risk retention through diversification** • Enterprise diversification (e.g., livestock and crops) • Off-farm employment

	Objective of the policy	
	Stabilize prices	*Cope with price instability*
Short term	Support stockholding** • Emergency reserve • Public stocks in landlocked countries • Support private stockholding Use border measures and trade policies** • Protect domestic market (e.g., reduce tariffs) Stimulate short-term production** • Input subsidy	Promote short-term risk retention through access to finance** • Improved access to credit • Promote savings Support targeted safety net programs*** • Cash and food transfers • Grain price subsidies • Safety net programs for producers

Expected effectiveness of the policy measure:
*** Can be highly effective on average with important variations from country to country
** Can be moderately effective and likely to induce market distortions on average with important variations from country to country

Moreover, the time dimension matters, as some policies have immediate impact while others have a long-term impact. Finally, policies may be mainly market based or government based, but it appears that all policies require private–public partnerships (PPP) to be effective.

Building on available evidence, this chapter proposes a qualitative assessment of the effectiveness of different policies adopted by governments to reduce price volatility and/or mitigate the effects of excessive volatility in developing countries. In particular, the chapter examines the challenges faced by governments attempting to manage price volatility and achieve food and nutrition security.

2 Policy measures to stabilize price

In low-income countries (LICs), price volatility that results from variability of agricultural production is often made worse by market failures that result from insecure property rights, incomplete information, inadequate access to essential public goods (infrastructure, logistics, essential regulations, etc.), and limited export and import options (FAO et al., 2011). Production shocks due to extreme weather, pests, and other natural calamities are exacerbated by poor infrastructure including storage facilities, high transport costs, inadequate support services, and weak institutions (World Bank, 2008).

Policy measures designed to stabilize prices in LICs therefore include facilitation of arbitrage by market actors (private sector) through improving infrastructure and logistics. But they also consider strengthening market institutions through direct intervention primarily intended to increase food availability, access, and stability such as stockholding, changing trade policies, and promoting a sustainable production increase (Galtier, 2013; Cummings, 2012).

Poor infrastructure, high transport costs, absence of credit or insurance markets, and various policy and governance failures may compound the initial difficulty. A relatively minor climatic incident in these conditions can become a serious food crisis at a local or regional level. Again, those most affected will be poor consumers and rural dwellers, mainly smallholders in less-developed countries or regions, heavily dependent on their own production.

2.1 Market infrastructure and logistics

The importance of a good transport infrastructure, storage logistics, and port facilities in reducing transport costs and facilitating the flow of food from surplus to deficit areas is widely recognized (Konandreas, 2012). Better marketing infrastructure not only reduces transport costs but also minimizes short-term food price volatility and facilitates price transmission. Improving rural roads and market facilities such as warehouses is also important in linking smallholders to markets, thus increasing market supply and contributing to more stable prices (FAO et al., 2011).

Food and agricultural markets in developing countries lack the ability to absorb domestic shocks, even when international prices are stable, because of severe challenges in marine and inland transport. Food imports fail to stabilize prices where freight costs are high and transit delays are significant because of shortages of container terminals, inadequate and obsolete equipment, excessive bureaucracy, and lack of competition in port management and dock services. Where inland transport systems are inadequate and spatial market integration is poor, increasing market production and marketable surpluses may result in declining and volatile prices, while other areas of the same country may suffer from deficits and rising prices. In most low-income countries, price changes in urban areas or the world market are not fully transmitted to producers (Pinstrup-Andersen and Shimokawa, 2006). All of the above is particularly common in landlocked countries of sub-Saharan Africa.

As a result, the major policy objective of developing market infrastructure and logistics is to address the barriers to the movement of grains from the point of production to the point of consumption. Increasing public investment in port and transport infrastructure has the potential to reduce price volatility (World Bank, 2005), but it would take a long time for this to have a major impact in poor countries where resources are limited. Landlocked countries are unlikely to have any influence over investment in ports and the inland transport infrastructure of other countries.

2.2 Market institutions

Warehouse receipt systems (WRSs), commodity exchange, and market information systems are among the major market institutions necessary for reducing transaction costs and facilitating marketing and trade of agricultural products.

WRSs protect farmers and traders from seasonal price risk variability by giving them access to secure and reliable storage and a documentary title for their produce, which can be used to obtain finance. With the WRSs, farmers can access inventory credit, avoid selling immediately after harvest, and potentially contribute to smoothing seasonal price variations. Small farmers can transact directly with larger-scale buyers, such as wholesalers, processors, and exporters, without going through multiple layers of middlemen, thereby minimizing the risk of getting unfair, low, or volatile prices (FAO et al., 2011; World Bank, 2005).

Major challenges in implementing WRSs include: (a) lack of well-established grades and standards to classify products on the basis of their quality and maintain them through adequate storage facilities; (b) absence of reliable trading platforms to ensure fair and transparent transactions and facilitate the sale of the stored commodities; (c) lack of well-developed and affordable financial markets to scale-up promising experiences and ineffective legal environments to enforce contracts. These limitations need to be addressed for WRSs to be widely utilized and provide immediate relief to problems of short-run price instability.

Commodity exchange systems

Commodity exchanges provide options to simplify title transfers, perform the "price discovery" mechanism, and deal with price risk and market uncertainty. Price discovery, a major benefit of futures markets, allows market agents to be informed of the true market clearing price quickly and efficiently, thus contributing to price stability. The futures markets provide a transparent price that can be used by traders as a benchmark to determine spot prices for a vast array of cash market contracts. Traders also make forward contract offers to farmers based upon contemporaneous futures prices. However, effective commodity exchanges to manage food system risks are rare in developing countries (though they are beginning to emerge in LICs like Ethiopia and Malawi). Small-scale farmers are also less likely to participate due to high fixed costs associated with the large underlying volumes customary in futures and options trading (World Bank, 2005). Lack of comprehensive and frequently published supply-and-demand information is also a critical bottleneck for futures markets to operate effectively in developing countries (McKenzie, 2012). It requires a sustained effort to build capacity to the point where decision makers are comfortable with the use of price risk management tools (FAO et al., 2011).

Market information systems

Agricultural market information systems (AMISs) refer to a process and tools to collect and deliver market information in order to reduce the risks and lower the transaction costs of farmers, traders, processors, and other market participants. It is widely believed that a lack of reliable and up-to-date information on prices, crop supply, demand, stocks, and export availability contributed to the 2007–2008 high food price volatility (FAO et al., 2011). In particular, international responses to both the 2007–2008 and 2010–2011 price shocks were hampered by the lack of reliable information in relation to the level and availability of grain stocks (Gilbert, 2011). AMISs are also a major prerequisite for effective operation of commodity exchanges, contract farming, and warehouse receipt systems.

Despite the progress in the use of information and communication technology (ICT), agricultural market information systems in many countries lack key market data. Information providers often do not include data on trade volume, quality/grade of commodities, location, prices at various stages of the value chain and price trends, and production forecasts in their market information systems. Information on stocks is an essential component of food market information systems, yet reliable data on stocks of grains is often unavailable partly because it is considered commercially sensitive information and because stocks are dispersed and difficult to track among farmers, traders, and other actors (World Bank, 2012). Producing consistent, accurate, and timely agricultural market data and analysis, especially in response to weather shocks, is particularly challenging in developing countries. Because market information has a public good nature and is necessary to better adjust and respond to market price signals, governments in developing countries need to invest in sustainable and effective AMISs by supporting private operators or developing public–private partnerships (FAO et al., 2011).

2.3 Stockholding or buffer stock policies

In an attempt to stabilize prices, a government agency may buy grain when prices are low (and build up stocks) and sell (and deplete stocks) when prices are high. Government policies may also subsidize the private sector to hold stocks (Gouel and Jean, 2012). Depending on how they are managed, stocks can have positive or negative effects on markets. Stocks can have a more direct and immediate impact in reducing excessive volatility in agricultural commodity markets (Wright, 2011). For example, it is shown that low or uncertain stock levels are among the major reasons for excessive volatility to occur (Wiggins and Keats, 2012; Maunder, 2013). A well-managed reserve can be a powerful tool against price volatility, in addition to supporting more remunerative prices for producers, averting and responding to food emergencies, providing a market for small-scale producers, and creating a reliable source of food for social safety nets such as school lunch programs. Food reserves can compensate for shortfalls in foreign currency, a common problem in poor countries (Sampson, 2012).

Public interest in buffer stocks has changed over the last 20 years. Public stocks were considered expensive because raising producer prices above market levels and lowering consumer prices below market levels entailed considerable fiscal costs. Intervention through stocks is said to distort the market since procurement and release levels and prices often involved guesswork and created uncertainty in the market. Public stocks can also crowd out private stocks and private trade, especially when the volume involved is substantial. In some LICs, especially in Africa, using buffer stocks failed to achieve price stability mainly due to bad governance (World Bank, 2012; Sampson, 2012). Moreover, the direct costs of stockholding programs, which include costs related to storage, transport, distribution, management, and spoilage, are high and escalate with increase in stock sizes (Deuss, 2014). These considerations led to the dismantling, downsizing, or divesting of public agencies managing public stocks in the 1980s and 1990s (Mittal, 2008).

The 2007–2008 food crisis, however, highlighted the inadequacies of relying on the market as the only strategy for addressing volatile prices in the grain markets. There has been a renewed interest in grain reserves for other reasons, such as maintaining at least a minimal level of food security, the increasing incidence of food emergencies (e.g., due to climate change), and the tendency to restrict export by several key agricultural exporters during the most recent food crisis (Sampson, 2012). As a result, public stocks in LICs have been growing since 2008, while they have been declining in HICs (World Bank, 2012).

Public stocks can play an important role in improving food security and are most effective in the short run, especially for bridging the time needed for food imports. The importance of public stocks is also greater in LICs and landlocked nations where import options are constrained by high access costs (Gouel, 2011; Gilbert, 2011). Because credit, insurance, and forward markets are incomplete in LICs, public stocks can augment private stocks and make food prices less sensitive to short-term shocks (World Bank, 2012).

In all cases, stocks need to be incorporated into a coherent long-term strategy that combines the use of trade, investments in agricultural productivity, and well-managed targeted safety net programs. For a more positive impact, policy makers need to make sure that stocks are managed with a level of autonomy similar to that of central banks, within a framework of clear and well-defined objectives and implementation arrangements. Clear triggers for market interventions and releases should be used to avoid market disruptions. As demonstrated by the experience of some countries (e.g., BULOG of Indonesia), public stocks should be limited in size to avoid a dominant position in the market (World Bank, 2012; Crola, 2012).

2.4 Border measures and trade policies

Trade is an excellent buffer for fluctuations originating in the domestic market. Year-to-year variations in domestic production can be more effectively and less expensively smoothened by adjustments in the quantities imported or exported. International and regional trade is a powerful tool to even out supply fluctuations across countries and, as a result, to reduce market price volatility. More precisely, regional trade can help reduce domestic food price volatility by allowing the flow of food staples from areas where local markets are unable to absorb surplus production to food-deficit regions.

Despite ongoing reforms, restrictive border measures have hampered trade in agricultural commodities among developing countries and between developing and OECD countries. Tariff and nontariff trade barriers have contributed to some of the grain price volatility experienced in recent years (Valdes and Foster, 2012). Among the major trade barriers are import and export bans, nontransparent licensing of importers, unrealistic import requirements in terms of price and quantity, release of subsidized food onto domestic markets (see buffer stocks above), and failure to deliver on announced state-to-state contracts. Average tariffs on agricultural and food products are estimated at 25% for MICs and 22% for HICs, higher than in LICs (Prakash and Stigler, 2011). Protectionism on agricultural products is not only higher than on nonagricultural products, it is also much more volatile (FAO et al., 2011).

In principle, border measures can be applied to insulate domestic markets from international price fluctuations. However, hampering the flow of grain between nations, as highlighted by the adoption of measures by some countries to insulate themselves from regional or international markets, can exacerbate price volatility (Anderson et al., 2014). An extreme approach is to opt for complete self-sufficiency with the use of trade only to smooth out fluctuations originating in the domestic market. However, keeping the domestic price level completely delinked from international price levels can be a very costly policy approach, greatly reducing economic welfare in the country concerned. An alternative approach can be to engage in international or regional trade, but to adjust border measures so that domestic markets are insulated from international price swings. For importing countries, tariffs are raised (if applied tariffs are not yet at their bound level) when world prices decline and vice versa when prices rise. Import subsidies can be used to counteract very high prices, but the fiscal costs can be prohibitive and unsustainable for most low-income food-deficit countries. Exporting countries have less scope for counteracting declining world market prices as export subsidies are tightly constrained by the WTO (for its member countries). However, when world prices rise, they can tax or restrict exports and the WTO imposes essentially no effective limits on these policies. In other words, governments of both importing and exporting countries can, within given limits, use trade policies to protect their domestic markets. However, using trade policies to stabilize domestic market prices could mean aggravating volatility on international markets (Tangermann, 2011).

2.5 Production support measures

Increasing and stabilizing food supply can mitigate price volatility in LICs. For production to increase, it is essential to provide the right incentives for producers and other private investors to invest more and at reduced risks and costs.

Priority areas of institutional and policy development in this regard include: (a) overall improved governance (e.g., stable macroeconomic conditions, sound structural policies, human capital development, and public services) of rural areas; (b) improved infrastructure, technology, and services, including irrigation facilities; (c) support to pro-smallholder innovations in financial markets, which often require public–private partnerships; and (d) an enabling legislative and policy environment for small producer organizations, which can greatly mitigate the risks faced by individual producers and help thicken markets and, as a result, reduce volatility (FAO et al., 2011).

The impact of production support measures on price volatility depends on whether a self-sufficiency or self-reliance strategy is adopted. Governments may pursue a policy of self-reliance or importing food from the world market when prices are cheaper than growing at home.[1] However, this strategy came under pressure during the food price crisis of 2007–2008, when importing countries found it difficult to import the food they needed because of export bans and other restrictions by exporting countries. A self-sufficiency strategy (growing domestically all the food the country needs) has gained popularity in recent years (Demeke et al., 2014). However, it may not be necessary for policy makers to choose between self-sufficiency and self-reliance options. Rather, the focus needs to be on establishing an efficient (undistorted) and sustainable agriculture sector and identifying the extent to which this meets food needs (Deb et al., 2009).

3 Policies aimed at coping with the effects of price instability

Policy measures that accept price volatility as a given and attempt to cope with it can be implemented through the market or through government interventions. The aim of market-based instruments is to prevent (using market mechanisms) price instability from causing income instability for producers. Economic agents can protect themselves against the risks of price variations through access to finance and financial hedging instruments such as forward contract, futures, and put options. Government-based instruments support households through public subsidies and transfers when prices are too high (for vulnerable consumers) or too low (for vulnerable producers) (Galtier, 2013).

3.1 Market-based price risk management

A market-based price risk management instrument is a financial contract that allows the parties involved to reduce their exposure to risk or alleviate its consequences. It may range from a simple risk retention using bank loans, which can smooth variable income flows, to more complex risk transfer instruments such as the purchase of a weather derivative (World Bank, 2005).

Credit services are coping mechanisms to help individuals or firms mitigate the negative consequences of shocks. They are a low-cost risk-retention strategy for less severe risks that occur more frequently. Farmers absorb less severe losses using self-insurance strategies, such as credit and savings, as well as on-farm risk management strategies, such as crop diversification, intercropping, and plot diversification. Access to credit markets allows farmers to maintain consumption levels when incomes fall and avoid distress sales of assets.

Farmers can cope with price risks (downside price risks) if they have access to short-term loans (World Bank, 2005) or formal saving mechanisms to draw down their own savings (during bad years). Many institutions provide grace periods for loans of clients affected by disasters, while others give small and standardized loans to help clients cover basic needs. Loans issued under emergency situations may also require a grace period before repayments start (Buchenau, 2003). Farmers' savings are likely to expand with improved access to institutions such as banks, savings and loan associations, and microfinance institutions.

Nonetheless, smallholders have limited access to finance in many developing countries. Several factors have hindered the establishment of viable rural financial systems in developing countries. Low population density, small farm sizes, and inadequate transport and communication services have translated into high transaction costs for financial institutions contemplating an entry into rural areas. Exposure of agricultural production to various risks has also affected rural financial services, including both weather and price risks, which significantly influence the outcome of farmers' investment. Grain trading and processing are also affected by these risks (World Bank, 2005). Therefore, measures designed to promote the establishment of a well-functioning rural finance system should focus on improving: (a) policies including an enabling legal, regulatory, and supervisory framework; (b) financial sector and real sector infrastructure; and (c) financial institutions.

Diversification

Diversification allows farmers to use their resources in different activities and/ or assets instead of concentrating them on one particular enterprise. Since the returns to different activities or assets are not perfectly correlated – i.e., not all farm enterprises and operations are likely to be affected in the same way by risk factors – the variance of the overall return is reduced. Hence, diversification spreads risk and is a successful risk management strategy. Some of the diversification strategies include managing multiple farm enterprises together at any one time (same season) or engaging in the same farm enterprise but in different locations. Many farmers often integrate crops and livestock to reduce risk as well as improve their efficiency and sustainable use of their natural resource base. Farmers may also take part-time work to generate income from off-farm activities (FAO et al., 2011; OECD, 2009). Diversification may entail some disadvantages, including lack of economies of scale or specialization (because of doing many different activities). However, the advantages of averting or minimizing risk and the importance of growing staple crops for home consumption outweigh the disadvantages of diversification in Tanzania (Mutabaz et al., 2013).

Risk transfer strategies: hedging instruments and insurance

Price and production risks that are likely to be widespread and substantial can in theory be transferred from farmers to financing institutions via financial hedging instruments or insurance.

Hedging instruments (forward contracts and futures markets)

Contract farming agreements are forward contracts specifying the obligations of the sellers (farmers) who promise to supply and the buyers (processors/traders) who promise to off-take agricultural produce as agreed. Contract farming is intended to solve the problems of imperfect product and input markets, price uncertainties, and credit market failures. The description of the contract agreement may remain quite vague or be well-defined obligations with remunerations for tasks done, often with specifications of pre-agreed price, volume, quality, and time of delivery. Contract farming may carry the risk of default (due to weak enforcement mechanisms) and contract prices could be slightly below prevailing market prices, but farmers agree to these conditions because they prefer consistent and foreseeable pricing to a highly volatile informal market situation (Kaganzi et al., 2009).

In developing countries, contracting with a large agribusiness firm may be the only way for farmers to access higher-end markets, receive higher returns, and have easier access to inputs along with credit from sponsors. It is a fact that the food supply chain has increasingly become vertically coordinated in developed and emerging countries, with contract farming as the main instrument of coordination for most traditional commodities, and this trend is also likely to affect less developed economies. Over the last two decades, contract farming in the production and marketing of agricultural products has seen a rapid expansion. In particular, livestock products such as dairy, poultry, and pigs have attracted a lot of attention by agroprocessing enterprises. Contract farming has also been a useful mechanism to help farmers diversify into new, high-value crops such as horticulture, cotton, tea, and tobacco.

Hedging via forward and futures markets protects producers against price reduction, but it does not allow them to benefit from price increases. Options, on the other hand, allow producers to protect themselves against declining prices (put option or selling option) while taking advantage of price increases. The strike price (a specified price) of the put option guarantees a price insurance to producers in the form of a minimum price floor at which they can sell their product. The main cost involved in the purchase of put options is the price of the options premium, which is paid up front. The value of the premium depends on the strike price relative to the underlying value of the options futures contract, the duration of the contract, and the volatility of the underlying commodity market prices.

It is clear that better functioning of futures markets can have an indirect impact on smallholders by mitigating international price volatility. However, this is beyond the reach of smallholders due to access costs, poor access to information, lack of training, and the usually lower quality of crops produced by smallholders. There are few relevant commodity markets in low-income countries to manage food systems through futures markets and options (FAO et al., 2011; World Bank, 2005).

Forward contracts are potentially more flexible and useful than future contracts for small-scale farmers and traders. However, future contracts are low-cost, highly liquid, and easily transferable financial instruments with no default risk. Failure to enforce forward contracts, especially for staple food crops, has meant that default risks are too high to support viable forward markets in many developing countries (World Bank, 2005). Government policies need to support the establishment of an enabling legal and regulatory framework and promote forward contracts and futures markets as complementary systems. Producer organizations need to be promoted to reduce the transaction costs of dealing with small farmers.

Insurance products: weather index and other risk management instruments

Insurance schemes are instruments designed to pool risks from a large population to cover payouts encountered by a small portion of that population. Innovative insurance schemes have become a useful tool for poor farmers in managing climatic risks, which tend to affect large number of farmers in a given area. Insurance coverage also improves creditworthiness of participating farmers. However, smallholders in developing countries have no real access to formal insurance coverage. Crop insurance, originating from either the private or public sector, is rarely offered in LICs, especially in sub-Saharan Africa, but is growing in many Asian and Latin America LICs and MICs. The main constraints are the large informational asymmetries and the high transaction costs of dealing with many small farmers.

Recent new innovative approaches in agricultural insurance markets have the potential to address the challenges of conventional insurance in the agricultural sector. Amongst the most promising "new" insurance mechanisms is the weather-based index insurance. Index insurance products apparently offer a practical solution to many of the barriers to conventional crop and livestock insurance for smallholders: adverse selection, moral hazard, high transaction costs, and high loss assessment expenses (Roberts, 2005). However, the development of index-based weather insurance will require public investment and policy support to develop the institutions that are needed to support viable insurance markets (World Bank, 2005).

Governments often have farm safety net programs aimed at alleviating credit, savings, and liquidity constraints, providing certainty, and thus insuring households against production and market risks. Such safety net programs prevent people from adopting coping strategies, which result in depletion of assets and capital divestment. In that sense, they help poor and vulnerable households to build long-term resilience to shocks and ensure sustainable food security. Supporting households to build their asset base, including financial support for livestock production, can improve the resilience of poor households.

There are different formal or informal risk management systems, but these cannot credibly offer full protection to farmers against catastrophic risks. The purpose of farm safety net interventions is to provide protections against catastrophic risks, such as devastation from natural disasters, as well as risks due to limited access to inputs or lack of resources. Many governments create specific calamity funds, which are accumulated every normal year to provide assistance whenever a calamity or a natural disaster strikes.

3.2 Government-based consumer-oriented safety net programs

Safety net programs enable governments to meet the immediate needs of vulnerable households as a result of market or production shocks or natural disasters. They are critical in minimizing the negative effects of large price and production shocks in both urban and rural areas.

Consumer support schemes are mainly designed as food and cash transfer programs that can be distributed through food vouchers or in-kind distributions. Price subsidies as a means of protecting consumers from high prices are also common in many developing countries.

It is now increasingly well accepted that, to be effective, safety net programs need to be targeted and based on an analysis of the different risks and specific vulnerabilities of households and duly designed to address any gender-specific constraints. For example, a school feeding program increases attendance and reduces malnutrition, but it may include the nonneedy (difficult to feed only the poor in a given classroom) or miss the most needy (children too poor to attend school). Similarly, an unrestricted general food or input price subsidy benefits everyone, but is more costly than targeted programs.

When an economic crisis strikes, governments need effective tools and methods both to rapidly identify groups and areas in need of external assistance and to design cost-effective policies (Compton et al., 2010). One of the benefits of the safety nets is that they avoid the negative effects of tariff adjustments (i.e., price-volatility spillovers onto international markets). Given the limited effectiveness of government interventions on markets, emphasis should be placed on establishing well-designed and -managed safety nets (Tangermann, 2011). However, many low-income countries cannot implement effective safety net policies due to limited resources and institutional capacity. Targeting the poor requires information that may not be available and is expensive to collect. Administering safety net programs requires management, accounting, and supervision skills, which could be in short supply in developing countries (IFPRI, 2004). Another priority area for successful safety net programs may include promoting integrated measures that combine different safety net instruments with other sectoral interventions in nutrition and agricultural investment (Grosh et al., 2011).

4 Conclusions

In developing countries, the two episodes of high food price volatility of 2007–2008 and 2010–2011 have caused a significant change in the orientation of policies affecting the food and agricultural sectors. In many cases, and in contrast with their behavior in preceding decades, many governments demonstrated mistrust in markets, especially international markets and were less inclined to rely on the private sector alone to achieve food security. Therefore, they often decided to react to the global price spikes by intervening in markets. For the most part, policies in response to rising and volatile food prices have included a combination of measures targeting producers, consumers, and trade.

It is unrealistic to try to separate stockholding policies from other domestic policies. Any government program that involves buying or releasing cereals requires the creation of public stocks. The connection between stockholding programs and trade instruments becomes apparent when analyzing price volatility in countries that hold buffer stocks. Countries that reported lower overall price volatility often also implemented drastic changes in their trade policies. The fact that buffer stocks appeared to stabilize prices in countries that have isolated their economies is not surprising. Buffer stocks can only function in countries that are able to insulate their own economies from the world market; otherwise, the stabilization effects of the buffer stock dissipate into the international market. Even though buffer stocks seem to justify the presence of trade barriers, openness to international trade usually offers more price stability because it pools production risk and because international markets generally exhibit lower price volatility than domestic markets.

In retrospect, it appears that governments have generally favored short-term interventions to mitigate the effects of the high food price crisis for consumers, including through food safety net programs, over long-term development policies to stabilize prices for producers through improved market institutions or measures to support production. Indeed, many policy responses, such as border measures targeting consumers, have adversely affected incentives to production

(Demeke et al., 2014), while others reduced welfare as they significantly restricted international or regional trade (Short et al., 2014). Although a number of these interventions have managed to insulate domestic markets (e.g., in Indonesia, India, and China) from price volatility emanating from international markets, they have also tended to exacerbate instability of international markets (Anderson et al., 2014; Dawe et al., 2015).

Moreover, the policy decisions taken by countries after the crisis remained largely consistent with those adopted during the crisis, although they also tended to give more importance to long-term policy objectives. Trade policy decisions were significantly reversed compared to measures taken in the wake of the 2007–2008 crisis. Less emphasis was placed on export restrictions and more support was given to agricultural production, for example, by facilitating access to inputs through subsidized prices or improving infrastructures. Infrastructures were improved by bettering smallholders' access to food and developing price and policy information systems (Maetz et al., 2011).

It also appears that a number of more innovative and promising policy options have remained insufficiently exploited by governments of developing countries. These included measures aiming at either mitigating the effects of food price volatility through risk retention or risk transfer measures, including insurance or even forward contracts and opportunities offered by futures markets, or stabilizing prices through more ambitious investments in market institutions and infrastructure. In most cases, these options could not be exploited because the basic requirements of improved governance and provision of fundamental public goods could not be met. For LICs to more effectively respond to new episodes of high food price volatility, the most urgent priority remains to tackle these fundamental obstacles to overall development.

Note

1   This would release land and other resources for other uses in which the country has comparative advantage.

References

Anderson, K., Ivanic, M., and Martin, W. (2014). Food price spikes, price insulation, and poverty. In Chavas, Hummels, and Wright (Eds.), *The economics of food price volatility* (pp. 311–339). Chicago: The University of Chicago Press.

Buchenau, J. (2003). Innovative products and adaptations for rural finance. Lead theme paper at the Paving the Way Forward for Rural Finance, An International Conference on Best Practices. Retrieved from http://www.microfinancegateway.org/sites/default/files/mfg-en-paper-innovative-products-and-adaptations-for-rural-finance-2003.pdf

Compton, J., Wiggins, S., and Keats, S. (2010). *Impact of the global food crisis on the poor: What is the evidence?* London: Overseas Development Institute.

Crola, J.D. (2012). Preparing for thin cows: Why the G-20 should keep buffer stocks on the agenda. In IATP (Ed.), *Grain reserves and the food price crisis: Selected writings from 2008–2012.* Minneapolis, MN: IATP (Institute for Agriculture and Trade Policy).

Cummings, R.W. (2012). Experience with managing foodgrains price volatility in Asia. *Global Food Security, 1*(2).

Dawe, D. (2001). How far down the path to free trade? The importance of rice price stabilization in developing Asia. *Food Policy, 26*, 163–175.

Dawe, D., Morales Opazo, C., Balie, J., and Pierre, G. (2015). How much have domestic food prices increased in the new era of higher food prices? *Global Food Security, 5*.

Deb, U.K., Hossain, M., and Jones, S. (2009). Rethinking food security strategy: Self-sufficiency or self-reliance. UK Department for International Development, May.

Demeke, M., Spinelli, A., Croce, S., Pernechele, V., Stefanelli, E., Jafari, A., Pangrazio, G., Carrasco, G., Lanos, B., and Roux, C. (2014). *Food and agriculture policy decisions: Trends, emerging issues and policy alignments since the 2007/08 food security crisis*. Rome: Food and Agriculture Organization of the United Nations.

Deuss, A. (2014). Review of stockholding policies, OECD. Background document for the OECD Global Forum on Agriculture: Issues in Agricultural Trade Policy, 2 December.

Díaz-Bonilla, E. (2008). Global macroeconomic developments and poverty. IFPRI Discussion paper No. 00766.

FAO, IFAD, IMF, OECD, UNCTAD, WFP, the World Bank, the WTO, IFPRI, and the UN HLTF. (2011). Price volatility in food and agricultural markets: Policy responses. June. Retrieved from http://www.oecd.org/tad/agricultural-trade/48152638.pdf

Galtier, F. (2013). Managing food price instability in developing countries: A critical analysis of strategies and instruments. AFD, CIRAD. April.

Gilbert, C. (2011). Food reserve in developing countries: Trade policy options for improved food security. ICTSD, Issue Paper No. 37.

Gouel, C. (2011). *Agricultural price instability and optimal stabilisation policies*. Unpublished PhD thesis. Paris: ÉcolePolytechnique.

Gouel, C., and Jean, S. (2012) Optimal food price stabilization in a small open developing country. CEPII, WP No. 2012–01.

Grosh, M., Andrews, C., Quintana, R., and Rodriguez-Alas, C. (2011). *Assessing safety net readiness in response to food price volatility*. Social Protection discussion paper no. 1118. Washington, DC: World Bank.

IFPRI. (2004). Linking safety nets, social protection, and poverty reduction – Directions for Africa. 2020 Africa Conference Brief 12. Washington, DC: IFPRI.

Kaganzi, E., Ferris, S., Barham, J., Abenakyo, A., Sanginga, P., and Njuki, J. (2009). Sustaining linkages to high value markets through collective action in Uganda. *Food Policy, 34*, 23–30.

Konandreas, P. (2012). Trade policy responses to food price volatility in poor net food-importing countries. ICTSD Programme on Agricultural Trade and Sustainable Development, Issue Paper No. 42, June.

Maetz, M., Aguirre, M., Kim, S., Matinroshan, Y., Pangrazio, G., and Pernechele, V. (2011). *Food and agricultural policy trends after the 2008 food security crisis – Renewed attention to agricultural development*. Rome: FAO.

Maunder, N. (2013). *What is known about the impact of emergency and stabilization reserves on resilient food systems?* London: Overseas Development Institute, March.

McKenzie, A. (2012). Prefeasibility study of an ASEAN rice futures market. ADB Sustainable Development Working Paper Series, No. 19, March.

Mittal, A. (2008). Food price crisis: Rethinking food security policies. G24 Technical Group Meeting, September 8–9, United Nations Headquarters, Geneva, Switzerland.

Mutabaz, K., Wiggins, S., and Mdoe, N. (2013). Commercialization of African smallholder farming: The case of smallholder farmers in central Tanzania. Future Agricultures, Working Paper 072.

OECD. (2009). Managing risk in agriculture: A holistic approach. (Extracts).

Pinstrup-Andersen, P., and Shimokawa, S. (2006). Rural infrastructure and agricultural development. Paper prepared for presentation at the Annual Bank Conference on Development Economics, May 29–30, Tokyo, Japan.

Poulton, C., Kydd, J., Wiggins S., and Dorward A. (2006). State intervention for food price stabilisation in Africa: Can it work? *Food Policy, 31*(4).

Prakash, A., and Stigler, M. (2011). The economics of information and behaviour in explaining excess volatility. In Parakash (Ed.), *Safeguarding food security in volatile global markets*. Rome: FAO.

Roberts, R.A.J. (2005). *Insurance of crops in developing countries*. Rome: FAO Agricultural Services Bulletin, No. 159.

Sampson, K. (2012). Why we need food reserves? In IATP (Ed.), *Grain reserves and the food price crisis: Selected writings from 2008–2012*. Minneapolis, MN: IATP (Institute for Agriculture and Trade Policy).

Short, C., Barreiro-Hurle, J., and Balie, J. (2014). Policy or markets? An analysis of price incentives and disincentives for rice and cotton in selected African countries. *Canadian Journal of Agricultural Economics*, 1–29.

Tangermann, S. (2011). Policy solutions to agricultural market volatility: A synthesis. ICTSD, Issue Paper No. 33.

Timmer, P. (1989). Food price policy: The rationale for government intervention. *Food Policy, 14*, 17–42.

Valdes, A., and Foster, W. (2012). Net food-importing developing countries: Who they are and policy options for global price volatility. ICTSD, Issue Paper No. 43.

Wiggins, S., and Keats, S. (2012). Grain stocks and price spikes. In IATP (Ed.), *Grain reserves and the food price crisis: Selected writings from 2008–2012*. Minneapolis, MN: IATP (Institute for Agriculture and Trade Policy).

World Bank. (2005). *Managing food price risks and instability in an environment of market liberalization, agriculture and rural development department*. Washington, DC: World Bank.

World Bank. (2008). *World development report 2008*. Washington, DC: World Bank.

World Bank. (2012). *Using public food grain stocks to enhance food security*. Washington, DC: World Bank.

Wright, B.D. (2011). The economics of grain price volatility. *Applied Economic Perspectives and Policy, 33*(1), 32–58.

14 Price volatility perceptions, management strategies, and policy options in EU food supply chains

Tsion Taye Assefa, Miranda P. M. Meuwissen and Alfons G. J. M. Oude Lansink

1 Introduction

In the last decade, agricultural prices have been increasingly volatile at a global level (FAO et al., 2011). In the European Union, the rise of volatility of international agricultural commodity prices has intensified the debate about the role of agricultural policies in mitigating risks. This debate among others resulted from the several reforms of the common agricultural policy (CAP) since the early 1990s that increased the exposure of EU domestic prices to international price signals (Tangermann, 2011). The reforms included the reduction of import barriers, export subsidies, production quotas, and intervention buying (European Commission, 2009; Bardají et al., 2011; Tangermann, 2011).

Price volatility, which includes unexpected price falls, entails risk to farmers who may react by reducing output supply and decreasing investments in productive inputs (Seal and Shonkwiler, 1987; Rezitis and Stavropoulos, 2009; Sckokai and Moro, 2009; Piot-Lepetit, 2011; Tangermann, 2011; Taya, 2012; Haile et al., 2015). The downstream sector of food supply chains is also subject to sourcing uncertainties arising from unexpected price fluctuations in agricultural production inputs (Rabobank, 2011). The food security of consumers spending a large share of their income on food can also be affected by price volatility (Hernandez et al., 2013). These assertions suggest that risk due to price volatility should be managed at all levels of the food supply chains.

Currently, little is known about the actual price volatility management strategies used by food chain actors. Recent studies are limited to the farm sector and focus on few volatility management strategies, such as insurance, futures markets, and income diversification (see for instance Meuwissen et al., 2001; Hall et al., 2003; Greinier et al., 2009; Bergfjord, 2009; Gebreegziabher and Tadesse, 2014). The current farm-level studies also fail to explore the strategies farmers use in practice. This is because these studies are based on structured questionnaires with a prespecified list of strategies that farmers have to evaluate based on their perceptions of the strategies' effectiveness to deal with price volatility. To address gaps in price volatility management strategies within EU food supply chains, policy makers need to be informed about the range of strategies chain actors use in practice.

According to Bardají et al. (2011), governments should intervene in a market when an "abnormal" or an "excessive" level of volatility is observed. Although characterizing volatility as excessive is not an easy task, the depth of a price change relative to the long-term trend and the duration of the depth are two important elements that could characterize "excessive" volatility (Bardají et al., 2011). In addition to objective measures of historical price volatility, understanding chain actors' perceptions of price volatility could help define what can be termed as excessive price volatility, at least from the market agents' perspective. Investigating chain actors' perceptions of price volatility can therefore inform policy makers about the timing of the market intervention.

The aim of this chapter is to present readers with price-related policy measures under the CAP (both reformed and maintained) and the price volatility perceptions and management strategies in selected EU food chains. Strategy gaps in the chains are then identified together with the opportunities for policy measures. The price volatility perceptions and management strategies were identified through interviews conducted with 42 actors in six EU food supply chains. Farmers, wholesalers, processors, and retailers were interviewed in the Bulgarian and French wheat, German pork, Dutch cheese, and Dutch and Spanish tomato supply chains.

2 CAP price stabilization policy measures

To date, a number of measures have been used within the CAP to stabilize agricultural markets. The measures can be classified as market management measures (including both internal and external measures and trade measures) and as those that are intended to increase the competitiveness of food supply chains. Table 14.1 lists and briefly defines each of the instruments that fall into these categories. The objective of the measures within the CAP has generally been to support EU farm prices and reduce their downward variability. While some measures listed in Table 14.1 are still being implemented, others have been discontinued or are scheduled for discontinuation. Increasing pressure from trading partners through WTO negotiations has been a major factor behind the discontinuation of CAP measures that supported prices. Export subsidies for all agricultural products have been completely removed since the end of 2013 (Netherlands Government, 2013); the production quotas for milk, sugar, and wine are scheduled for removal in 2015, 2017 (Meijerink and Achterbosch, 2013; European Commission, 2015a; European Commission, 2015b), and 2030 (Eurocare, 2013), respectively. The production quota for milk was removed in April 2015.

The increasing pressures to discontinue some of the market measures triggered the implementation of policy measures that do not distort the market, such as increasing the competitiveness of food supply chains. Under this measure, producer and interbranch organizations are granted exemption from a series of competition rules (Tothova and Velazquez, 2012). Collusive behavior,

Table 14.1 Price-related measures under the CAP

Policy measures	Description
Market management measures	
External measures	
Export refunds[1]	Subsidies provided to exporters to encourage the export of excess production to world markets at a competitive price.
Border protection	The use of import quotas and levies to restrict imports to the EU.
Internal measures	
Intervention buying	Government buys at intervention prices and stores certain agricultural products or provides aid to private storage when prices fall below a threshold and release the stock when the need arises. Private storage aid is currently in place for cereals, rice, sugar, olive oil and table olives, beef and veal, milk and milk products, pork, sheep meat, and goat meat. Public intervention buying is currently in place for cereals, rice, skimmed milk powder, butter, and beef. Because the current intervention prices are very low, the impact of this instrument on market prices is limited.
Production quotas[1]	Limiting production levels of certain agricultural products to support prices.
Measures that improve the competitiveness of the chain	
Producer organizations (POs)	Encouragement of POs is aimed, among other things, at improving the bargaining position of member farmers and helping them secure fair and stable prices.
Inter-professional organizations (IPOs)	IPOs, which coordinate vertical actions (such as supply concentration and marketing) are encouraged because they lead to stable prices through the use of contracts, the setting up of minimum upstream prices, and controlled supply.
Contract standardization	Standardization helps to specify the basic elements to be included in the contract, eases negotiations, reduces transaction costs, enhances better organized market transactions, and minimizes unfair practices.

[1] Export subsidies for all agricultural products have been completely removed since the end of 2013. The production quotas for milk, sugar, and wine are scheduled for removal in 2015, 2017, and 2030, respectively. The production quota for milk was removed in April 2015.

such as price fixing, is prohibited in the EU in Articles 101 of the Treatment on the Functioning of the EU (TFEU) (Bardají et al., 2011). However, Articles 175 and 176 of EC regulation 1234/2007 allow for exemptions to the agricultural sector provided that, among other things, the negotiation among farmers involves sharing production or marketing facilities (Bardají et al., 2011;

European Commission, 2011). An example of such an exemption is the proposal that enables dairy producer organizations to collectively negotiate contract terms, including prices (Bardají et al., 2011). Such an exemption not only allows farmers to get a fair price for their produce, but also helps stabilize prices both for the farmers and the buyers. A precise definition of the types of producer and interbranch organizations that qualify for legal protection from competition is crucial for these organizations to flourish (Bardají et al., 2011). Another policy option within the CAP is to learn from other countries' policy measures. An interesting example is Mexico's commodity hedging program called ASERCA (Agency for Commercialization and Development Services for Agricultural Markets) (see Box 14.1). This program is aimed at encouraging contracts between buyers and sellers in grain markets. Given the resistance of EU wholesalers and processors to engage in long-term price-fixing contracts (see section 3.2 for more detail), Mexico's hedging program can provide a valuable example of the action EU governments can take to encourage such contracts.

The further reduction of border protection and the removal of export subsidies are expected to increase the downward variability in EU prices. On the other hand, the reduction of intervention prices and the abolishment of production quotas might make imports uncompetitive in the EU because they lower EU prices. However, such an effect greatly depends on world market prices and exchange rate conditions. As a result, the exposure of EU farm gate prices to world price signals might increase and prices may be less stable than they were in the past decade. All this implies that the downstream sector will also be increasingly exposed to price instability, because volatility of farm prices can transmit to the downstream parts of the chain and vice versa.

Box 14.1 Mexican government commodity hedging program

ASERCA program by the Mexican government

Every year, about four months before harvest, the Mexican government opens a program called ASERCA. This program has been implemented since 2010. In the program, farmers and millers can enter into contracts for durum wheat of the new crop at a price that is calculated on Soft Red Winter futures prices (on three different expiration dates) plus a basis fixed by the government. This calculated price will serve as a strike price of the call options offered to the farmers who signed the contract and of the put options offered to the millers that bought the durum wheat. The put and call options are offered for free by the government. The farmers or the millers can exert their options when the market conditions are favorable. An explanation of a call option in the ASERCA program is provided next.

(Continued)

Box 14.1 Continued

Call option

The farmer enters into a contract with, say, a miller to sell durum wheat. The contract price is equal to the Soft Red Winter futures price plus a basis fixed by the government. The farmer then buys a call option from the government (for free) with a strike price equal to the price specified in the contract the farmer and miller entered into. If the spot durum wheat price at time of harvest is higher than the strike price, then the farmer will exercise his call option. The government will then have to pay the farmer the difference between the spot and the strike price. The farmer will thus receive this price difference from the government and still sell his wheat to the miller at the contracted price. But the total price received by the farmer will be equal to the spot price. If the spot price at time of harvest is less than the strike price, a call option is not exercised. Then the farmer's selling price will stay fixed at the government set contract price and the government does not need to pay anything to the farmer. In this way, the farmer is able to benefit from all spot wheat price increases, but is also protected from all price falls below the government set contract price.

---

3 Chain actors' price volatility perceptions and management strategies

We conducted in-depth interviews with 42 actors in five European countries and six food supply chains. Four categories of food products (dairy, meat, cereals, and vegetables) and four food products (cheese, pork, wheat, and tomatoes) are represented in the sample. The choices for the country/food chain combinations were based on the importance of the individual food products in the respective countries. Indicators, such as the share of area used for tomatoes in total land for fresh vegetables, share of pigs' production in total livestock production, share of cheese production in raw milk collected, and share of wheat in total cereal consumption, were used to rank the countries and determine the level of importance of each product in each country. Table 14.2 reports the number of participants per chain and chain stage.

The interviews focused on two items: how actors perceived price volatility and what the strategies are to manage the risk from price volatility. The chain actors' perception of price volatility was assessed by asking them about (1) the percentage price deviation from an expected price level, which they perceived as volatility, and (2) the factors that determined whether a certain level of price volatility is perceived as risky. The chain actors' perceptions can guide the definition of "extreme" volatility that can signal the timing of policy intervention. The price volatility perceptions and management strategies are presented in the following sections.

Table 14.2 Interview participants (n = 42)

Chain stages	Investigated chains					
	Dutch cheese	German pork	Spanish fresh tomatoes	Bulgarian wheat	French wheat	Dutch fresh tomatoes
Farm	3	2	3	2	2	3
Wholesale[1]	3	2	4	3	1	2
Processing[2]	5	0	N/A[3]	3	1	N/A
Retail	1	0	2	0	0	0

[1] Wholesalers are Dutch cheese: cheese wholesalers; German pork: pig wholesalers (one is a cooperative); Spanish tomatoes: fresh tomato wholesalers (two are cooperatives); Bulgarian wheat: wheat grain wholesalers (mainly focused on exports); French wheat: a cooperative wheat grain wholesaler; Dutch tomatoes: fresh tomato wholesalers.
[2] Processors are Dutch cheese: cheese processors (four of them cooperatives); Bulgarian wheat: two millers and one bakery; French wheat: one miller.
[3] Not applicable.

3.1 Price volatility perceptions

Past experience with price volatility

Chain actors were asked about their past experiences with price volatility before proceeding to the questions on the percentage price deviations perceived as price volatility and the factors that determined whether such volatility is perceived as risky. The responses revealed that price volatility has been a challenge to actors in all investigated supply chains. A common finding obtained from all interviewees was that price volatility was perceived to be high from 2007 onwards. The 2007 price spike was felt more pronounced by the actors in the cheese and wheat supply chains than in the pork and tomato chains. The difference in the 2007 price spike in the Bulgarian wheat and Spanish tomato farm prices can be seen in Figure 14.1. Farmers were the most affected actors, as the spike resulted in major investments being undertaken with the belief that the high price would stay for a long time. In the Dutch tomato chain, investments in glasshouses and other equipment made during this period were perceived to have negative effects until present day. The large investments during the price spike are believed to have led to today's overproduction and low tomato prices. In the pork chain, a different picture emerged as the 2007–2008 crisis was not perceived as a volatile period as it was in the other chains. In the pork supply chain, detection of diseases or news of diseases were responsible for the price volatility that was perceived by farmers and wholesalers. The detection of dioxin in feed in 2011 and the more recent detection of African Swine Fever in Poland and Russia were the reasons indicated by the stakeholders for the observed volatility.

Percentage price deviations perceived as price volatility

Simple averages of the percentage price deviations that chain actors perceived as price volatility were calculated per chain and chain stage. These percentage

Bulgarian wheat farm prices

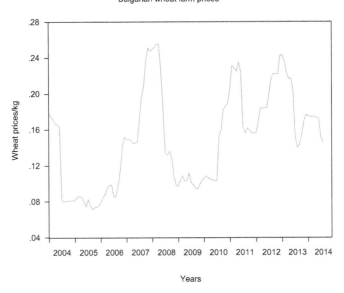

Spanish tomato farm prices

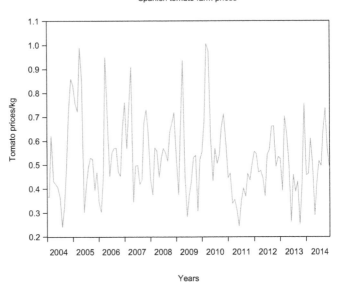

Figure 14.1 Plots of Bulgarian wheat and Spanish tomato farm prices.

price deviations could serve as the lower bound of excessive volatility that could require policy interventions. Table 14.3 provides a summary of the average percentages per chain and chain stage. A more than 10%–15% change in prices from their expected values is perceived as price volatility by a majority

Table 14.3 Percentage deviations in prices perceived as price volatility[1]

Farm	Wholesale	Processing	Retail
• Wheat grain: 10%	• Wheat grain: 10%	• Wheat grain and flour: 10%	• Cheese: 3%
• Pig feed: 10%	• Pigs: 10%	• Milk and cheese[2]: 10%	• Tomatoes 20%
• Pigs: 10%	• Cheese: 10%		
• Cattle feed: 15%	• Tomatoes: 20%		
• Milk: 10%			
• Tomatoes: 20%			

[1] Percentage deviations from an expected price level that exceed the specified percentages are perceived as price volatility by the chain actors. The percentages are averages across respondents. Percentages are expressed relative to the price in the previous price settlement period in each chain, i.e., month in the Dutch milk and cheese chain and week in the remaining chains. Percentages for wheat grain and flour are averages for the French and Bulgarian wheat chains. Similarly, percentages for tomatoes are averages for the Dutch and Spanish tomato chains.
[2] Note that only one cheese processor perceived a price deviation greater than 20% as volatility; the remaining processors perceived a price deviation less than 5% as volatility.

of the respondents. Actors in the Dutch and Spanish tomato chains are an exception to this as the majority perceived as price volatility a more than 25% price change. A similar perception is that of Dutch dairy farmers, who argue that feed prices (maize in particular) are volatile if prices change by more than 20% from their expected values. Recurring large changes in the prices of fresh tomatoes and cattle feed justify the price volatility perceptions of the tomato and dairy farmers. A comparison of perceptions along the chain reveals that processors and retailers seem to perceive lower magnitudes of price changes as price volatility than the farmers and wholesalers.

When defining the magnitude of price change perceived as price volatility, it is important to define what expected prices refer to. The interviews revealed that the minimum period for which actors form price expectations coincide with the frequency at which prices are set in the chain. For instance, because milk prices are set on a monthly basis in the Dutch cheese supply chain, dairy farmers form milk price expectations on a month-to-month basis or for longer time intervals. Since milk prices serve as a main reference to set cheese prices, Dutch cheese processors, wholesalers, and retailers also form milk and cheese price expectations on a month-to-month basis. In the tomato and pork chains, price expectations are made on a week-to-week basis or for longer time intervals. In the wheat supply chains, though high frequency trading can take place at the wholesale stage, weekly price expectations seem to be the norm.

Factors determining the riskiness of price volatility

Price volatility, defined as a percentage price deviation from the expected level, is not perceived as risky by all interviewed actors. The persistence of price deviation was found to be one of the factors that determines whether price volatility is perceived as risky. The degree of persistence of price volatility perceived as risky is summarized in Table 14.4 per chain and chain stage. A finding common to most of the interviewed farmers is that high input price or low output price levels persisting for one year/production cycle (i.e., a year for wheat and dairy farmers and one production cycle for pig and tomato farmers) or longer are perceived to be most problematic. Though higher frequency price changes with shorter durations occurring during the year/production cycle are also not desirable by farmers, these are seen as less problematic because the farmers cannot easily respond to these price changes anyway. Similar to farmers, retailers tend to be more concerned about the trend in yearly average prices. Price changes occurring during the year are perceived as more problematic to the wholesale and processing stages. Fixed-price sales contracts unmatched with fixed-price purchase contracts (and vice versa) and storage are at the roots of the challenges. For instance, it is problematic when output prices drop during the period the input price is fixed through a contract (and vice versa for input prices). Sudden output price drops are also problematic for actors having goods in stock.

The factors causing prices to deviate from their expected values are also seen as the factors that determine the perceived significance of the price deviations. Price changes caused by sudden changes in local weather conditions and changes in global demand and supply conditions (caused for instance by conflicts in major producing countries and by border restricting policy measures) are perceived as problematic by actors in the cheese and wheat supply chains. Actors in the tomato supply chains mainly consider price changes caused by changes in local weather conditions as problematic. In the pork supply chains, the most challenging price changes are those caused by contagious animal disease outbreaks. Predictable seasonal price changes and price changes that actors attribute to speculation are not considered as alarming by most of the actors. The minor importance attributed to volatility caused by speculation and the

Table 14.4 Persistence of price volatility perceived as risky

Farm[1]	Wholesale	Processing	Retail
• A production cycle[2] (DC, DT, BW, GP, ST) • Depending on stock level and position in forward contract[3] (FW)	• Depending on stock level and position in forward contract (BW, DC, FW) • One week and longer[2] (GP, DT, ST)	• Depending on stock level and position in forward contract (BW, DC)	• A year (DC, ST)

[1] BW: Bulgarian wheat chain, FW: French wheat chain, GP: German pork chain, DC: Dutch cheese chain, DT: Dutch tomato chain, ST: Spanish tomato chain.
[2] Price volatility is perceived as risky if a high input or low output price level persists for the specified period or longer.
[3] Price volatility is perceived as risky when output prices drop (input prices rise) and stay low (high) during the period that input prices (output prices) are fixed through contracts at a high (low) level. Price volatility is also perceived as risky when output prices drop while the actor holds goods in stock.

major importance attributed to volatility caused by weather shocks contradicts the finding of Brümmer et al. (2013). In their literature review, they find that the majority of studies attribute volatility to speculation and only a minority attribute volatility to weather shocks. The effect of news related to animal diseases is not indicated at all in their review as a factor affecting price volatility.

Finally, the results of the interviews show that the stability in margins determines whether price volatility is perceived as risky. All interviewed actors argue that an extreme decrease in an output price is not a concern if is matched by a proportionate and immediate decrease in the input prices (and vice versa). In practice, this rarely happens due to, among other things, time lags in production, contracts (either on the buying or selling side), or price influences of retailers (for instance, retailers keeping the processor's selling price low while the processor's input price is increasing).

3.2 Price volatility management strategies

Following Hardaker et al. (2004), we classified the price risk management strategies adopted by the chain actors into two categories: as on-farm/within-business and risk-sharing strategies. The list of the identified strategies is presented in Table 14.5. As the labels of the categories imply, on-farm or within-business strategies are strategies implemented at the discretion of the farm or company concerned. On the other hand, the implementation of risk-sharing strategies involves the participation of other parties.

Most of the farmers' on-farm strategies were found to be loss-minimizing strategies in response to adverse price movements. The loss-minimizing strategies are, among others, the reduction of physical production, reduction of major investments, improvement in efficiency, diversification, and selling produce quickly to avoid loss of quality and therefore lower prices. A notable new development in farmers' on-farm strategies is to create added value through a selection of better varieties to plant, production with less pesticide residues, product promotion, and collaboration with the retail sector to develop improved products. Some farmers are looking into the commercial side of farming as a way to manage the risk from the increasingly volatile prices of agricultural products. That is, these farmers are moving from supply-oriented to demand-oriented farming by shifting their focus away from maximizing production volume towards satisfying customer demands. Focusing on the production and trade of quality produce and targeting niche markets is also a within-business strategy adopted by wholesalers, processors, and retailers. These actors believe that such strategy helps to secure stable and high prices under less favorable market conditions.

Examples of risk-sharing strategies are forward and futures contracts. From Table 14.5, one can see that the use of long-term fixed price contracts is losing popularity in particular among wholesalers and processors. These actors prefer instead to engage in shorter contracts or in contracts with flexible prices, as long-term fixed price contracts are believed to be risky in a volatile environment.

Table 14.5 Price volatility management strategies

Chain stages[1]	On-farm/within-business strategies	Risk-sharing strategies
Farm	• Substitute or cut production (DC, ST, BW) • Substitute expensive ingredients (DC) • Increase production efficiency, reduce costs, and increase productivity (DC, BW, DT) • Avoid major investments (DC) • Wait a bit and sell at whatever price (ST, GP, BW) • Diversify production (BW, FW) • Closely follow market development, improve price predictions, and concentrate production in high price weeks (ST, DT) • Improve output quality (BW,[2] DT, ST)	• Promotion of product by producer organization in times of sudden price drop caused by excess production (DT) • Shorter contracts with small quantities per contract (FW) • Fixed price forward contract for inputs (DC, GP) • Backward integration to produce own maize (DC) • Better marketing/promotion of produce by producer organization to add value to the produce (DT) • Use average seasonal price offered by cooperatives (FW) • Hedge in futures market (GP,[2] FW) • Fixed price forward contract for outputs (FW, DT[2]) • Forward integration to process own milk[2] (DC) • Closer relationship with retailers for improved product development and with long-term fixed price contracts[2] (DT)
Wholesale	• Wait a bit and sell[3] (ST) • Ask farmers to wait a week or two weeks more before harvesting the plant[3] (ST) • Increase production efficiency[3] (ST) • Diversify suppliers (ST) and buyers (DT)[3] • Sell quickly at whatever price[3] (GP, DC) • Cut purchases during overproduction as prices are too low to sell back (ST) • Switch production among alternative products (DC, BW)	• Agree with competitors to throw away excess production and raise back prices (ST[3], DT) • Sell excess production through retail promotion (ST, DT[3]) • Shorter contracts (DC) • Renegotiate fixed price contracts (DC) • Long-term contracts with flexible output prices (DC) • Fixed price forward sales contract with 100% advance payment[2] (BW)

[1] BW: Bulgarian wheat chain, FW: French wheat chain, GP: German pork chain, DC: Dutch cheese chain, DT: Dutch tomato chain, ST: Spanish tomato chain.

[2] Strategies not yet implemented, but planned for the future.

[3] Strategies used by cooperative wholesalers whose main objectives are to minimize the losses that member farmers face in times of sudden drop in prices.

Chain stages[1]	On-farm/within business strategies	Risk-sharing strategies
Wholesale	• Adjust production volume (BW) • Agree on input and output price on same day (FW, BW) • Avoid storage/buy only for daily needs (BW) • Buy spot milk to take advantage of volatility (sudden drop in milk prices) (DC) • Trade quality produce (ST, BW) • Pay farmers an average of 2 weeks' prices (GP)	• Fixed price forward contract for outputs (ST) • Closer relationship with retailers for better marketing/promotion of produce to add value to the produce (DT) • Hedge with options (FW) • Merger among wholesalers to gain more market power[2] • Hedge in futures market[2] (DC, GP, BW)
Processing	• Diversify production (DC) • Cut production (BW) • Switch production among alternative products (DC, BW) • Adjust production volume (BW) • Agree on input and output price on same day (FW, BW) • Avoid storage/buy only for daily needs (BW) • Buy spot milk to take advantage of volatility (sudden drop in milk prices) (DC) • Produce quality product (DC, BW) • Do not overreact: fix milk price at moderate level (DC) • Store (BW)	• Use milk pools to set output prices[3] (DC) • Shorter sales contracts (DC) • Contracts with flexible output prices (flexible with milk prices; use output price bands to share price risk with retailer; cost-plus pricing) (DC) • Transmit price changes to customers (BW) • Renegotiate fixed price contracts (DC) • Hedge in future market[2] (DC) • Over-the-counter contracts for milk[2] (DC)
Retail	• Diversify suppliers (ST) • Secure supply at whatever price (DC) • Secure quality product (DC, ST)	• Transmit price changes to consumers (price decreases in particular) (DC, ST) • Fixed price purchase contract (ST)

[1] BW: Bulgarian wheat chain, FW: French wheat chain, GP: German pork chain, DC: Dutch cheese chain, DT: Dutch tomato chain, ST: Spanish tomato chain.
[2] Strategies not yet implemented, but planned for the future.
[3] A cooperative producing only cheese can pay farmers a competitive milk price that is based on a "weighted-average" of final dairy prices of competitor.

This is particularly true if there is a fixed price long-term contract on the buying side with no contracts on the selling side (or vice versa). Other risk-sharing strategies that are gaining popularity are horizontal and vertical coordination in the chain. Interest for horizontal and vertical coordination is particularly observed among tomato farmers. These farmers are interested in collaborating among themselves and the downstream stage of the chain to be able to market their produce and develop quality products that meet consumers' requirements. This in turn helps them survive in times of sudden drops in prices. In spite of common belief, much interest for futures and options contracts was not observed among the interviewed actors.

4 Conclusions

Food and agricultural commodity prices have been increasingly volatile both at the global and EU levels within the last decade. Although the current literature proposes alternative strategies to deal with price volatility, proposed strategies have often targeted the farm stage. The scope of the proposed strategies has also been limited to a few strategies, with forward contracts, futures, options, and diversification being the main ones. In this study, we took a broader approach and explored the strategies used both at the farm and beyond the farm stages of the food supply chain.

Results show that a deviation in prices by more than 10% to 15% from their expected levels is perceived as price volatility by a majority of the respondents. Although these percentages are based on a small number of interviews, they can still serve as thresholds to define "extreme" volatility that requires policy measures. Three main factors determined whether price volatility is perceived as risky by the chain actors: the persistence, the reason, and the stability of margins. Whereas farmers and retailers perceive persistent price deviations as risky, wholesalers and processors perceive short-term price changes occurring during the year or production cycle as risky. Farmers' strategies are mostly survival strategies through output and cost reduction in response to adverse price movements. Wholesalers and processors focus on adaptive strategies that allow them to secure stable margins regardless of price movements. Retailers' main focus is to secure a continuous supply of quality produce for their customers rather than to reduce price volatility. Overall, the findings suggest diversity in perceptions and strategies along EU food chains and challenge current assumptions that price volatility management strategies are limited to a few traditional instruments. This study also showed that price volatility leads to the development of nontraditional types of strategies and to changes in the structure of the chains and in the competitive landscapes of EU food markets.

Actors' perceptions of price volatility can suggest when market interventions are needed. For instance, the gaps in the strategies used in the chains inform policy makers on how they can address these strategy gaps through policy interventions. The interview results showed that many actors in the chains were interested in further cooperation within the chain. The CAP measures encouraging producer organizations and interbranch organizations are useful policy measures to increase cooperation in the chain. Another area of policy support concerns futures markets. Actors in the Dutch dairy and Bulgarian wheat sectors expressed an interest in a futures market, and policy makers could therefore consider investigating the needs and possibilities for the establishment of such markets.

A further opportunity for policy intervention concerns the timely dissemination to chain actors of improved and accessible data and predictions on market prices. This study shows that some actors rely on such information for their production and sales decisions. Given the confidentiality of price data in the private sector, collecting and disseminating such information becomes a responsibility of the public sector. The interviews revealed that many actors consider contracts as being risky in a volatile environment. The Mexican government's hedging program can be a learning experience to encourage contracts in EU food chains. Besides informing on threshold volatility levels, actors' perceptions of price volatility showed that risk management for weather events, geopolitical risks, and animal health risks need to be prioritized.

Acknowledgments

We would also like to thank Mr. Emilio Ferrari from Barilla G. e R. Fratelli for providing us with information on the Mexican government's hedging program.

References

Bardají, M., Garrido, A., Iglesias, E., Blanco, M., and Bielza, M. (2011). What market measures in the future CAP after 2013? Retrieved from http://www.europarl.europa.eu/studies

Bergfjord, O.J. (2009). Risk perception and risk management in Norwegian aquaculture. *Journal of Risk Research, 12*(1), 91–104.

Brümmer, B., Korn, O., Jaghdani, J., Saucedo, A., and Schlüßler, K. (2013). Food price volatility drivers in retrospect. Retrieved from http://www.fp7-ulysses.eu/publications/ULYSSES%20 Policy%20Brief%201_Food%20price%20volatility%20drivers%20in%20retrospect.pdf

Eurocare. (2013). European Parliament votes in favour of wine quotas till 2030. Retrieved from http://www.eurocare.org/library/updates/ep_wine_quotas

European Commission. (2009). "Health check" of the common agricultural policy. Retrieved from http://ec.europa.eu/agriculture/healthcheck/index_en.htm

European Commission. (2011). Common organisation of agricultural markets. Retrieved from http://europa.eu/legislation_summaries/agriculture/agricultural_products_markets/ l67001_en.htm

European Commission. (2015a). The end of milk quotas. Retrieved from http://ec.europa. eu/agriculture/milk-quota-end/index_en.htm

European Commission. (2015b). Sugar. Retrieved from http://ec.europa.eu/agriculture/ sugar/index_en.htm

FAO, IFAD, IMF, OECD, UNCTAD, WFP, the World Bank, the WTO, IFPRI, and the UN HLTF. (2011). Price volatility in food and agricultural markets: Policy responses. Retrieved from http://www.oecd.org/dataoecd/40/34/48152638.pdf

Gebreegziabher, K., and Tadesse, T. (2014). Risk perception and management in smallholder dairy farming in Tigray, Northern Ethiopia. *Journal of Risk Research, 17*(3), 367–381.

Greinier, R., Patterson, R., and Miller, O. (2009). Motivations, risk perceptions, and adoption of conservation practices by farmers. *Agricultural Systems, 99*(2), 86–104.

Haile, M.G., Kalhuhl, M., and von Braun, J. (2015). Worldwide acreage response to international price change and volatility: A dynamic panel data analysis for wheat, rice, corn and soybeans. *American Journal of Agricultural Economics*. doi: 10.1093/ajae/AAV013

Hall, D.C., Knight, T.O., Coble, K.H., Baquet, A.E., and Patrick, G.F. (2003). Analysis of beef producers' risk management perceptions and desire for further risk management education. *Review of Agricultural Economics, 25*(2), 430–448.

Hardaker, J.B., Huirne, R.B.M., Anderson, J.R., and Lien, G. (2004). *Coping with risk in agriculture.* Wallingford, UK: CABI Publishing.

Hernandez, M.A., Ibarra, R., and Trupkin, D.R. (2013). How far do shocks move across borders? Examining volatility transmission in major agricultural futures markets. *European Review of Agricultural Economics, 41*(2): 1–25.

Meijerink, G., and Achterbosch, T. (2013). CAP and EU trade policy reform, assessing impact on developing countries (report no. 2013–023). The Hague, Netherlands: LEI.

Meuwissen, M.P.M, Huirne, R.B.M., and Hardaker, J.B. (2001). Risk and risk management: An empirical analysis of Dutch livestock farmers. *Livestock Production Science, 69*(1), 43–53.

Netherlands Government. (2013). Europe stops export refunds for agricultural products. Retrieved from http://www.government.nl/news/2013/07/25/europe-stops-export-refunds-for-agricultural-products.html

Piot-Lepetit, I. (2011). Price volatility and price leadership in the EU beef and pork meat market. In I. Piot-Lepetit and R. M'Barek (Eds.), *Methods to analyse agricultural commodity price volatility* (pp. 85–106). New York: Springer Science+Business Media.

Rabobank. (2011). Rethinking the food and agribusiness supply chain: Impact of agricultural price volatility on sourcing strategies. Retrieved from http://hugin.info/133178/R/1549493/476482.pdf

Rezitis, A., and Stavropoulos, K. (2009). Modelling pork supply response and price volatility: The case of Greece. *Journal of Agricultural and Applied Economics, 41*(1), 145–162.

Sckokai, P., and Moro, D. (2009). Modelling the impact of the CAP single farm payment on farm investment and output. *European Review of Agricultural Economics, 36*(3), 395–423.

Seal, J., and Shonkwiler, J. (1987). Rationality, price risk, and response. *Southern Journal of Agricultural Economics, 19*(1), 111–118.

Tangermann, S. (2011). Risk management in agriculture and the future of the EU's common agricultural policy. Retrieved from http://ictsd.org/downloads/2011/12/risk-management-in-agriculture-and-the-future-of-the-eus-common-agricultural-policy.pdf

Taya, S. (2012). Stochastic model development and price volatility analysis, OECD food, agricultural and fisheries working papers, No. 57, OECD Publishing. Retrieved from http://dx.doi.org/10.1787/5k95tmlz3522-en

Tothova, M., and Velazquez, B. (2012). Issues and policy solutions to commodity price volatility in the European Union. Paper presented to the 2nd IFAMA annual symposium: The Road to 2050, the China Factor, Shanghai.

15 Book summary and ULYSSES project's conclusions

Plamen Mishev, Alberto Garrido, Nedka Ivanova and Milkana Mochurova

1 Introduction

In this chapter, we summarise the main messages of the previous chapters and include a list of the starkest policy conclusions that emerge from the ULYSSES project's additional publications, all of which are accessible from the project's webpage.[1] The two sections should be read complementarily. However, since the sources of the comments differ, the authors thought that only the sources of section 3 should be listed at the end (ULYSSES project publications). The sources of section 2 are obviously the book's previous chapters, which are referred to by the chapter number, instead of by the authors' names used in section 3. This will make it easier to find the original source for those readers interested in seeking more elaboration and support of the ideas presented in this chapter.

2 Chapters' summaries and main lessons

After the introductory chapter, **Part 1** includes six chapters devoted to a review of the literature on short-term volatility drivers (**Chapter 2**); updating empirical volatility assessments and spillovers (**Chapter 3**); reviewing the mid- and long-term drivers of market volatility (**Chapter 4**); examining the implications and regulatory issues associated with the transparency of food pricing (**Chapter 5**); delving into contextual factors of volatility transmission in food supply chains (**Chapter 6**); and reviewing the literature about the impacts of increased food prices and volatility on consumers and households (**Chapter 7**).

Chapter 2 reviews the most recent empirical literature devoted to analysing short-term volatility drivers. The chapter covers empirical studies addressing price volatility drivers, theoretical aspects of volatility analysis, and spillover effects (focusing specifically on macroeconomic factors within commodity markets, between energy and agricultural markets, and between spot and futures markets, and on the role of the index fund speculation). None of these subtopics and areas of work yields clear consensus in the literature. But, it is perhaps instructive to establish two groups of results: those that gather more support, and those in which the competing results are more balanced or nuanced.

From Chapter 2, it appears that market fundamentals are the primary causes of price volatility and among these the major causes of recent events of wide price movements are low stocks-to-use and supply shocks. In a second level of statistical significance and consideration by the authors stand the macroeconomic factors (including exchange rates and money supply), trade policies, unexpected market information and spillovers from the energy markets. These four groups of drivers are not considered by all authors, and of course they result from different hypothesis-testing exercises. The fact is that some authors reject hypotheses about these drivers' effects, whereas other fail to reject them.

There is some disagreement about the interaction between spot and future price volatility. First, the direction of causes can be bi- or unidirectional; second, it can be found in some products but not in others; and third, it can occur across products spreading to different markets (e.g. cotton and wheat). One final aspect reviewed in Chapter 2 looks at the impact of index fund speculation on the level of volatility of futures prices. The literature appears to conclude that the impact is not significant. The authors conclude that 'reforms to the regulatory framework for futures markets should hence be applied rather carefully, so as not to hamper the price discovery and hedging functions of those markets, although additional transparency requirements should be imposed as swiftly as possible' (p. 24).

Building some consensus of value to policy makers about what causes price volatility is a complex task. This is because primary drivers give rise to or trigger drivers of a second level, and these, in turn, exacerbate the impact of others. Technically, studying this sequence of drivers' impacts involves careful modelling of the time each driver changes and how its effect on price can be identified. Note also that correlations between some drivers and prices (e.g. oil price and basic agricultural commodities) grew stronger and more intensely during the crisis. Therefore, it is very likely that the process leading to an episode of accelerated instability may be caused by, in general terms, fundamentals 1 and 2 (e.g. supply shock and low stocks to use) exacerbating driver 1 which, together with unexpected news, gives rise to policies among key countries that, in turn, activate fundamental 3 (panic hoarding) perhaps stimulated by drivers 2 and 3 (e.g. cheap dollar and low interest rates). This process raises expectations of price increases among fund managers, pushing up futures and options markets, which consecutively make some countries adopt drastic policy decisions, which together with driver 4 (oil prices now entering the strong correlation phase) add more tension that spills over to other markets, and so on.

Chapter 3 first reviews the concepts and measurement approaches of price volatility. To the extent that there are various types of measurements, time frames, estimation methods and assumptions, ex-ante vs. ex-post perspectives, as well as price data, volatility assessments will vary significantly. This has a direct bearing on at least one of the questions raised in Chapter 1: Who do policy makers want to protect and from what? Because one can observe prices moving widely and rapidly, that does not mean that the targeted sector and its agents will be forced to engage in unprofitable or undesired market changes. Farmers, for instance, may not be too concerned about daily or even weekly price variations. The time frame of price volatility can vary significantly across agents in the value chain (see Chapter 14).

In its second part, Chapter 3 reviews selected empirical analyses showing the spillover effects covering groups of related markets (*grains*, including wheat, maize, bioethanol and ammonia; *oilseeds*, including rapeseed and soybean; *vegetable oils*, covering palm, sunflower, soybean, and rapeseed oil and biodiesel; *sugar*, with sugar and bioethanol; and *meats* with pork, maize and soybean meal). Although the products in these groups of commodities are tightly connected, authors find cases of clear effects in some groups (palm oils over all other products) and no spillover effects in others (sugar over bioethanol and vice versa). Therefore, even though substitution possibilities would support the hypothesis of multi-directional effects among related products, empirical results give a very heterogeneous picture. The chapter ends by concluding that, based on the recent literature on the analysis of volatility of major crops (maize, rice, wheat and soybean), there is a clear distinction between the period of lower volatility before 2006–2007 and higher volatility after that until today.

Chapter 4 offers a medium- and long-term perspective of volatility, identifying some drivers that have potential for making prices more unstable or volatile. Using agroeconomic models, Chapter 4 shows that by 2030 crude oil prices and macroeconomic indicators, especially exchange rates, might be the main sources of price variability, though GDP and consumer price index, as well as weather shocks and climate change, will also be important drivers. The chapter also shows that oilseeds and meat/dairy markets will become more volatile due to their connections with macroeconomic indicators and fossil fuels. It seems also that price changes will attenuate the effect of climate change, but there will be differences across regions and products. Concerning the impacts of climate change on agriculture, both biophysical and economic results vary widely across scenarios, regions and sectors, but the carbon fertilization may lead to price decreases. Market projections to 2030 are sensitive to changes in crop productivity variability and, therefore, to climate change uncertainties.

Chapter 5 summarises the main findings and policy conclusions of the Project Transparency of Food Prices (TRANSFOP)[2] that looked at the functioning of the food supply chain and the imbalances in the bargaining power of participants in the EU. The results reveal the considerable heterogeneity across supply branches and Member States of the food supply chain in the EU. Two main policy messages are worth mentioning. First, a large concentration in a given stage of the chain does not necessarily mean that food pricing should be considered noncompetitive; it is behaviour rather than number of firms that really matters for addressing competition. Second, food supply consolidation occurs via horizontal and vertical mergers, whose results on price transmission may have offsetting effects. But the authors state that 'to the extent that consolidation may improve the functioning of the supply chain, removing barriers to promoting an active market for corporate control is an important consideration for providing a more unified policy space throughout the EU' (p. 79). Chapter 5 concludes by making four recommendations for the EU food supply chain: (a) Maintain and strengthen the current commitment to monitor prices; (b) enhance monitoring of the structure and the functioning of the food supply chain in different Member States and for critical food products; (c) explore the potential of scanner data to increase the transparency of food pricing in the EU; and (d) continue to improve the functioning of the food supply chain.

Chapter 6 reviews the literature of price level and volatility transmission among the supply chain. Price level and volatility transmission are similar in that they both deal with price linkages along the chain and may be affected by similar factors. However, an important distinction is that price transmission refers to the linkages between the conditional mean prices, while price volatility transmission refers to the linkages between the conditional variance of prices. Factors affecting level and volatility transmission can have desirable effects on one type of transmission, but they may have the opposite effect on the other type of transmission. This indicates that different market measures that complement each other could better handle the two types of transmissions. An example is the encouragement of market competition to enhance price transmission while at the same time encouraging contractual relations among chain actors. The chapter argues that contractual mechanisms help reflect the predictable portions of market prices while they do not account for the unpredictable portion of price movements. The downside of the use of forward contracts among competitive chain actors is that they can reduce price volatility transmission while enhancing the transmission of the predictable portion of price changes.

Chapter 7 reviews the literature on the impacts of increased consumer prices and volatility in both the EU and low-income countries (LICs). A significant finding is that consumer prices of food and staples behaved quite differently across countries, regardless of their income level or whether they share a common currency (e.g. euro). Consumer prices grew more rapidly during and after the crisis in all EU Member States than the general price indices. They became more volatile during Jan. 2007–Nov. 2014 than in Jan. 2000–Dec. 2006 in most Member States. More expensive food had a significant impact in the segment of the lowest income quintile, reaching almost to the median households in Bulgaria and Romania. Food price increases and positive deviations from the general inflation are associated with increases in the proportion of poor households in the EU that declare suffering food deprivation. This in turn can be anticipated by the share of food expenditures over the household's disposable income. A rise in food prices may have long-term health consequences among the poorest households, not only in the poorest Member States but also in the rich ones.

In low-income countries, the impacts are also varied. In the short term, net consumers suffered more than net producers, but in the medium term increased prices may have had a poverty reduction effect. How to cope immediately and during events of price spikes of the basic staples is still subject to considerable debate. From a purely national interest, price insulation may be easier to institute, but targeted safety nets may be more effective and less distortive. It appears that poor households value more the protection against price rises than against unstable prices.

Part 2, with five shorter chapters, presents the views of an officer of the European Commission about markets financialisation (**Chapter 8**); two representative organisations of EU agricultural producers, German pigs (**Chapter 9**) and European cereals (**Chapter 10**); an EU dairy processor (**Chapter 11**); and an NGO with intense activity in sub-Saharan Africa (**Chapter 12**).

Chapter 8 discusses the implications of the recent surge of financialisation with agricultural commodities, especially the growth of derivative contracts. The author's view is that the major measures on both sides of the Atlantic, namely, Dodd-Frank in the US and the EU package Markets in Financial Instruments Directive (MIFID) and the Market Abuse Directive (MAD), which was followed by the European Market Infrastructure Regulation (EMIR), cover a small percentage of the use of financial instruments. This is because they leave out over-the-counter (OTC) contracts, which represent 15 to 20 times the amount of regulated finance. The chapter concludes by highlighting the need to promote research about the use of financial contracts, with a view to discuss how the regulatory framework can be improved.

Chapter 9 offers the particular view of the interest group of pig farmers in Germany (ISN).[3] The chapter briefly reviews the recent and successful evolution of the German pork sector. The view of ISN is clear in asking for a no-intervention policy in the EU: no price support, no subsidies to storage and no trade barriers. Pig growers in Germany manage their margin risks primarily with hedging with the price of feed or purchasing it through larger associations. The price of piglets and slaughter pigs 'complies with weekly price announcements of more than 30 producer associations within Germany' (p. 125), which consist of a uniform price mask fixed weekly. The political requests of ISN include, among others: (a) Free market without any trade barriers, quotas, export subsidies, or public stock-keeping, which is thought to lead to greater problems in future; (b) the need to transpose simultaneously the EU directives into national laws in all MS in order to avoid competitive disadvantages for certain farmers within Europe; (c) the protection of high EU standards – the requirements for keeping pigs in the EU are described as being significantly higher than in most other regions in the world; (d) transparency of the market should be a priority; when fewer and growing companies influence or even determine the market the distribution channels disappear, having a negative effect on competition and deterring pig farmers from engaging in market activities; and (e) not only is price volatility a predominant issue that farmers have to cope with, but also the absence of predictability concerning political decisions.

Chapter 10 offers the view of European cereal growers.[4] The chapter reviews the evolution of price management tools and strategies of French producers since 2000. Before the reform of the CAP in 2003, growers relied primarily on 'pool pricing', which is one way of transfering risk from the producer to the collector, because the agent pays an average selling price of split sales and hedges the price commitments using futures and derivatives markets. However, as markets and prices became more volatile, producers began using fixed price contracts: spot price contracts and fixed price forwards, both also offered by collectors. This permitted disconnecting selling (chosen day) from physical delivery, storage being either on farm or a service specifically charged for by collectors. Of increasing use by French growers are forward contracts, where the price is not fixed but determined at delivery time with reference to financial markets. It appears that producers have been stimulated to switch from pool pricing to various types of forward contracts with the goal to beat the pool price, but the author doubts this has actually been accomplished.

Overall, the use of financial instruments faces three limitations: (a) No protection against consistently low prices over a long period; (b) a cost of €5 to €20 per tonne of cereals for options; and (c) the limited scope of futures markets for grains, both in terms of products and geography. In view of these limitations, the author turns to other instruments like revenue farm insurance and farm savings accounts, whose potential seem beyond the present legal, institutional and political realities in the EU. This shifts the focus of the chapter to the CAP post-2020 that the author envisions as having less budget, as somewhat renationalised, and as more legitimate in the eyes of citizens. The latter implies, in the author's view, that the CAP has to bring about environmental benefits and farmers' income support in the form of counter-cyclical schemes. The author concludes that subsidised farm insurance and savings accounts are seen as promising instruments for the consideration in the next CAP reform.

In **Chapter 11**, attention is paid to the EU dairy sector, and the particular view of a large EU dairy cooperative.[5] The perspective in this case is of a sector with good European and international reputation and significant scope to grow by diversifying the products and catering to the nutritional needs of consumers of all ages and incomes around the world. After milk quotas were removed in the EU, the sector's standpoint seems to be in favour of ex-post measures to make the industry more resilient, although the author does not specify exactly what type of measures should be desirable. The dairy sector is heterogeneous in Europe, with large cooperatives in northern EU states with a large share of the market, and much smaller companies in southern Member States. In addition to the improved regulation of the supply chain, making obligatory the use of written contracts, it appears that there is not any commonly desired instrument for the EU dairy sector, although hedging in the input markets, revenue insurance and fiscal measures to build reserves, in the author's view, deserve some consideration.

Finally, **Chapter 12**, authored by representatives of a global NGO, changes the focus and looks at the role of local food reserves (LFR) in LICs. Even if one admits that holding local food reserves involves a certain degree of market distortions, the authors claim that they can secure food availability in delicate moments and help farmers manage supply and market risks in isolated regions. There are other ancillary benefits of LFR, including the promotion of mechanization, credit and the improvement of agricultural practices. LFR can also empower women, allowing them to undertake new economic activities, decreasing dependence on middlemen and promoting social cohesion. LFR face the risks of supply shocks, especially in drought prone areas; bad design and management; and price cycle inversion (paying higher prices when building stocks than those cashed when drawing them down). The authors convey a warning against food aid interventions, which can cause economic losses and even destroy credit culture. These risks can be overcome with better coordination between national food reserves and local initiatives and supporting local reserves through structured demand: targeting food aid to school feeding and other social protection programmes.

Part 3, consisting of two chapters, focuses on business and policy strategies to manage and cope with agricultural and food price instability. **Chapter 13** is focused on LICs and **Chapter 14** on business strategies for supply agents in the EU.

Chapter 13 reviews policies to prevent, manage and cope with food markets instability in LICs. The chapter proposes two main groups of policies: those that attempt to stabilise markets (including improved market infrastructure and logistics, market institutions, stockholding and buffer stocks, border and trade measures and production support measures) and policies aimed at coping with the effects of price instability (including market-based risk management and safety net programmes). Despite the wide choice of instruments implemented by LICs during and after the crisis, it appears that governments have preferred making short-term interventions to mitigate the effects of high prices, including the implementation of food safety net programmes over long-term development policies to stabilise prices for producers through improved market institutions or measures to support production. The chapter concludes that stockholding policies must be accompanied by trade measures, because in the absence of domestic price insulation, the effect of the buffer stocks would be neutralised in the international markets. The authors highlight the insufficient use and development of insurance, risk retention and risk transfer schemes and the scarce attention paid to building market institutions and infrastructure. The authors recommend that 'for LICs to more effectively respond to new episodes of high food price volatility, the most urgent priority remains to tackle these fundamental obstacles to overall development' (p. 173).

Chapter 14 looks at price volatility perceptions, management strategies and policy options in EU food supply chains. The authors summarise the main findings of in-depth interviews with 42 actors in five European countries and six food supply chains, covering four categories of food products (dairy, meat, cereals and vegetables) and four food products (cheese, pork, wheat and tomatoes). Results show that the stability in margins determines whether price volatility is perceived as risky. Interviewees were asked to rate three key elements of perceived price risks: persistence, the reason behind the price movements and the stability of margins. Each sector, stage in the chain and product has quite different concerns about these three elements. For instance, 'extreme' volatility implies price changes above 25% from week to week for fresh tomato producers, 20% for dairy farmers and 10% for wheat growers. For processors of flour, milk and cheese, 10% is considered a large price movement. Risk perceptions are also quite different: farmers and retailers are concerned with persistent price deviations but wholesalers and processors fear more short-term price changes occurring during the production cycle. Strategies vary significantly across sectors too: Farmers focus on survival strategies, through output and cost reduction; wholesalers and processors focus on adaptive strategies to stabilise margins; and retailers care to secure a continuous supply of quality produce for their customers. Overall, the findings suggest diversity in perceptions and strategies along EU food chains and challenge current assumptions that price volatility management strategies are limited to a few traditional instruments. This study also demonstrates that price volatility may lead to the development of nontraditional types of strategies and to changes in the structure of the chains and in the competitive landscapes of EU food markets.

The main policy conclusion of the chapter is that actors' perceptions of price volatility can suggest when market interventions are needed. 'For instance, the gaps in the strategies used in the chains inform policy makers on how they can address these strategy gaps through policy interventions. . . . results showed that many actors in the chains were interested in further cooperation within the chain. The CAP measures encouraging producer organizations and interbranch organizations are useful policy measures to increase cooperation in the chain. Another area of policy support concerns futures markets. Actors in the Dutch dairy and Bulgarian wheat sectors expressed an interest in a futures market, and policy makers could therefore consider investigating the needs and possibilities for the establishment of such markets' (p. 188).

3 Main policy implications of the ULYSSES project

3.1 Policy implications of the drivers affecting price volatility

- ULYSSES results (Brümmer et al., 2013) and the literature reveal much heterogeneity. The development of price volatility over time differs a lot, as does the impact of the potential drivers. This suggests that there is no general approach for managing and coping with excessive levels of price volatility in agricultural markets.
- One common pattern across all groups of commodities and markets within each group is the strong role played by lagged own price volatility. Price volatility on agricultural markets is largely driven by factors which are

specific to each market (Brümmer et al., 2014b). Thus, policies for limiting price volatility would have to be fine-tuned to the market in question.

- Empirical results show that different volatility measures indeed capture different aspects of price volatility (Brümmer et al., 2014a).

- Price formation for the most important agricultural commodities takes place primarily on a global scale (Brümmer et al., 2014b). This represents a considerable barrier for effective policy and suggests that a more promising approach relies on policies focused on helping producers and consumers to cope with price volatility, instead of preventing price volatility.

- There are significant variations of maize, wheat and rice domestic volatility in developing countries (Pierre et al., 2014). Maize is the most volatile, and Africa is the most unstable region. Looking at potential volatility drivers and quantifying their impact by commodity or by continent, the results highlight the influence of international prices volatility, oil prices volatility and yields on domestic price stability.

- Price volatility and level for rice were higher in Africa than in Asia (except in the Philippines) (Pierre et al., 2014). This is a problem especially for some countries in western Africa, where rice is one of the most important staple foods.

- Implied volatility estimators reveal more valuable information about future price moves than historical estimators (Brümmer et al., 2014a). Policy makers who are interested in foreseeing volatility can use market expectations (Geman and Ott, 2014). Forward-looking volatility can be derived from option contracts traded on markets of agricultural derivative contracts. This implied volatility reveals market information regarding the risk aversion to future agricultural price developments and hence contains useful information for policy makers.

- The application of implied risk measures still faces different challenges, especially for early warning systems (Brümmer et al., 2014a): (a) the choice of an appropriate threshold level that defines 'large' price moves, which should be made in light of potential consequences of a price change and may be a complex market specific issue – the threshold could be considered as a free parameter that can also change over time; and (b) a clear limitation is the requirement of having reliable option prices, which limits the number of commodity markets that qualify for an application of implied risk measures.

3.2 Long-term drivers

- Uncertainty in the macroeconomic environment in large exporting countries can translate into competiveness losses or gains due to exchange rates; thus, imports can increase or decrease, and third countries can benefit from an excess in the world supply to increase their stocks when prices are low (Araujo Enciso et al., 2014).

- Specific sensible policy variables, such as the self-sufficiency rate, are not exempt from increasing uncertainty in the future. Specific policy goals might not be met and world markets would need to adjust to the new situations. Findings suggest that agricultural policies, as well as the uncertainty around key market drivers (macroeconomic environment and yields), have a significant impact on future price levels and volatility, which is in line with the literature (Araujo Enciso et al., 2014).

3.3 The role of financialisation

- ULYSSES results do not provide evidence that financialisation and speculation are among the most important drivers of increasing agricultural price volatility (Brümmer et al., 2014b). In consequence, findings do not support the notion that the introduction of position limits, a key element of the MIFID reform, would help in curbing price volatility on agricultural markets.

3.4 Biofuels

- Biofuel mandates have an influence on the price variation by establishing a link among the different domestic markets and the world market (Araujo Enciso et al., 2014). Analysis suggests that biofuel policies do indeed contribute to higher volatility spillovers from the oil market to key agricultural products (Saucedo et al., 2015). In episodes of amplified volatility, the impact of oil price volatility on agricultural markets, which are already suffering from higher price levels and inflated uncertainty, exacerbates the situation.
- Analysis of volatility spillovers suggests that mitigating measures, which have the potential to limit the transmission of price volatility from oil to agriculture, might constitute a politically feasible approach (Saucedo et al., 2015). These measures could include a more flexible handling of blending requirements for biodiesel and bioethanol, an approach which is already partially in use in Brazil and the United States. Developing countries contemplating a stronger support to biofuels should take this into account when designing their policies (Saucedo et al., 2015).
- The 2030 scenario with abolished biofuel mandates reveals that the mandates appear to be reducing uncertainty by setting strict consumption obligations. Without them, the strong uncertainty around crude oil prices is partially transmitted particularly to biodiesel, since it is less competitive than bioethanol (Artavia et al., 2014).
- With respect to biofuel mandates, although the results show a negative trend in biodiesel price volatility, at least in a short run, it should be admitted that this is possibly a consequence of the policy framework driven

by the EU renewable energy directive (Artavia et al., 2014). Therefore, maintaining the current renewable energy policy could slightly reduce the price volatility of biodiesel.

- Results also show that an adjustment of biofuel prices could be expected with the removal of the mandates in the major pricing countries (EU, US, Brazil, Argentina, Australia and Canada), which is particularly noticeable for biodiesel (Artavia et al., 2014). While removing the mandates has a minor impact on the consumption of bioethanol as well as on its price level and uncertainty (since bioethanol prices are relatively competitive), for biodiesel the incentive for consuming at mandate levels would disappear and the price uncertainty in case of biodiesel would increase.

3.5 Market spillovers

- If considered in isolation, the oil volatility spillovers are higher especially in the after-crisis episode and affect mainly the maize market for the ethanol group and all the vegetable oils for the biodiesel group (Saucedo et al., 2015).
- In the ethanol group, maize is most strongly affected by oil price volatility spillovers (Saucedo et al., 2015). Shocks from the oil market may also be transmitted indirectly to wheat because of its high degree of acreage competition in production with wheat and the (limited) substitutability in consumption between maize and wheat.
- In the case of the biodiesel feedstocks, oil price volatility is found to affect all main vegetable oils (Saucedo et al., 2015), especially at the beginning and at the end of the post-crisis period. This suggests that the high values of the spillover index for the biodiesel group come mainly from the shocks to soybean oil and palm oil and the interaction between them.
- Rapeseed prices are much more stable in the observed period. Rapeseed oil is the main raw material for the EU biodiesel production (Saucedo et al., 2015).
- The analysis of volatility spillovers has clearly indicated that these spillovers between the products rarely follow a simple pattern (Saucedo et al., 2015). Episodes with notoriously high oil price fluctuations induce additional volatility in key agricultural markets.

3.6 The role of stocks

- A wide consensus in the literature emerges for the role of stocks in explaining price volatility (Brümmer et al., 2014b). This does not necessarily imply that storage polices are a viable policy option. It should be noted that there is no statistically significant impact of the stocks kept in a single country (the US stocks, which were included in several cases) (Brümmer et al., 2014b). This might point to the futility of country-specific buffer stocks.

- Holding global buffer stocks is unlikely to be viable because of their relatively high costs and the incentives for free-riding (Brümmer et al., 2013). Furthermore, given the drastic difference in the relative size of oil and agricultural markets, when oil markets drive agricultural price volatilities, holding national stocks would have very limiting effects (Saucedo et al., 2015).
- The importance of improving the access to public information on stocks is supported by the findings on the explanatory effect of revisions of stock projections on maize's price volatility (Brümmer et al., 2014b).

3.7 Supply shocks and climate change

- Comparing simulation scenarios, results show that the magnitude of the carbon fertilization effect strongly influences the direction of projected price movements (Artavia et al., 2014). Results show less positive (or more negative) yield effects across EU regions compared to the world average, in line with findings from other studies. However, agri-food market projections to 2030 are sensitive to changes in crop productivity (Araujo Enciso et al., 2014) and climate change uncertainties, in particular to climate projections and the magnitude of the carbon fertilization effect.
- Economic simulations highlight that positive yield effects will be counterbalanced by crop price decreases and vice versa (Artavia et al., 2014). As a consequence, market forces and changes in competitive advantages can reverse the effects of yield changes and even attenuate the effects of climate change at the global level. They would have divergent effects across regions and sectors, depending on the magnitude and direction of yield changes and their impact on productivity (Araujo Enciso et al., 2014).
- However, results should be interpreted cautiously, because climate change simulations only considered the effects on average yields and did not take into account a full adaptation to climate change (management practices adjustments, technical change, structural change) but only partial market-induced adaptation (cropland allocation, input adjustments) (Artavia et al., 2014).

3.8 Early warning systems

- The methodology built up in the project (Brümmer et al., 2014b) allows for estimating the normal and unexpected price moves. Because the results show that the magnitude of large price increases is expected to be larger than the magnitude of large price decreases, and the mean probability of a large price move is well above 0.5 for all markets analysed, efforts to develop tools to predict the expected price spikes would provide a sound basis for developing early warning systems.
- Results suggest that the measure of volatility should be adapted to the targeted economic agent (Geman and Ott, 2014). As policy makers are concerned with the welfare of farmers and consumers, the realized volatility of

agricultural commodities should be measured on the price level instead of the return of the price. Furthermore, differentiating volatilities on the time horizon of the risk borne by agents – within the crop year (intraannual volatility) and beyond the crop year (interannual volatility) – is also relevant.

3.9 Value chain perspectives

For the EU

- Policy measures and instruments targeted at improving markets' information and transparency, training to improve farmers' ability to manage risk and developing risk management instruments, as well as appropriate frameworks (economic, institutional, legislative), may lower the barriers to promote futures markets (Assefa et al., 2014; 2015).
- Opportunities for policy intervention are identified at the farm stage where a gap in risk management seems to exist (Assefa et al., 2014). Although farmers can respond to price drop persistence for one year/production cycle or longer, their responses are of limited value if the directions of price changes are suddenly reversed between years/production cycles. Income stabilisation tools are useful policy tools in this respect. The single farm payment scheme currently in place is one such tool. Future policy support for whole-farm income insurance can be a future policy option.
- Further support of farmers to organize themselves in producer organizations and cooperatives is another policy option to allow farmers to invest in the production of specialty products and create closer links with retailers, bypassing the wholesale stage (Assefa et al., 2014). This can empower farmers vis-à-vis the downstream sector and help secure good and stable prices for their produces.
- Absence of active futures markets in relevant market sectors (e.g. the German pork, Dutch cheese and Bulgarian wheat) is another risk management gap that could be filled with policy intervention (Assefa et al., 2014). Interest for these hedging instruments was expressed among wholesalers, farmers (German pig farmers) and processors (Dutch cheese processors) in these sectors.
- Better prediction of short- and long-term drivers of price volatility and timely dissemination of price predictions can be useful to help chain actors better manage the risk from price volatility (Assefa et al., 2014). While predictions of long-term trends in prices are particularly useful for farm investment decisions, predictions of short-term price changes can support the downstream sector's decisions on whether and when to enter into contracts and on whether to raise stock levels.
- Price transmission mechanisms vary across member states in cointegration significance and levels, long-term elasticities and the speed of adjustment (García-Germán et al., 2014). The differences are striking, even among MS whose economies are closely integrated (for example, Benelux and Germany, Spain and Portugal, and France and Italy).

- Transmission elasticities of world agricultural prices to domestic consumer prices also vary significantly across countries (García-Germán et al., 2014). It tends to be at around 0.25 in the Eurozone and above 0.5 in the nonmember countries of Eurozone, suggesting that monetary policy and exchange rate stability provide a stronger cushion for world food price instability.
- Many of the strategies identified in field work and interviews with value agents involved following the spot market prices without fixing prices (Assefa et al., 2015). As a result, many of the strategies adopted do not reduce the price volatility faced by the chain actors. Results show nevertheless that price-fixing contracts and hedging in derivative markets are effective instruments to reduce the price volatility faced by the chain actors. Encouraging the use of these two instruments could be an effective policy option.

Low-income countries

- The appropriate policy response to food price risk and instability will vary across and within countries because of differences in geography, patterns of food production and consumption and institutional capacity to implement alternative policies (Demeke et al., 2014).
- Policies should address structural problems, among which the most important are (1) the widening gap between domestic cereal supply and demand, (2) marketing constraints and (3) political instability and policy uncertainties (Demeke et al., 2014).
- There are six significant options for reducing price risks in sub-Saharan African countries (Antonaci et al., 2015): warehouse receipt systems (WRS), commodity exchanges, contract farming, agricultural information systems (market information systems and weather forecast and early warning systems), grain stock management and trade policies. The options to support producers are the following: financial services, insurance, technology development and adoption, and farm safety nets. No developing country has successfully reduced poverty without first increasing agricultural productivity, which in turn depends on effective management of price and production risks. Policies should contribute to designing a policy framework for the mitigation of the negative effects of volatile prices and production shocks.
- Market-based approaches are very important for dealing with unstable markets, but their implementation requires a series of preconditions and an enabling policy environment (Antonaci et al., 2015). The country experiences highlighted show that these tools are not in place or are not fully developed in most African countries. Farmers are not sufficiently protected, and this emphasises the critical role that governments should play in agricultural risk management.

- Governments should create a supportive institutional environment where modern risk management tools can thrive (Antonaci et al., 2015). Investments in basic services, such as definition of grades and standards, contract enforcement and market information, will help sustain long-term market development. An effective legal framework and a conducive business and economic environment would facilitate the development of solutions for risk pooling/sharing. Policy makers need to adopt an integrated and holistic approach in support of risk management interventions through incentives and by strengthening agricultural markets and financial institutions.

- Most African governments have yet to include agricultural risk management policies in their national development plans (Antonaci et al., 2015). Risk management tools need to be mainstreamed into agricultural policies and programmes in order to promote a paradigm shift towards an integrated approach of managing 'development' and 'emergencies'. Enabling an efficient response to systemic risks, components of disaster risk management should be incorporated into national strategic plans. Besides large-scale emergency operations, they can improve farmers' capacities to adapt to changing environmental pressures.

- Training of extension officers and farmers in hazard-affected communities is critical to encourage crop diversification, counter-season production, water harvesting and water conservation, the adoption of resistant seeds (against drought or floods) and generally to improve existing production techniques (Antonaci et al., 2015). The recent move by the New Partnership for Africa's Development (NEPAD) Planning and Coordination Agency (NPCA) to mainstream risk management policies and resilience-building programmes into the Comprehensive Africa Agriculture Development Program (CAADP) investment plans is a step in the right direction.

- Information about modern risk management strategies in Africa is scarce, and governments generally lack the capacity to manage agricultural risks (Antonaci et al., 2015). Combined with high levels of price and production risks in Africa, the weaknesses provide a good case for comprehensive studies into risk profiles, assessment of risk management tools, a legal framework and policy environment, the role of social protection, and risk management policies and strategies which best suit the different political and economic contexts of African countries.

- Structural problems have affected price levels and volatilities in sub-Saharan Africa (SSA) (Demeke et al., 2014). First, maize production variability has increased markedly in recent years in most countries with available data. Cereal production has also declined significantly in recent years in countries affected by political or civil conflicts. Because of commercial links (formal and informal trade), staple grain prices in some countries are affected by production declines and political turmoil in neighbouring countries. At the same time, demand has steadily increased due to high population growth and rapid urbanisation in nearly all African countries.

High income growth in many countries has also contributed to the widening gap between demand and variable supply. Attempting to bridge the deficit through commercial import has widened the food trade deficit, raised the cost of staples and increased vulnerability to international price volatility.

- Inadequate national and regional markets in SSA exacerbate the problems of price rises (Demeke et al., 2014). High transport costs, inappropriate and high cost of storage, small-scale operations, high cost of finance and limited access to information, among others, have contributed to price volatility and high price levels for consumers but low prices for producers. Neither the public nor the private sector maintains enough stock of grains to offset the impact of production variability on prices. Because of poor roads, lack of bulk transport systems, high cost of operating and maintenance costs, the cost of transport is significantly higher in SSA than elsewhere.

- The performance of food and agriculture is better in countries where the public and private sectors work together to stabilise prices (Demeke et al., 2014). Policy makers should also have a regional perspective to market development as grain trade ties are relatively strong among neighbouring countries. It is also important to realize that regional trade could help reduce price variation by spreading supplies across geographically dispersed markets.

4 Impacts on consumers and households

4.1 European Union

- Poor households in the EU are vulnerable to food deprivation (not affording a meal with meat, chicken, fish or vegetarian equivalent every second day) and face difficulties in consuming healthy food items (García-Germán et al., 2015).

- Results reveal that there is a significantly negative relationship between the probability of being less food deprived and the consumer food price index, even if the household's disposable income, size and Member State are taken into account. Positive deviations of the index of consumer food prices above the general consumer food prices do also explain the probability of a household in the lowest income quintile suffering food deprivation (García-Germán et al., 2015). Since wages and pensions are usually pegged to inflation rates, these results suggest that Member States should keep an eye to food prices and provide income, food or social assistance to the most vulnerable households when food prices rise consistently above inflation rates.

- Income and social support to children and vulnerable households should be a major policy goal, although it is not clear that the European policy level is the most appropriate to address the problem of malnutrition and obesity.

- Based on the importance given by many authors to the percentage of food expenditure, it is clear that increasing food prices must have had notable impacts in the households within the lowest income quintile in Romania, Lithuania, Bulgaria, Malta, Poland, Slovakia and Estonia, reaching possibly to the median income household in Romania and Bulgaria (García-Germán et al., 2015).

- From a policy perspective, it is important to delve also into the retailers' strategies, learning more about how the poorest urban consumers make use of the wide food choices they can find in EU cities and by rural households in less densely populated areas (García-Germán et al., 2015).

4.2 Low-income countries

- Households would benefit more from preventing or limiting an increase in the level of the cereals/food prices, rather than in reducing their volatility (Magrini et al., 2015). The greater impact of a price change should not be a surprise as it has multiple direct and indirect effects on the daily lives of agricultural households, influencing both their production and consumption strategies. Conversely, the impact pathway of price volatility is less clear and evident because it is connected to the dynamic concept of risk and the unobservable household capacities to manage and cope with it. The recommendation naturally arising from this finding is to focus more on policies mitigating and coping with the effects of price surges.
- Domestic markets of different countries have responded differently to this surge in international price volatility (Pierre et al., 2014). The sources, size and consequences of food price instability vary substantially across and within countries. The appropriate policy response to food price risk and instability will also vary across and within countries because of differences in geography, patterns of food production and consumption, and institutional capacity to implement alternative policies.
- Policy responses in the wake of the food crisis have focused on short-term coping mechanisms rather than addressing key structural problems, production variability and market underdevelopment and failure (Demeke et al., 2014). Greater attention has been given to protecting consumers through policy measures such as reducing tariffs and VAT, releasing stocks, banning export and undermining the private sector thorough ad-hoc interventions with little regard to the impact of such measures on producers and traders. Unpredictable changes in policy and high price volatility have raised the cost of doing business in the area of grain marketing.
- Increasing agricultural productivity and preventing a food crisis 'rather than trying to cope after the fact with their impact on the poor is the only way to avoid substantial, perhaps permanent, damage to the welfare of poor households'(Demeke et al., 2014). Protecting consumers should not be done at the expense of addressing structural problems of increasing production and developing markets. Support to producers and market improvement have long-term benefits of increasing domestic supply and lowering prices for consumers.

- Welfare of farmers who rely on cereals-based food systems is determined by the interaction of several complex and interconnected factors, namely, consumer and producer price dynamics, the market structure and the policy environment (Magrini et al., 2015). Understanding how these factors operate together is essential for policy makers engaged in delivering food security as part of their mandate. Hence, a deeper understanding of the forces influencing household responses to price shocks at the micro level is a necessary step to better support policy intervention with evidence-based suggestions.

- The impact of price changes and price volatility on welfare should be analysed at the domestic level, because the country-specific structure of the economy plays a fundamental role (Magrini et al., 2015). Results suggest key variations across countries for the same price shocks, and this heterogeneity depends on differences in the share of food expenditure over total consumption, the specific budget share devoted to cereals, the substitution effect among food items and the relative number of net sellers and net buyers accessing the market.

Notes

1 http://www.fp7-ulysses.eu/
2 http://www.transfop.eu/
3 Interessengemeinschaft der Schweinehalter Deutschlands e.V. (http://www.schweine. net)
4 Association Générale des Producteurs de Blé et autres céréales (http://agpb.fr/)
5 http://www.frieslandcampina.com/
6 All of these references can be downloaded from ULYSSES's web page: http://www. fp7-ulysses.eu/publications.html

References[6]

Antonaci, L., Demeke, M., and Vezzani, A. (2015). The challenges of implementing price and production risk management in sub-Saharan Africa. Scientific Paper 9B, ULYSSES project, 35 pp.

Araujo Enciso, S., Blanco, M., Artavia, M., Ramos, F., Fernández, F., Van Doorslaer, B., Fumagalli, D., and Ceglar, A. (2014). Volatility modelling: Long-term challenges and policy implications. Scientific Paper 5, ULYSSES project, 39 pp.

Artavia, M., Blanco, M., Araujo Enciso, S.R., Ramos, F., Van Doorsaer, B., Fumagalli, D., Niemeyer, S., Fernández, F.J., and M'Barek, R. (2014). Production and crop roots (causes?) of volatility measures including partial stochastic simulations of yields and macroeconomic variables. Scientific Paper 2, ULYSSES project, 36 pp.

Assefa, T.T., Meuwissen, M.P.M., and Oude Lansink, A.G.J.M. (2014). Price volatility perceptions and management strategies in European food supply chains. Scientific Paper 6, ULYSSES project, 26 pp.

Assefa, T.T., Meuwissen, M.P.M., and Oude Lansink, A.G.J.M. (2015). Quantifying the effectiveness of price volatility management strategies in reducing price volatility. Scientific Paper 9A, ULYSSES project, 35 pp.

Brümmer, B., Korn, O., Schlüßler, K., and Jaghdani, T.J. (2014a). On historical and implied risk measures for major agricultural commodity markets. Scientific Paper 4, ULYSSES project, 49 pp.

Brümmer, B., Korn, O., Schlüβler, K., and Jaghdani, T.J. (2014b). Volatility analysis: Causation impacts in retrospect (2007–2011) and preparing for the future. Scientific Paper 1, ULYSSES project, 41 pp.

Demeke, M., Morales-Opazo, C., and Doroudian (2014). Staple food prices in sub-Saharan Africa the context of a crisis: Challenges and policy options. Scientific Paper 7B, ULYSSES project, 32 pp.

García-Germán, S., Bardají, I., and Garrido, A. (2015). Analysis of material deprivation in the EU under food price volatility and rise. Scientific Paper 10, ULYSSES project, 29 pp.

García-Germán, S., Garrido, A., and Bardají, I. (2014). Evaluating transmission prices between global agricultural markets and consumers' food price indices in the EU. Scientific Paper 7A, ULYSSES project, 29 pp.

Geman, H., and Ott, H. (2014). A re-examination of food price volatility. Working Paper 6, ULYSSES project, 68 pp.

Magrini, E., Morales-Opazo, C., and Balié, J. (2015). Price shocks, volatility and household welfare: A cross-country inquiry. Scientific Paper 11, ULYSSES project, 51 pp.

Pierre, G., Morales-Opazo, C., and Demeke, M. (2014). Analysis and determinants of retail and wholesale staple food price volatility in developing countries. Scientific Paper 7, ULYSSES project, 23 pp.

Saucedo, A., Brümmer B., and Jaghdani, T.J. (2015). The dynamic pattern of volatility spillovers between oil and agricultural markets. Scientific Paper 8, ULYSSES project, 31 pp.

Index

Note: Italicized page numbers indicate a figure on the corresponding page. Page numbers in bold indicate a table on the corresponding page.

For Product Safety Concerns and Information please contact our EU
representative GPSR@taylorandfrancis.com Taylor & Francis Verlag GmbH,
Kaufingerstraße 24, 80331 München, Germany

Printed and bound by CPI Group (UK) Ltd, Croydon, CR0 4YY
08/05/2025
01864355-0004